Praise for *The Gandhian Iceberg*

"I've been waiting twenty years for this book. Concise, in-depth, and challenging, *The Gandhian Iceberg* reweds strategic and principled nonviolence, to unveil the unimaginable power and potential of integral nonviolence. Chris Moore-Backman, courageous practitioner and brilliant scholar both, lays out a clear and full effort response to the current world emergency. (Incidentally, if the ideas and invitations in this book were not terrifying its subject would not be integral nonviolence.) I encourage us all to read this seminal work and put its wisdom into practice immediately. It can help us transform fear into an unstoppable force of love and action." —Ethan Hughes, co-founder of the Possibility Alliance

"I first sat down with *The Gandhian Iceberg* at 8:30pm, intending to read for a half-hour or so. It was 3am when I turned the final page. That's how good it is." —Jim Douglass, Catholic Worker and author of *JFK and the Unspeakable*

"An engrossing manifesto. Chris Moore-Backman's careful and imaginative examination of Gandhi's teaching yields an impressive, compelling call to nonviolent struggle. Readers who resonate may realistically prepare for direct action." —Kathy Kelly, co-coordinator of Voices for Creative Nonviolence and author of *Other Lands Have Dreams*

"Moore-Backman's project is at once both sweeping and eminently practical, and it takes on its formidable goals with compassion, lyricism, a vast knowledge base, and a lot of heart. Full of nuance and insight, *The Gandhian Iceberg* is a searing call to action in the face of global crises—and a fascinating read, to boot." —Maya Schenwar, editor-in-chief of Truthout and author of *Locked Down, Locked Out*

"A powerful exploration of how people today can relate to nonviolence and how nonviolence today can relate to the urgency of our time. *The Gandhian Iceberg* lays out the costs of staying on the sidelines and the exhilarating potential of individual and collective nonviolent transformation. The stakes could not be higher." —Kit Miller, director of the MK Gandhi Institute for Nonviolence

"Chris Moore-Backman has done a job I've wanted someone to take on for years. *The Gandhian Iceberg* grapples in earnest with the legacy of Gandhi's life and thought to begin to answer the question of our times: Is there a nonviolent path to a livable future? Practical and visionary, anyone in whom lives the fire of making the world work for all of life will find companionship, solace, and challenge." —Miki Kashtan, author of *Reweaving Our Human Fabric: Working Together to Create a Nonviolent Future*

"Chris Moore-Backman has plumbed the depths of integral nonviolence to create a vital roadmap for cultural and ecological transformation. This is a crucial book for a crucial moment in history." —Tom Benevento, founder and co-director of New Community Project, Harrisonburg, Virginia

"In the year 1930, in the part of the planet we call India, 78 people with a deep personal transformation practice skillfully changed the course of humanity. Now, Chris Moore-Backman is inviting us to tap into that same immense source of courage, wisdom, and compassion to ignite a movement of movements for the liberation of the Earth. A much needed adaptation of integral nonviolence today and a must read for any citizen of the world in the 21st century." —Pancho Ramos-Stierle, full-time ServiceSpace volunteer and co-founder of Casa de Paz, Oakland, California

The Gandhian Iceberg

A Nonviolence Manifesto
for the Age of the Great Turning

Chris Moore-Backman

BE THE CHANGE PROJECT
RENO, NEVADA

Published by the Be the Change Project
2055 McCloud Avenue, Reno, Nevada 89512

Copies of *The Gandhian Iceberg* are available on a gift economy basis.
Visit www.gandhianiceberg.com or write to the above address for details.

ISBN 978-0-692-75636-2

Cover and interior design: Vanessa Mendozzi
Interior artwork: Sarena Kirk
Author photo: Yousef Natsheh

Permissions:
Mary Oliver, "The Summer Day," from *House of Light*, by Mary Oliver. Published by Beacon Press, Boston. Copyright © 1990 by Mary Oliver. Reprinted by permission of the Charlotte Sheedy Literary Agency Inc.

St. Theresa of Avila, "The Sky's Sheets," from *Love Poems From God: Twelve Sacred Voices from the East and West*, by Daniel Ladinsky. Published by Penguin, New York. Copyright © 2002 by Daniel Ladinsky and used with his permission.

Hafiz, "The Sun Never Says," from *The Gift: Poems by Hafiz*, by Daniel Ladinsky. Published by Penguin, New York. Copyright © 1999 by Daniel Ladinsky and used with his permission.

Excerpts from Jesus' beatitudes, from *The Essential Jesus: Original Sayings and Earliest Images*, by John Dominic Crossan. Published by Castle Books, Edison, NJ. Copyright © 1994 by John Dominic Crossan and used with his permission.

for Vincent and Isa

CONTENTS

PREFACE

OUR HUMAN FAMILY stands at an unimaginably perilous and promising cross-roads. In defense of life and with a great thirst for justice, a global movement of movements is beginning to coalesce. It may soon be poised to launch the largest, most momentous social crusade in human history.

This book is born of the simple contention that within this emerging and beautifully vast movement of movements, a small, disciplined, and deeply committed band of U.S.-based integral nonviolence practitioners will play a distinct and crucial role. While I trust that a wide spectrum of changemakers will take a sincere interest and find value in the book, it has been addressed primarily to those who will comprise this as yet unformed submovement.

At the time of this writing, we are farflung throughout the nation, still seeking each other out, still longing to cohere. Some of us, already well-anchored by the core principles and inspiration at the heart of Gandhi's teaching, have known for a long time that what usually passes as nonviolence in our society has little if anything to do with it. We have been preparing with great love, creativity, and one-pointedness to correct this near universal misunderstanding, not through argument, but through courageous, protracted action on the frontlines—and behind the scenes—of nonviolent revolution.

There are others out there as well, equally called to and made for this sub-movement, who have yet to be introduced to the great power and possibilities of integral nonviolence. When they are—and I hope *The Gandhian Iceberg* might play some small part in this—their experience will be one of unmistakable recognition and homecoming.

In this age of inconceivable, imminent danger—and opportunity—an age many changemakers are calling the Great Turning, I doubt it would be possible to overstate the importance of our pulling together, and of our doing so immediately. All to say, my basic purpose in writing this book has been to help us find one another and to give us a common point of reference, connection, and generative debate as we come to know how—at this most critical moment—we are best called to serve the unfolding struggle for justice, wholeness, and redemption.

The Gandhian Iceberg

The good news is that not everybody agreed to forget.

—Naomi Klein, *This Changes Everything*

INTRODUCTION

"GANDHI IS OUR GREATEST FAILURE."

Definitely not the response I was expecting. Anand Mazgaonkar's parents had worked and walked with Gandhi. He was now following in their footsteps, a steady and respected advocate and friend of the Gujarati poor. His grin accented the irony of his statement.

"Consider Gandhi's principal goals," he said, then he listed them one by one, slowly and deliberately:

Hindu-Muslim unity
The end of untouchability
The uplift of women
The revitalization of a human-scaled village-based economy
Sobriety
Economic equality
Nonviolence

A pregnant pause, then, "Failures each and all."

Mazgaonkar's words spoke of failure but his face glowed with admiration and respect, the eyes adding the dimension of a deep and complex sadness. "What are we to say of Gandhi in an India still divided, an India drunk on the values and trinkets of the West, and arming herself with nuclear weapons?"

That conversation happened in 2005, during my sole visit to India—an experience which provided ample evidence to support the ironic claim: "...our greatest failure."

Earlier on the trip, amidst the frenetic bustle of downtown Cochin, I tried to tune out the deafening din of the traffic as I gazed at one of India's thousands upon thousands of statues of Gandhi. There he was again, the mahatma seated in meditation, eyes closed, face serene. I had simply stopped for a moment to pay my respects, but I found myself moving closer, intrigued by what I guessed was a deep black lacquer coating the monument. When I reached out to touch Gandhi's shin, I was puzzled. I lifted my hand and, transfixed, stared at the smudge of grime on my index finger.

Inhaling, I could taste at the back of my throat the acrid-sweet pollution of modern, urban India. I looked up into Gandhi's soot-covered face and found myself flashing to a still earlier scene from my trip: a cow, a sacred cow of India loping along the center divider on a busy roadway. As buses, cars, motorcycles, bicycles, and pedestrians rushed passed in a blur, she gracefully lowered her head into a pile of trash, took a plastic shopping bag in her mouth, and slowly, methodically chewed it down.

In the sight of that cow, the blackened statue, and Anand's sad smile you can feel the imprint of horrors that defy all. In our minds, certain place names, events, and images stand at attention, like dutiful envoys for the Unspeakable: the ovens of Auschwitz, the bomb descending on Hiroshima, the Killing Fields of Cambodia, Burma, or Rwanda, the Trail of Tears, the Middle Passage.

Keep tugging that thread and our biosphere appears, in its entirety, edging towards a rolling boil. Our civilization wandering lost, addicted to all manner of things disconnecting, dealing out untold suffering and irreversible extinction, bringing an end to indescribable power and beauty. Were we to allow ourselves vulnerability enough to fully feel the weight of it—the finality—would it be too much for our hearts to bear?

Rewind a little more: February 16th, 2003.

By that time, my own experiments with nonviolence had formed my lukewarm (at best) opinion of the marches and rallies currently in fashion. But February 16th was not a day to let skepticism reign. War was imminent and people were taking to the streets. I knew I ought be among them.

Not to say that I stepped out on that winter morning with every bit of my hard-earned skepticism left at the door, but I did step out. My heart earnest and open.

Downtown, I met up with a small group of friends and we wove ourselves among the gathered thousands of our fellow Bay Area activists, adding our voices to the resounding "NO!" collectively and clearly pronounced in the face of the looming re-invasion of Iraq. It was a sweet taste of "people power"—an experience of a great underlying solidarity binding us together. It was an unforgettable day. And one of the loneliest days of my life.

It wasn't that my skeptic shadow caught up with me and wrestled me to the pavement. In fact, I believe it was the relaxed grip of my skepticism that opened me to the truth I encountered that day. Defenses down, I had that singular experience of clearly seeing something for the first time that at some level I had known all along.

Amidst the day's exhilaration it was plain to me that something essential was missing—that there was a blank space, a deadness, in the center of what we were doing. Deep down I knew that this marvelous day was a day of certain failure. I knew that our massive mobilization to stop the war would inevitably and necessarily fade, and that it would do so quickly.

———

Up on your pedestal Gandhi! That's where we like you, where we get to revere you as the patron saint of nonviolence, as a larger-than-life figure we can never hope to fully emulate. A comfortable distance is a helpful thing. We get to feel impressed and inspired, while remaining free and clear from what you actually taught. We get to paint your pithiest slogans on cardboard rectangles, hold them aloft at the rally, and call it good.

Gandhi himself bristled at the thought of being called mahatma, or "great soul"—the epitome of the pedestal—straight out denying his worthiness of the accolade and knowing full well that such veneration only distracted people from what he was actually doing. Instead of exalting him, Gandhi urged his fellow Indians to get busy with the nuts and bolts of nonviolent transformation. By and large they ignored the request, as we'll discuss.

When the treachery and death of Shock and Awe loomed early in 2003, I had already been searching for Gandhi (sans pedestal) for more than a decade. Following February 16th, though, the quest hit an altogether different pitch. The children of Iraq compelled me to understand the blank space I beheld that day and the nature of what might fill it in.

On February 27, 1930, two short weeks prior to launching the Salt Satyagraha, one of the most iconic touchstones in the history of nonviolence, Gandhi wrote a short article for *Harijan*, his national publication. Characteristic of his quirky, forthright writing style Gandhi called the article "When I am Arrested." Given that the Salt Satyagraha is arguably the most pivotal episode in India's struggle for independence from British rule, it's been the subject of immense interest to historians, social change theorists, and activists. Nevertheless, "When I Am Arrested" has gone mostly unnoticed. Drowned out, safe to assume, by the high drama of the "great march to the sea": the 240-mile trek to the seashore, Gandhi lifting the iconic, Empire-busting fistful of salt above his head, and the massive civil disobedience that followed throughout the nation.

It's easy to get swept up in the theatrics and personality of the Salt March. But if we take time to look closely at "When I am Arrested" we catch a behind-the-scenes glimpse of the inner workings and design of India's independence movement, and of its leader's revolutionary rationale. Gandhi published the article to put the masses of India on alert and to give them a final set of instructions. Just imagine being there, reading Gandhi's impassioned battle cry, culminating with his declaration that with this campaign not a single nonviolent devotee in the struggle "should find himself free or alive at the end of the effort."

Just prior to that statement, there's a particular paragraph in "When I Am Arrested" that's profoundly significant for those of us deeply committed to nonviolence. It centers on Gandhi's spiritual community, Satyagraha Ashram, which was the starting point of the march to the sea:

So far as I am concerned, my intention is to start the movement only through the inmates of the Ashram and those who have submitted to its discipline and assimilated the spirit of its methods. Those, therefore, who will offer battle at the very commencement will be unknown to fame. Hitherto the Ashram has been deliberately kept in reserve in order that by a fairly long course of discipline it might acquire stability. I feel, that if the Satyagraha Ashram is to deserve the great confidence that has been reposed in it and the affection lavished upon it by friends, the time has arrived for it to demonstrate the qualities implied in the word satyagraha. I feel that our self-imposed restraints have become subtle indulgences, and the prestige acquired has provided us with privileges and conveniences of which we may be utterly unworthy. These have been thankfully accepted in the hope that someday we would be able to give a good account of ourselves in terms of satyagraha. And if at the end of nearly 15 years of its existence, the Ashram cannot give such a demonstration, it and I should disappear, and it would be well for the nation, the Ashram and me.

———

What struck me that day in San Francisco, on the eve of war, was that we who opposed it were entirely unprepared for the battle at hand. Our "movement" lacked the depth necessary to sustain itself. After the bombs started dropping, we simply and forlornly returned, with a few exceptions, to our lives, to business—"progressive" though it may have been—as more or less usual. And we have re-staged this scene again and again in the years since Shock and Awe. While the pace of our collective return to normalcy has varied, this has become our consistent, entrenched response.

That said, the few exceptions to the above withering must be acknowledged. While so many millions of us were marching, singing, and sloganing, Kathy Kelly and her friends from Voices in the Wilderness (now Voices for Creative Nonviolence), for example, had placed their bodies smack dab in the heart of Baghdad. Yes, right there with the Iraqi people, right there under the bombs, a witness to all of us of the kind of love and courage Gandhi was talking about.

A few of us with a similar calling dappled the crowd on February 16th, 2003. Nevertheless, despite that fact and despite the well-known presence of the Voices contingent in Baghdad, the marching thousands were not grounded by the power and intention of a core group like that which added such depth to India's independence movement. Or, to bring it home for those of us in the U.S., we weren't grounded by the power and intention of a core group like that which gave the civil rights stage of the African American Freedom Movement its similar umph. Try as we might to organize full-throttle nonviolent resistance, if we proceed as though the battle doesn't require the same, our efforts will necessarily continue to come up short.

But where, we ask, does such umph come from?

Kathy Kelly and her friends certainly know something about it. Kathy's*

* To feel at home in my own writing I often cite people I know personally by first name, while citing those I haven't yet had the privilege to meet, or who I have only met in the context of an interview, by last name.

book, *Other Lands Have Dreams*, offers some powerful clues. Foremost among them, I'd argue, are presence and stories. Nonviolence doesn't happen in the stands. It's a commitment to direct exposure and the sharing of stories—true stories revealed in places bowed down with injustice, shared by those who bear the scars of that injustice. Such stories carry great power. As do those of pilgrims who voluntarily embed themselves in such situations, as an expression of loving, embodied solidarity. As restorative justice pioneer Dominic Barter says: "You're only changed by the world if you're willing to feel it." Direct exposure and stories help us feel the world.

But there's more, of course, to this umph, and "When I Am Arrested" offers us a solid lead. Consider the article's fascinating two-part proposition: 78 people, 15 years preparation. Gandhi chose 78 emissaries from his ashram to form the nucleus of the Salt Satyagraha. These 78 had undergone the rigorous training of spiritual discipline and hands-on community-based social uplift as members of the ashram, which at that point had been devoted to the cause of personal and national liberation for just shy of 15 years. Only after that "fairly long course of discipline," Gandhi said, had the ashram and those 78 emissaries attained the level of "stability" needed to adequately demonstrate the true meaning of satyagraha—nonviolent resistance—for the Indian nation.

Obviously that corps of 78 did not carry out the Salt Satyagraha on their own. The campaign's power was many-layered, involving literally millions of individuals responding to the direction of a trusted and almost entirely undisputed leader. But the role of the 78 was nevertheless essential to the Salt Satyagraha's deep impact, and to the energy that infused India's independence struggle.

It follows, I believe, that to truly benefit from Gandhi's guidance here we need to enter into a soulful investigation of what Gandhi meant when he said that the Salt Satyagraha would only be started by those who had "submitted to [the ashram's] discipline and assimilated the spirit of its methods."

It was in the ashram, Gandhi argued, not in Delhi, that the key to India's freedom would be discovered. The ashram was Gandhi's "laboratory" for nonviolent resistance, and in it the objective was nothing less than full-blown transformation—a trading in of old lives for new. It's an assignment that few are willing to genuinely, fully consider taking up. But for those who do, the systematic approach to nonviolence that Gandhi practiced and taught—and which was the compass for daily life at his ashram communities—can be an invaluable aid.

Gandhi's nonviolence approach indicates three interrelated, mutually supportive areas or modes of experimentation. Pioneering nonviolence scholars Gene Sharp and Robert Burrowes were probably the first to distill these three categories from Gandhi's teaching and action. Sharp described them like this: "(1) the improvement of individuals in their own lives and ways of living; (2) a constructive program to begin building a new social order even as the old one still exists; and (3) the practice of various forms of nonviolent action against specific social evils." Burrowes like this: "personal nonviolence as a way of life, constructive work to create the new society, and nonviolent resistance to direct and structural violence."

I was first introduced to this threefold description by Joanne Sheehan, who, with John Humphries, had been using a condensed version of the Sharp-Burrowes formulas in Gandhi workshops they were leading in New England around the turn of the century. They called the threesome personal transformation, constructive program, and political action. I began following suit in my own Gandhi workshops beginning in 2004, utilizing a simple Venn diagram.

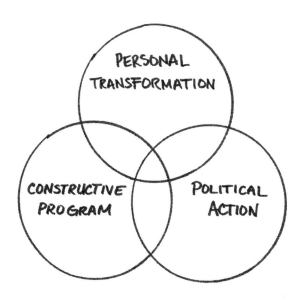

The diagram had a knack for catalyzing *ah ha* moments for workshop participants—moments that almost invariably occurred at the same point during the process. Indicating the center of the model, the place where all three areas merge, I would quickly deconstruct the Salt Satyagraha. It was easy enough to see that within that one campaign all three spheres of the Gandhian approach were intrinsic, and that their interplay lent the movement a depth and power beyond our ken. Looking at the Venn diagram, at a certain point, workshop participants could see that the Salt Satyagraha elegantly illustrated an integral form of nonviolent revolution.

According to Gandhi the great march to the sea was first and foremost a "sacred pilgrimage." "Nonviolence is impossible without self-purification," he said, so the march, like everything else of Gandhian design, was geared for transformation at the personal level. This meant that the entire adventure was punctuated by the spiritual practices and observances that characterized life at the ashram. Such disciplines grounded practitioners in the spirit of self-emptying prayer, and reminded them day in and day out of the true nature of their motivation for action, and the depth of their capacities.

But make no mistake, such personal practice, according to Gandhi, had immeasurably powerful effects far beyond the individual:

> Unfortunately a belief has today sprung up that one's private character has nothing to do with one's public activity. This superstition must go. Our public workers must set about the task of reforming society by reforming themselves first. The spiritual weapon of self-purification, intangible as it seems, is the most potent means of revolutionizing one's environment and loosening external shackles. It works subtly and invisibly; it is an intense process though it might often seem a weary and long-drawn process, it is the straightest way to liberation, the surest and quickest and no effort can be too great for it.

The Salt Satyagraha was also a potent expression of constructive program. Not to be confused with the well-meaning but often tepid social enterprises we may associate with non-profit organizations, constructive program is the stuff of radical, self-reliant, community-based nation-building. Through the Salt Satyagraha, the Indian people concretely enacted the reclamation of an indigenous industry that had been forfeited to their imperial occupier. But, by way of the illegal grassroots manufacture and distribution of sea salt harvested directly from India's shoreline, the salt satyagrahis were out to reclaim far more than just one forfeited industry. They were out to reclaim their autonomy and their faith in collective self-reliance.

"We brought the English, and we keep them," Gandhi insisted. "Why do you forget that our adoption of their civilization makes their presence in India at all possible?" Constructive program, Gandhi taught—and the Salt Satyagraha demonstrated—enacts true civilization. That is, it enacts the establishment of a free and self-reliant society founded on justice and nonviolence.

Finally, the breach of the salt laws and the widespread ancillary forms of civil disobedience it catalyzed across the nation were dramatic expressions of nonviolent resistance in the political realm. This was the demonstration of satyagraha: nonviolent resistance; self-sacrificial, non-vilifying, militant love-in-action. This was the demonstration for which Satyagraha Ashram had been "deliberately kept in reserve"—the demonstration for which the 78 had been diligently preparing. In the end, the direct action sparked by the Salt March carried on for a full year—during which time thousands of resisters were imprisoned. With Gandhi's signing of the Gandhi-Irwin Pact, which marked the end of the campaign, many Indians were deeply disappointed by the lack of concrete gains from their year of ardent struggle. Nevertheless and indisputably, the Salt Satyagraha was a major tipping point for the movement. When the campaign finally came to its close, the proverbial writing was on the wall. Louis Fischer, one of Gandhi's first and best biographers, explains:

> India was now free. Technically, legally, nothing had changed. India was still a British colony… [But] Gandhi…made the British people aware that they were cruelly subjugating India, and he gave Indians the conviction that they could, by lifting their heads and straightening their spines, lift the yoke from their shoulders. After that, it was inevitable that Britain should some day refuse to rule India and that India should some day refuse to be ruled.

Eventually I began to favor Gandhi's own language in the Venn diagram, substituting "satyagraha" for "political action," and—to some people's consternation—"self-purification" for "personal transformation." The phrase self-purification has an uncanny ability for hitting tender nerves. It tends to remind people of certain other hyphenated phrases starting with self, each it's own unique shade of off-putting—self-preoccupation, self-mortification, and self-loathing, for example.

We certainly have every right to be suspicious of Gandhi's puritanical tendencies. Truth be told, though, were he alive today I very much doubt Gandhi would use the phrase self-purification as he did a century ago. But the phrase is spread liberally throughout his teachings and writings, and I've chosen to let it stand. At bottom, Gandhi taught that something profound needs to happen at the level of the individual for the full power of nonviolence to be experienced and unleashed. If, for you, "self-purification" doesn't serve as a helpful marker for this essential piece of the puzzle, I hope you'll take this opportunity to do some in-house translating, resting assured that this facet of Gandhi's nonviolence approach, while certainly not devoid of his puritanism (which we'll discuss), invites us into an expansive and fundamentally positive and empowering world.

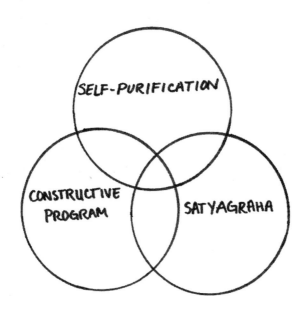

In 2010, Michael Nagler and his friends at Metta Center for Nonviolence added another rendering of Gandhi's threefold approach to the mix, which is well worth checking out too. They call it the Roadmap.

Then, just last year I discovered that Joanna Macy, beloved Buddhist author, teacher, and visionary, was working a strikingly similar three-part construction into her prophetic Work That Reconnects writings and gatherings. The Work That Reconnects boldly asserts that our collective and diverse efforts to transition from our exploitative and destructive "industrial growth society" to a truly "just and life-sustaining society" represent a new and pivotal epoch in our human evolution. Joanna suggests that this monumental shift might best be called the Great Turning, a phrase I feel perfectly answers our current need for an overarching visional statement. During this period of civilizational do or die, with its unfathomable depth of suffering and possibility, Joanna observes that the Great Turning is "happening simultaneously, in three areas or dimensions that are mutually reinforcing": (1) Holding Actions in Defense of Life; (2) Transforming the Foundations of Our Common Life; and (3) A Fundamental Shift in Perception and Values. (Loosely translated: (1) satyagraha; (2) constructive program; and (3) self-purification.)

When I asked Joanna if she was aware of the remarkable similarity between her model and the various descriptions that Sharp, Burrowes et al had devised for the Gandhian approach to nonviolence, she told me that she had no idea, but that she wasn't at all surprised to learn of it. "I think the model must be archetypal," she said, and I agree. All those *ah ha* moments I've witnessed over the years when folks are exposed to this simple recipe suggest to me that this formula resides in us, waiting only to be recognized and put into practice.

Out of the blue, a third evolution of my own presentation of this three-part model came to be. It was the day before I was scheduled to facilitate a daylong workshop, when a young man phoned to inquire about it. He had heard that I was conducting a nonviolence training. The workshop was called "Gandhi and the Call to Integral Nonviolence."

"A training for nonviolent direct action, right?" he asked.

In answer, the well-worn cliché jumped from my mouth: "That's just the tip of the iceberg." Then I went on to explain that the phrase *integral nonviolence* was meant to denote Gandhi's holistic and comprehensive nonviolence philosophy and way of life. While the workshop would certainly consider direct action, I explained, the day would be devoted to giving an overview of the whole Gandhian Iceberg. I briefly described the three essential areas of Gandhian experimentation, and explained that they were three expressions of one, integrated whole, each sharing the same fundamental nature, and each blending into and enriching the others.

As soon as I was off the phone I grabbed a pen and paper and drew the Gandhian Iceberg for the first time. A bit of a twist on the common metaphorical depiction of an iceberg, which only indicates two parts—the huge, hidden mass of ice under water and the much smaller, proverbial tip of the iceberg above water—my sketch made room for all three elements of the Gandhian approach by locating the iceberg's tip (satyagraha) on the outermost edge of the ice. A simple re-working of the Venn diagram I had been using previously, the drawing added a helpful element of scale and showed that the three parts of the model don't merely overlap, they're all of one indivisible substance.

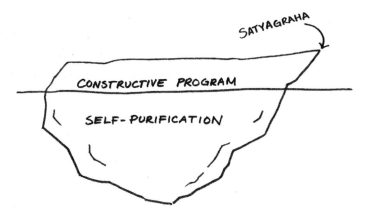

This sketch gives this book its basic structure, with chapter 1 tackling what's common to the entire iceberg, and chapters 2, 3, and 4 treating its three not so distinct parts one at a time. In chapter 5, I offer up several concrete proposals as to how we might pull the whole thing together in immediate, radical service to the Great Turning.

Whereas the Venn diagram conveyed the interconnectedness of the model's three parts in the overlapping center of the illustration, with the iceberg we can picture those aspects of the Gandhian approach that represent a combination of two or all three of the model's elements as being located at the waterline, where the water rises and falls. And yes, often the swells will even lap up and over the tip of the iceberg. The main point is that the boundaries between the three categories are meant to be amorphous. Because of that, and though it may seem counterintuitive, don't feel distressed if you sometimes get confused about which chapter you're in. In a strange way, that may actually be a good sign.

Integral nonviolence is leery of compartmentalization. While writing this book I've often caught myself thinking of the inner as separate from the outer, of the political and the spiritual as somehow mutually exclusive. But of course the personal and the social, the physical and the mystical, are all interwoven. To a large degree, that was Gandhi's entire point.

Therefore, despite the fact that the iceberg provides a map for our journey together, I encourage you to not take it or any of the aforementioned variations of this three-part model too seriously. A model's a model after all, and some of the best practitioners of an integrated and comprehensive nonviolence have done fine without this one. Always, the work is to mine for the riches underneath.

The three-part description is a tool with the express purpose of illustrating that Gandhi's approach to social change is based on his understanding that the building blocks of a nonviolent society are the vibrant, productive, nonviolent lives of individuals. Effective nonviolent political action does not spring from a vacuum. It grows out of daily living grounded in personal and communal spiritual practice. It grows out of constructive service to one's community. Nonviolence on the political stage is only as powerful as the personal and community-based nonviolence of those who engage in it. For this reason, while again acknowledging their fundamental interconnectedness, Gandhi clearly prioritized constructive program above resistance in the political realm, and self-purification above all.

The importance of the ashram experience flows from this understanding, a fundamental aspect of the Gandhian design that almost entirely eludes those of us in the United States. Here, we most often employ the reverse order of Gandhi's threefold approach, seeking a political response first, the building up of a constructive alternative second, and the stuff of all-out personal reformation third, if at all. This reversal allows even the most dedicated activists to sidestep foundational aspects of Gandhi's nonviolence recipe: not least among them, radical simplicity, disciplined spiritual practice, and the forging of solidarity and heart unity across bitter lines of social division. Because we do not believe that nonviolence requires these of us, we miss the significance of the ashram experience.

No one can build a nonviolent life as an individual. I may be able to practice some measure of piecemeal nonviolence more or less on my own. But if I'm going to pluck the seeds of war, inequality, and climate change from each part of my life that I possibly can, if I am going to renounce and abandon the violence inherent in my first-world way of life, I need the accompaniment of others whose knowledge, wisdom, and experience will complement mine, and whose example and company will inspire me to stay the course.

The members of Satyagraha Ashram who were the cadre of "foot soldiers" Gandhi chose to be the nucleus of the Salt Satyagraha were doing this for one another over a period of nearly 15 years. Lest we romanticize this, they were doubtlessly years fraught with the full spectrum of ups and downs, comings and goings, betrayals and beauties that typify life in community. The point is that all that it was, as imperfect and incomplete as it must have been, proved enough to prepare the 78 for the high level of sacrifice that Gandhi foresaw: "Not a single believer in nonviolence* as an article of faith

---

* I've taken it upon myself to remove the hyphen from Gandhi's mentions of nonviolence, in hopes of curtailing some very understandable confusion. Today, the hyphenated version of the word, non-violence, which was the version Gandhi and his contemporaries used, is increasingly understood to represent the most rudimentary expression of nonviolence, which is merely the abstention from the use of physical force. Whereas nonviolence (no hyphen) has come to denote the holistic and comprehensive approach to nonviolent living and struggle that Gandhi sought to model.

for the purpose of achieving India's goal should find himself free or alive at the end of the effort."

Should find *himself* free or alive?

Yes, throughout this book I've allowed the sexist language in Gandhi's (and Martin Luther King Jr.'s) quotations to remain as is. On one level this simply cues what by now has become for most of us a routinized inner translation process, where we revise antiquated language to better reflect our respect for *everybody*. On a deeper level, however, the presence of such language in this book signals a different and far more complicated challenge.

I've produced this book about Gandhian nonviolence from the only vantage point I have—that of a white U.S. heterosexual male with lots of formal education. There's quite a bit more to me, of course, but that doesn't alter the fact that each of those characteristics leaves an indelible imprint on my thinking and writing. There's also no altering the fact that white supremacy and patriarchy have seen to it that most of the individuals who have worked out the going theories on nonviolence, its relevancy and implications—at least the theories that are widely known and easily accessible—come from the same or a similar demographic as mine.

Preceding and during this writing process, I have made a diligent effort to stay awake to and observant of the secret side of nonviolence history, where the voices and wisdom of women, people of color, and otherwise marginalized individuals and communities can and must be heard. I'm nevertheless painfully aware of my limitations, and I anticipate that many a reader will find me stumbling here and there as a consequence of my blind spots. I hope such readers will both bear with me and lovingly call me to task.

A great many of us have been immersing ourselves in anti-oppression work, in recent years especially, recognizing that a bold, honest, and often acutely uncomfortable effort to understand and take on racism, sexism, heteronormativity, and a host of other embedded systems and patterns of oppression is utterly crucial right now. Like dauntless active nonviolent resistance in the public arena, the transformative work of undoing oppressions from a root causes level—spanning as it does the intrapersonal, interpersonal, and systemic—clearly exemplifies where Gandhian nonviolence and the Great Turning are calling us. I hope that in some small way this book and the questions it raises will help move this critical process forward.

Before shifting gears, one last flag: In addition to the sexist language in the quotes of Gandhi and King, the word *untouchable* also appears frequently in this book. Thankfully the term is now seen as derogatory and has passed out of common usage. Nevertheless, during Gandhi's time *untouchable* was the common referent for India's most oppressed and excluded castes, and the word appears universally in the source material I worked with throughout my writing process. I decided, therefore, that substituting *Dalit*, the popular self-chosen and contemporary political name for India's most oppressed classes, or *scheduled castes*, India's widely used legal term for the groups formerly known as *untouchables*, would have led to undue confusion.

Back to our story.

Gandhi's mention of "India's goal" in "When I Am Arrested" opens up an extremely important topic for us. We need to talk about success and failure. For those of us steeped in the conventional western success narrative, where winning (so-called) is everything, this may be disorienting and unsettling terrain. But, if we're true to Gandhi we see that his nonviolence standpoint fundamentally contradicts and rebukes what our culture teaches us to desire, feel, and see as success. I've come to believe that the shift in our understanding of what it means to be "successful" may be one of the most significant of our lives.

In an article about Jesus' botched career as an activist, Will Braun explores the theme of what he calls "holy failure." At the end of the piece he asks himself: "In all my efforts, how can I best nurture the holiness, tenderness and beauty that will live on even when the powers prevail?" In *Daring Greatly*, Brené Brown's powerful study of courage, shame, and vulnerability, she poses a question that cuts to the same chase: "What's worth doing even if I fail?"

I'm not bringing up the concept of "holy failure" in order to spin an apology for losing. I know that the desire to "win" is inextricably linked with the desire for justice, the desire to alleviate suffering, the desire to make our planet livable for ourselves and future human and non-human generations. But I've come to believe that we're so trapped in the dominant win-lose paradigm that we can't see the way it blocks our creativity, our vision, and our ability to respond with full integrity.

I've come to think of it this way: This thing we call nonviolence is the pearl of great price. Our job—and what an honor it is to be able to take it up—is to use it, to preserve it, and to pass it on. Picture a lit candle—providing an unfathomable, beautiful, and mysterious light of indescribable power. It dispels the darkest darkness, and yet, like most wonderful things, it's extremely modest and vulnerable. Preserving the light requires steady vigilance. Picture a small, motley, and earnest crew, raising their hands to shield the flame from whatever wind might blow it out. The flame is nonviolence, integral and unadulterated—nonviolence as Gandhi taught it. The people are those of us called to preserve it. Regardless of the seeming victories of Empire ("... even when the powers prevail..."), regardless of the failures and inadequacies of those of us who would like to see nonviolence launched full-power in response to any number of current crises and oppressions, regardless of whether or not nonviolence will ultimately prevail and "save us" or "save the planet," this remains our core intention: to protect the teaching—as best we can manage to interpret it—and to put it to use with full effort, because it reflects the beauty that is in us, regardless.

It also happens to be our best chance, our only chance really, at a future worthy of that beauty. I hope this book helps to illustrate why.

Reflecting on success and failure also invites us to recast or relinquish our notions of Gandhi's sainthood. The historians have unearthed far more than enough to prove that the "great soul" was, in fact, utterly human, with his fair share of blind spots, weaknesses, and mistakes. What we have of Gandhi's life narrative—which represents an unusually expansive and open book—is dappled with self-contradictions and plenty of evidence that Gandhi was not immune to the prejudices of his times and culture. He, like all of us, was a human being in process, deeply shaped by his conditioning, and profoundly redefining and reinventing himself along the full course of his life's path. We already noted Gandhi's consistent use of sexist language, which was obviously in keeping with the custom of his times. But from our present vantage point, in view of the ultimate vision of nonviolence, justice, and equality that so define his legacy, several other aspects of Gandhi's story are far more jarring.

We marvel, for example, and rightly recoil at Gandhi's imperial loyalism during his formative South Africa years, 1893-1914, when he pursued his bid for Indian civic recognition by way of Aryan racial and cultural solidarity with the British Empire. As predictable as it was for an Indian of his station and status at that time, Gandhi's attitude toward black Africans during this period was disturbingly racist and elitist. In 1908, for example, after his first stint in a South African prison, he wrote:

> We were then marched off to a prison intended for Kaffirs*... We could not understand not being classed with the whites, but to be placed on the same level as the Natives seemed too much to put up with.... Kaffirs are as a rule uncivilized—the convicts even more so. They are troublesome, very dirty and live almost like animals.

"In his battle to hold the empire to its 'promise' of equality for all who subscribed to its narrow, evolutionary notions of 'civilized culture,'" writes

---

* Kaffir is a derogatory word for black South African, sometimes likened to the word nigger.

South African essayist Thembisa Waetjen, "Gandhi both accommodated and deployed the worst of its premises." During the South Africa period, Waetjen continues, "Gandhi's humanism and moral radar excluded indigenous Africans and betrayed irrefutably racist views on human diversity." It would take some profound wake-up calls to eventually rouse Gandhi from his loyalty to the British Empire and its racist underpinnings—including his volunteer service as a nurse tending brutally wounded Zulus, both combatants and non-combatants, during the horrifically bloody Boer War.

Arguably, Gandhi's tendency toward loyalism was just as strong with regard to gender roles. From our vantage point today, Gandhi's devotion to India's traditional family structure and values likely appears in stark contrast to his professed commitment to the liberation and uplift of women. And, as we'll discuss in chapter 2, Gandhi's puritanism with regards to sexuality, which he never did shake, and which fueled his rigid objectification of women as agents of either shame or honor, is as much a part of his legacy as is his revolutionary pro-women advocacy. Gandhi's antiquated views on the Indian caste system (which we'll visit in chapter 3), set alongside his unwavering disavowal of untouchability, are similarly discordant and perplexing.

And of course, over the expanse of Gandhi's entire life, there are other areas where his views or his "experiments with Truth" were clearly misguided and hurtful to others—where, in other words, Gandhi seemed intent on opposing the very things he so passionately claimed to stand for. Some of these areas will be helpful for us to explore, while others would do little more than distract.

Gandhi was a mixed bag, and it's important to acknowledge it. This reminds us that he was a human being, for starters, but it also—I hope— gets us thinking about ourselves, our own relationship to leaders, and our attachment to the myths of our leaders' perfection. Perhaps, for some of us, it will also get us thinking about that part of ourselves that relishes in blasting leaders or tearing them down. This book seeks neither to rationalize Gandhi's wrongdoings, nor apologize for them. Rather, it seeks to welcome Gandhi down from the pedestal—strengths, weaknesses, historical and cultural contexts, and all—so we might learn something of his discoveries about nonviolence, and so we might improve the living of our own lives. In other words, so we might reinvent ourselves.

What I'm saying is that freeing Gandhi from the pedestal frees us too. How else would we be able to relate to him as an equal in both greatness and brokenness? It has proven especially meaningful to me, as someone who has walked many bitter miles with depression, to know that Gandhi too struggled mightily with despair, especially during his final years. In her lauded biography, *Gandhi: Prisoner of Hope*, Judith Brown writes: "Given his increasing frailty, his battles with himself, his suppressed anger and his isolation, it is perhaps little wonder that as he aged he suffered from bouts of extreme dejection and loss of confidence."

At the end of his life, Gandhi spoke frequently of his intense sense of isolation, remarking that he felt that no one had actually understood the essential meaning of nonviolence:

I see through them… I know India is not with me.

I deceived myself into the belief that the people were wedded to nonviolence.

I must confess my bankruptcy, not that of nonviolence… India has no experience of the nonviolence of the strong.

I failed to recognize, until it was too late, that what I had mistaken for ahimsa [nonviolence] was not ahimsa, but passive resistance of the weak.

In the India that is shaping today there is no place for me.

Gandhi's lifelong companion and beloved wife Kasturba had recently died, as had Mahadev Desai, arguably Gandhi's closest friend. And then, the partition of India and Pakistan—brokered by the British as a condition of Indian independence—broke his nation and his heart in two. Imagine it. In light of the tragedy of partition, Gandhi refuses to attend the ceremony when the British relinquish control, entrusting India to her own nationhood. The independence for which Gandhi is revered, hard-won over decades of nonviolent battle and perseverance, is followed by partition's fratricidal bloodlust, taking the lives of one million—yes, *one million*—men, women, and children, and displacing another *fifteen million*. The Indian people who in their quest for freedom had refused to inflict violence against the British, inflict it on one another the moment the British hand over the baton of governance.

Gandhi's seventy-eighth birthday fell a few short months after India's independence was made official. Birthday greetings, gifts, and congratulations flowed in:

> Would it not be more appropriate to send condolences? There is nothing but anguish in my heart. Time was whatever I said the masses followed. Today, mine is a lone voice… I invoke the aid of the all-embracing Power to take me away from this 'vale of tears' rather than make me a helpless witness of the butchery by man become savage.

Gandhi's despondency is mirrored twenty years later by Dr. King. Those close to King confess that during his final months (and intermittently before that) he battled depression, and that he too felt increasingly alone in his unshakable commitment to nonviolence. As the "triplet evils" of racism, materialism, and militarism bore down on the nation, King's nonviolence philosophy and commitment were drawn more and more into question by proponents of Black Power and black nationalism. Further, his stand against the war in Vietnam and his blistering condemnation of U.S. capitalism alienated him from friends and detractors alike.

People suffer in isolation. Gandhi and King were no exceptions.

"Our greatest failure."

Meeting Gandhi down from the pedestal forces us to wrestle with hard truths. Perhaps the hardest one of all, and the one that the pedestal tries best to conceal, is the one that Anand Mazgaonkar pointed to so matter-of-factly: Gandhi did not reach the most central goals he set for himself and for his nation. Far from it.

To illustrate, we can simply recall that the 78 who launched the Salt March did so in order to *demonstrate* satyagraha for the Indian nation. Gandhi knew that the people were in need of a demonstration because satyagraha was something they continually struggled to understand and adopt. The same was also true of constructive program and self-purification over the course of the entire struggle. Even with the powerful demonstrations Gandhi and his core followers were able to orchestrate, India as a whole never caught on to the comprehensive, life-encompassing nonviolence that Gandhi practiced and taught. The best he was able to wrest from the national movement was an acceptance of nonviolence "as a policy," but not—with the vital exception of a tiny band of serious practitioners—as "a life force" and "an article of faith." At bottom, the Indian independence movement was not a Gandhian movement. Gandhi-inspired, yes. A movement with Gandhian elements, definitely. But a Gandhian movement? No.

After partition, true to form, Gandhi credited this to his own failure as a leader, concluding, in effect, that he had moved too quickly for his nation. Whether Gandhi moved too quickly or the nation moved too slowly, it is painfully clear that India never caught up to her leader when it came to nonviolence.

But the same holds true the world over and across history. Our own present-day U.S. context provides a model illustration. Many in the U.S. today are actively engaged in one or two of the three elements of the Gandhian Iceberg, but seldom do we find nonviolence jugglers keeping all three torches up in the air. We also notice that many who might appear from a distance to be engaging with the Gandhian recipe actually remain deeply embedded in the dominant paradigm. That is, their efforts in the realms of personal transformation, community uplift, and political resistance do not stand in true opposition to the status quo, but are fundamentally beholden to it. By way of example, considering the element of resistance, we see that a great many people are up for old-line pacifism, rejecting violence, but mainly from the sidelines. Such activists rarely propose a viable alternative response to extreme oppression and heinous inhumanity, nor genuinely offer up their own minds—let alone their bodies—in service to developing such an alternative. We also see a great many others who are good to go with non-violence, the hyphenated kind—that is, non-violence as an expedient tactic—but who keep good old fashioned violence in their back pocket just in case. To such well-meaning activists as these, Gandhi said: "Nonviolence is not a garment to be put on and off at will. Its seat is in the heart, and it must be an insep-arable part of our being."

This reality check leads to a troubling and thrilling realization: The nonviolence of Gandhi's conception has only been experimented with to a limited degree. The impact of his efforts and the extraordinary witness of other nonviolence practitioners across the globe are incredibly impressive. But that doesn't change the fact that at this point Gandhian nonviolence remains largely theoretical. We have yet to see this stuff launched in real life at anything approaching full-power.

It may feel a bit surreal, but we're now called upon to go where Gandhi and his co-workers never went, and where all his successors to date have never gone. And I'm guessing you'll agree with me that in the age of the Great Turning that sounds just about right. It's going to take something more than we've seen up to now—ever—to turn this sucker around.

When I discovered the three-part Gandhian framework, the 78 foot soldiers, and the 15-year timeline, I figured I was really on to it. So much so that I took this 3/78/15 analysis on the road, along with some juicy history, concepts, and practices to further flesh out the Gandhian philosophy.

I led weekend workshops for lots of folks in lots of places, and they all built up to the same straightforward hypothesis: As soon as our own critical mass of serious integral nonviolence practitioners (our own 78) assembled themselves in community and committed themselves to a protracted period of concerted training, we'd have a corps ready to demonstrate for *our* nation the true meaning of the word satyagraha. Furthermore, went the second part of the hypothesis, such a corps, if located near the heart of a bona fide social movement, would generate enough joy, beauty, and power to create the gravitational pull needed to mobilize the numbers and support for seriously transformational struggle.

I facilitated such workshops off and on for ten years. The lay of the land being what it was, and what it largely remains, the 3/78/15 analysis resonated almost universally for participants, *and* something like one out of every one hundred of them seemed to genuinely wrestle with the possibility that s/he might actually *be* one of the hypothesized 78. Over the course of that decade those ones in a hundred never did cohere into a unified community experiment. They, and obviously a good number of others that I've never met, remain scattered all over the country.

But here's the rub folks: Time's up.

In recent years my own work has mostly been in support of the movement to end the U.S. system of mass incarceration. Zoom out from there and you can't miss the connection to mass deportation. Zoom out some more and you see how the prison-deportation industrial complex dovetails with the military industrial complex—private prisons, border walls, aid to Israel, perpetual war in Afghanistan, murderous drones and so much else bearing the same immoral signature. Zoom out a little more and the entire wide-angled context of U.S.-sponsored winner-loser capitalism comes into focus, epitomized most strikingly, perhaps, by one unimaginable statistic: The richest 62 individuals on the planet now control more wealth than half of the entire human population combined.

Zoom out from there, just a smidge more, and the full-blown existential crisis of climate change subsumes it all. As much as our internal defenses and denial might try to convince us otherwise, this isn't fictional.

Since 1970 we have melted 85 percent of the Arctic's summer ice. Atmospheric methane, which in 2014 reached 254 percent of the level it held prior to industrialization, is now being released by thawing Arctic permafrost. Because methane is eighty-four times more potent a greenhouse gas than CO^2, climate scientists warn that, unless checked, rising temperatures will result in a "permafrost carbon feedback loop" that will usher in global warming that only a new ice age could reverse. At the time of this writing, we're coming to the close of the hottest year ever in the 135 years since we began monitoring climate. The last thirteen of fourteen years were all record breakers. In June of 2012, a rainstorm hit Mecca, Saudi Arabia, despite temperatures of 109 degrees. It was the hottest downpour in recorded history, until just two months later, when the little town of Needles, California, was pelted with rain while the temperature soared to 115.

Scientific consensus asserts in no uncertain terms that we risk catastrophic consequences worldwide if the globe warms by more than two degrees Celsius.* In order to stay below that tipping point, humanity's estimated remaining carbon budget is roughly 565 gigatons of CO^2. The fossil fuel industry has five times that amount ready to extract and burn. They spend $90 million per day in exploration and project $27 trillion dollars of profit from their holdings. Yet eighty percent of these known reserves must stay in the ground if we're going to stay at or below the two degrees Celsius limit.

As I write this, thousands upon thousands of slash and burn-initiated fires, exacerbated by climate change weather patterns, are blazing across the full-length of Indonesia—a stark example of the type of capitalism / climate change feedback loop that will become increasingly commonplace in the months and years to come. Most of the Indonesian fires were started

---

* Scientists and climate change activists in our planet's drier, hotter bioregions—in Africa, for example—insist that 1.5 degrees Celsius represents a much more realistic upper limit.

deliberately by palm oil plantations, and their carbon emissions are currently accounting for ninety-seven percent of Indonesia's total emissions. While the fires burn, Indonesia surpasses both China and the United States as the world's worst emitter. (The U.S. is five times as big as Indonesia geographically and twenty times as big economically.)

In the twenty-four hours that make up this day an estimated one hundred-fifty to two hundred species of plant, insect, bird, and mammal will become extinct. This is roughly one thousand times the planet's natural rate of species extinction and is greater than anything the world has seen since the dinosaurs vanished sixty-five million years ago.

I'll say it again: As much as our defenses and denial might struggle to convince us otherwise, this isn't fictional. Under the circumstances it has become painfully clear that the only reasonable response must be utterly radical and immediate.

If I'm not mistaken, we're at the critical juncture—"the threshold"—that legendary teacher and mythologist Joseph Campbell describes in his rendering of "The Hero's Journey."

Here's a paraphrase:

A deep and resonant call is sounded and received. Preparations are made and a journey is begun. Mysterious and magical forces are unleashed. Unexpected guides step in to accompany and support.

A threshold is reached.

Most stop at it and proceed no further, knowing that crossing over would be an irreversible leap, the beginning of real and true death for the old self, the old life. But the choice to stop is the choice to enter a "wasteland." We might label it progressive. Those in this wasteland may have become more radical than the mother culture, but their fundamental devotion to conformity, accommodation, and safety remains. Familiarity and distraction still enjoy their allegiance. The maps of their true hearts remain unread, and they gradually become shadowlike. They gradually become simulations of themselves.

A few at the threshold, however, have the courage to cross over. A road of trials, death, and rebirth awaits them. They enter a new reality. They see the world more clearly than ever before. They risk all they've known and give their lives over to mystery.

They are tempted and tested.

They battle.

They summon as yet unknown powers and allies.

They atone.

They face a dragon, each of them—a dragon that is both personal and cultural. They let go, surrender, die to self, and are purified.

"You come then," Campbell explains, "to the final experience of discovering and making your own that which was lacking in the place from which you departed."

Those who have survived the journey this far receive, or on some occasions steal, a great and singular treasure. Along with it comes the duty to return. A great gift that was hidden can now be shared, and so the hero goes back to where she began.

It's the archetypal human struggle, this Hero's Journey, and it's known in one form or another to every culture in the world. Always and everywhere, despite benevolent accompaniment and aid, the journey is fundamentally an individual and solitary venture. We each receive our own unique call. We each set out alone. Campbell warns us, in fact, to steer clear of the tracks left by others, lest they lead us "astray entirely."

But the individual and the collective are nevertheless and utterly inter-twined. We know this foundational principle of integral nonviolence well. We are not islands. Until we who have come to experience the true meaning and promise of Gandhi's teaching make a bold and collective leap, some part of each us—even those among us who appear to have crossed over—will nevertheless remain on the wasteland side of what might be.

One of my principal motivations for writing this book is that enough of my fellow integral nonviolence practitioners have confirmed for me that our many and varied calls all bear the unmistakable imprint of the Great Turning. It's paradoxical, that while the Hero's Journey undoubtedly remains an individual and solitary venture, we nevertheless find ourselves here, together, at the threshold. And I've begun to think that our exodus now from the wasteland, as individuals and as a collective, may be the crucial requirement that marks the commencement of the Great Turning's first full-fledged action phase.

Theologian and author Walter Wink has a simple and profound label for the immense and deadly web of oppressive and destructive systems, forces, attitudes, and patterns that express and perpetuate human violence in all its forms. He calls it the Domination System. (It's a system, by the way, which is not separate from us. We're part of it.) I read Wink in the late nineties, but it wasn't until this year when I read Naomi Klein's book, *This Changes Everything: Capitalism vs. the Climate*, that I began to get what I experience as a true feel for the Domination System's reach. Klein's book, which of course is one of many that have done this, places all of us and all conversations in the context of the inconceivable danger and possibility of this moment in our species' evolution. It's terrifying how few acknowledge this definitive truth about our place in history.

We bring that with us as we attempt to understand Gandhi's contemporary relevance. There's no other conscionable choice.

And because there isn't, I've had to face the hard fact that Walter Wink and Naomi Klein have me fully convinced that the 15-year hourglass—the one for the collective nonviolence training period I was envisioning—got turned over long before I discovered "When I Am Arrested" and put two and two together. In fact, by now, the last grains of sand in that hourglass have already fallen or are in midair.

Which brings me to my bottom-line point: Ready or not, it's time for our dispersed community of serious integral nonviolence practitioners—many of whom *have* been at it for 15 years, or more, and many of whom, luckily, are really quick studies—to come together, to plant our collective feet on the solid ice beneath us, and to make our way out to the tip of the iceberg.

By design and necessity, self-purification and constructive program will of course imbue our action on the frontlines, and they will remain priorities one and two in our long-term vision. But, in answer to the signs of the times, as was the case when Gandhi and his co-workers launched the Salt March, the balance of our energy and focus must now shift to incorporate full-fledged satyagraha against the forces of the Domination System.

At the tip of the iceberg, we'll no doubt gain some extremely helpful perspective, not to mention some magnificent allies. Out there, it will become readily apparent that we are part of a vast movement of movements in the making—an as yet amorphous macro-coalition that is gradually coalescing in defiance of the Domination System and on behalf of the Great Turning. (We'll consider the movement of movements at some length in chapter 5.) My hope is that we'll come to see that we are called to serve this emerging and overarching Great Turning alliance, as a small but unified integral nonviolence submovement. My further hope is that, at the movement of movement's bidding, and with the knowledge that we are intrinsically interdependent with its great array of constituent communities of struggle, we—like Gandhi's 78—will demonstrate satyagraha, and through it the comprehensive and holistic nature of nonviolence. That is to say, when the time comes, I hope we'll give our full effort to demonstrating an integral form of love-driven revolution.

Okay. We're just about ready to turn to the iceberg.

But before we do, three key questions—one or the other of which you may very well be asking yourself—deserve some attention.

The first is this:

What about those of us who are committed to an integral Gandhian approach to nonviolence, and committed to the cause of the Great Turning, but who are called to take on something other than the frontlines role modeled by the 78?

This iceberg is by no means the private domain of those on the frontlines of direct action. Our integral nonviolence submovement will feature a beautiful array of harmonized and essential movement roles, just as a symphony orchestra features a beautiful array of harmonized and essential instruments. Deeply committed and prepared nonviolence practitioners, folks who are definitely as "all in" as the 78, have gifts to give the movement that will need to be offered from someplace other than the direct action vanguard. (The same orchestra metaphor wholly applies, by the way, to the overarching movement of movements.)

For starters, and lest we forget, individuals on the frontlines of a struggle are able to fulfill their role because they're backed by a community of support. When Gandhi and his 78 co-workers left the ashram for the coastline, an equally important but unsung contingent stayed behind to tend the hearth and the gardens, and to care for the children. As Gandhi and the 78 marched from village to village, other contingents prepared the food that nourished them along the way and the camps where they laid their heads at night.

Our 78 and those who will offer them direct and indirect support, however, will represent only two sections of the orchestra. That is, they will be just two of the many nonviolent cadres that carry forth the work of our submovement. We are each gifted in different ways, and we're each called to express nonviolence in our own unique fashion. That said, to practice Gandhian nonviolence is to work with the whole iceberg. And, in the age of the Great Turning, "time's up" applies to all of us. Regardless of whether you experience a genuine call to be at the vanguard of head-on engagement with Empire— risking life and limb, prison sentences, and other forms of punishment and repression—we are all, I believe, called to and needed at the tip of the iceberg. And we're needed there now.

To illustrate the multiplicity of roles that await us out there, I'll offer an imaginative scenario. None of the examples below should be viewed as mutually exclusive. Nonviolence cadres such as these overlap and blend in innumerable ways (if we wanted to, we could draw another Venn diagram). Depending on how we and the struggle develop, some of us might devote ourselves to one such cadre, and some of us might participate with several of them at once, or move from one to another along the way.

Picture this:

As **the 78** move into position (which we'll discuss in chapter 4), backed by **the 78's community of support**, a cadre of **monastics and other full-time spiritualists** tune their prayer practices to the struggle, and spiritually infiltrate their respective faith communities with the urgency of the Great Turning and the call to integral nonviolence. They gather to meditate in public spaces where direct engagement is happening or will happen, and in spaces where conflict resolution processes and movement strategy planning are taking place. They host prayer circles for those on the frontlines, and for all those with whom those on the frontlines engage.

After bowing in honor of past musical trailblazers, a cadre of **musicians and songwriters** contribute to the building up of a brand new repertoire for the Great Turning. As this living soundtrack for the movement comes into being, they play and sing it out into spaces of active resistance, sharing and teaching it as they go, in communities of struggle all over the nation. They often collaborate with a cadre of **visual and theatrical artists** who orchestrate powerful and artistically stunning public actions and movement recruitment events. These artistic satyagrahis also beautify movement spaces, design and illustrate call to action literature, and create stirring visuals to accompany and inspire the action phase of the movement.

A team of **simplicity and resiliency pioneers** (maestros with natural building, local food, car-free living and organizing, appropriate technology, etc.) guide the unfolding mass movement activism so it models material simplicity, responsible stewardship of resources, and radical community-centeredness. With their help, the action phase of the struggle reflects the principles and practices driving the transition to a just and life-sustaining society.

The integral nonviolence submovement raises up a cadre of **orators and writers** to serve as spokespersons, inspirers, and meaning imparters during the movement's action phase. They help craft and communicate the movement narrative, describing with passion and precision the necessity of nonviolent resistance, and placing the struggle in its larger historical context, rooting it to the ages-old struggle for freedom.

Social justice educators team up to guide the submovement, and the overarching movement too, in an effort to hold Great Turning change-makers accountable to their own internal work and transformation in the realms of racism, sexism, heteronormativity, religious intolerance, and the like. In close consultation and spiritual kinship with people of color, white folks in this group spearhead a national campaign of white atonement and reparations for the victims of white supremacy (both past and present). In tandem with this national atonement and reparations campaign, a cadre of **gift economists** hit the road to lovingly persuade the financially privileged to also direct their surplus wealth in support of the action phase of the Great Turning. As they go, they propagate the gospel of the gift economy, teaching any with the ears to hear how to renounce and abandon the practices and mindset of winner/loser capitalism.

These cadres work closely with **interpersonal communication trainers and group process pioneers** who facilitate decision-making, dialog, mediation, and restorative circles within the submovement and the wider mass movement, and between the movement and its various counter-players over the course of the protracted struggle.

Throughout the nation, a dispersed integral nonviolence cadre of **teachers and youth advocates** accompany **young changemakers** in their experience of witnessing and participating in the struggle. They listen deeply to the youth, serve them as mentors and advocates, collaborate with them, and take their lead in bold new directions of nonviolent action and expression. This intergenerational alliance works together to clear the path for youth leadership at all levels of the struggle.

And, finally, a cadre of deeply trusted **strategists, analysts, and servant leaders** hold key posts at Movement Mission Control—studying, listening, observing, debating, collaborating, directing, evaluating, and adjusting, adjusting, adjusting as the Great Turning turns.

We could envision several more such roles with little difficulty. But the point is clear enough: There's plenty of room at the tip of the iceberg.

One caveat remains, however—an important one—in response to this first question. Digging in deeper we recognize that it's more complicated than it may have first appeared. All the foregoing notwithstanding, I believe that we shouldn't presume to know whether at some point the Great Turning will require all of us who are wedded to integral nonviolence to stand shoulder to shoulder on the frontlines. It may be that at a certain moment in the struggle we will hear our own version of Gandhi's call, that "This time...not a single believer in nonviolence as an article of faith...should find himself free or alive at the end of the effort." That is to say, perhaps at some point the ranks of the 78 will need to swell to include us all—with each of us in the orchestra setting our particular instrument aside in order to raise our voice, or perhaps hold silence, in a unified act of great, unbroken solidarity and power.

The second question is this:

What about those of us who want to commit to this approach and to this cause but who simply aren't prepared for the struggle?

It wasn't long ago that my primary vision for this book was that it would act as an on-ramp—that it would provide a Gandhian blueprint for folks setting out for a long course of preparation for full-powered, long-term nonviolent struggle. *This Changes Everything*, however, changed that. Circumstances being what they are, as I've already discussed, I'm no longer looking to team up with nonviolence practitioners seeking to emulate Gandhi's ashram for a 15-year period of getting ready. Rather, I'm reaching out primarily to practitioners who have already done their "15 years."

I believe, nonetheless, that the book still captures the makings of an honest-to-Gandhi and sturdy on-ramp, and I'm hopeful that many readers will use it as such. While for those already steeped in and committed to the Gandhian approach the book will likely serve as a familiar touchstone, describing much of what we've already been wrestling with, living through, and cultivating, for newcomers I hope it will represent a challenging and inspiring introduction. To young people new to integral nonviolence and who feel called at the deepest level to serve and defend life, I extend a special welcome. Your readiness and your great capacity remind us all that "15 years" is far more metaphor than hard-and-fast rule.

And, finally, the third question:

Why the focus on U.S. nonviolence practitioners when we're clearly facing a global crisis in need of a global response?

The Great Turning will indeed be an Earthwide undertaking, orchestrated by an as yet undreamed constellation of peoples from all corners of the world. Nevertheless, this book focuses specifically on the U.S. for two main reasons. The first is that this is where I'm from and this is where I'm based. It's a choice that has everything to do with a word we'll begin talking about momentarily, in chapter one: swadeshi. Nonviolence beckons us home, in a sense, to focus our energy and our work in the place where our historical and cultural rivers run. The second reason is that, because of the central role the U.S. plays in global plunder, capitalism, and militarism, the emergence of our U.S. integral nonviolence contingent holds particular global significance. No national community on Earth bears as much responsibility to get its house in order as we do.

Our shared illusion of national borders epitomizes our tragic lack of human unity. But national and other kinds of borders also demarcate distinct histories, mythologies, and patterns. Obviously such invisible lines also demarcate distinct wounds. And these things bring more to bear on the character and emergence of movements than we could ever quantify. Simply put, nonviolent organizing here in the U.S. will look and needs to look different than it looks in other parts of the world. The nonviolent vision, as

I understand it, heralds a constellation of strong, autonomous place-based groups working in sympathetic, mutually strengthening partnership. It's my hope that every land will raise up a multifaceted integral nonviolence sub-movement in service to its own national movement of movements, which in turn will place itself in service to the overarching global macro-movement of movements. In my view, an interwoven, worldwide nonviolence coalition, embedded at every level of this massive movement structure promises to bring immeasurable gifts to the unfolding struggle. First thing being first, though, as a U.S. nonviolence practitioner, my purpose is to help ensure that if and when such a coalition comes into being, our home team will not only be trained and suited up—we'll already be in the game.

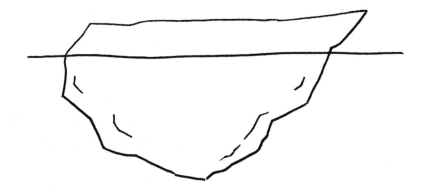

1.
THE ICE

LANGUAGE MATTERS. The words we use make a difference.

It matters that Martin Luther King Jr. and his co-workers made clear that the goal they sought was not adequately captured by the phrases "civil rights" or "racial equality." As important as those concepts were, and as truly as they represented core movement aims, King and others spoke of theirs as a struggle to build the "beloved community" and "to redeem the soul of America." It was a struggle for freedom itself, but our society favors the lowest common denominator. We look back on a "civil rights movement" and the far more spiritual, far more expansive, demanding, and promise-filled goals of beloved community and redemption are mostly lost—supplanted by what is, in comparison, a passionless legalistic tag.

It matters that a small handful of years ago the strong and steady voice of Michelle Alexander called the U.S. reality of mass incarceration by another name: the New Jim Crow. Those are words that reach in, words that get us more in the gut than between the ears. Words that locate the struggle in its appropriate context: the still-flowing and selfsame river of resistance, the African American Freedom Movement, that King was talking about.

The linguistic connection does not limit the struggle to African Americans, but roots what is a multiracial, multigenerational, multifaith struggle in the heritage and blessing of our nation's most powerful movement lineage.

I'm reminded as I share this that in the early stages of my own involvement in the movement to end mass incarceration, Michelle encouraged me to connect with Susan Burton, founder of A New Way of Life Reentry Project in South Los Angeles. Michelle could have recommended Susan to me as an expert in the field of re-entry for formerly incarcerated folks, which she is. But what Michelle said was different: "Chris, Susan's someone you need to meet. She's helping to build the new underground railroad." Again, Michelle is locating us in a particular place and in a particular way, through her careful choice of words. When I witnessed Susan and her work, the deeper truth was immediately evident. What Susan is doing to blaze a trail for disenfranchised and dispossessed former prisoners is indeed the building up of a new underground railroad. And that makes her, in a very real sense, a modern Harriet Tubman.

It matters to think and talk about things this way. It activates the heart. It inspires. And we need that.

Gandhi is credited with leading India to political independence from the British Empire through nonviolent means. The claim appears accurate enough, though there is a good deal of evidence to suggest that the shifting tides brought on by World War II had just as much if not more to do with forcing the Empire's hand than Gandhi ever did. Whichever the case, it turns out, the above synopsis of Gandhi's contribution is woefully incomplete. Unfortunately our tendency to link Gandhi so closely with the acquisition of political liberty does more to distract than enlighten. For starters, it tricks us into the political realm, where we are bound to underestimate if not entirely lose sight of Gandhi's own core goals. To be true to Gandhi, we are challenged to see political independence from Britain within the context of his primary personal motivation, which was to "see God face to face."

> What I want to achieve—what I have been striving and pining to achieve
> these 30 years—is self-realization, to see God face to face, to attain moksha
> [deliverance; liberation from the cycle of birth and death]. I live and
> move and have my being in pursuit of this goal. All that I do by way
> of speaking and writing, and all my ventures in the political field are
> directed to this same end.

Political independence must also be seen within the context of Gandhi's
overarching vision for the Indian nation, which was the establishment of a
social order in service to *sarvodaya*, "the uplift of all beings."

To see God face to face? The uplift of all beings? With aims as lofty as
these it's little wonder that we would opt to focus on the more manageable
and quantifiable realm of politics. But in so doing we all but lose Gandhi.

———

Ruby Sales was sixteen years old when she began working with the Student
Non-Violent Coordinating Committee in Lowndes County, Alabama. Voter
registration and community organizing in Lowndes' intense climate of racial
hatred was a deep plunge into the Southern Freedom Struggle. In August
1965, at age seventeen, Ruby stood beside her friend and co-worker Jonathan
Daniels—a white, Episcopal seminarian who had come to the South to join
the struggle—when he was shot dead without the slightest provocation. The
trauma of witnessing Daniels' murder sent Ruby into a period of complete
silence. It was several weeks before she uttered a word. Eventually, she stood
witness to testify at the trial of Daniels' murderer, a racist storekeeper named
Tom Coleman. Coleman, who shot Daniels at nearly point blank range, was
acquitted by an all-white jury after ninety-one minutes deliberation.

Ruby Sales' great depth of concern for others, the spiritual foundation of her upbringing within the embrace of the Southern black church, and what she describes as the spiritual accompaniment of Sojourner Truth, propelled her into a life of service and activism. She is described by her co-workers at SpiritHouse, a national organization that unites diverse people in the pursuit of peace and equality, as a "long-distance runner for justice."

I had the opportunity to interview Ruby in 2009, as part of my masters program. I was studying the African American Freedom Movement through the lens of Gandhian nonviolence, and the centerpiece of my self-designed program was an interview series with six veterans of the civil rights chapter of the movement. Ruby was gracious enough to participate, giving me the privilege of bearing witness to her hard-earned insight, and to the way she dances with language. It made sense to me, deep in, that one whose proximity to death and blind hatred had at one point moved her to utter silence, could teach me so much about the power of words. Language, Ruby argued, was capable not only of describing the motions of our hearts, dreams, and intentions. Language can catalyze and shape such as these. And language, she taught me, makes possible a common vocabulary of resistance. Ruby connected the boots on the ground nonviolence she participated in with the black folk theology she absorbed as a child reared within the Southern church community and tradition. This was the language and theology, she said, that Martin Luther King Jr. drew on to convey the nature of black people's experience, and which was the ground beneath the movement's feet:

> That theology infused the words of King when he talked about "a bright and morning star," "a lily in the valley," "a shelter in a raging storm," "a way out of no way," "captain of the ship"—all those metaphors that said that black people didn't give in to despair, because we recognized that while the Empire thought it was the architect of creation, we knew it was God that put breath in our bodies… Martin Luther King, and I, and other people who had grown up infused in that spiritual structure—we understood the response to be, the theology to be, "I am somebody… I might be poor, I might be black, but I'm somebody." "Poor little Jesus

boy, they didn't know it was you." That was a theology of somebodiness, a theology of justice and righteousness, a theology that said that we were somebody in a society that said we were nobody.

Ruby says that the individuals who formed the vanguard of the freedom struggle, most of them in their late teens and early twenties, were able to access a profound depth of courage because they stood on the solid ground of this vocabulary and theology of somebodiness.

In a different time, within a different culture, Gandhi and his co-workers stood on their own solid ground. As they carried forth India's freedom movement during the first half of the twentieth century, they too shared a common vocabulary of resistance and a theology of somebodiness. Whereas the mid-twentieth-century movement in the United States was rooted and propelled by powerful words from the Hebrew-Christian scriptures, often expertly blended by King with phrases from the U.S. Constitution and Declaration of Independence, the Gandhi-led movement in India found strength and direction in an array of words from India's rich Hindu spiritual heritage. This ancient vocabulary, along with a small number of deliberately chosen modern words, begins to bring Gandhi's teaching and example into focus and gives us a feel for the solid ground that he and his co-workers stood on as they went about their work to build a new society.

For those of us unaccustomed to Indian culture, making room for Gandhi the teacher makes room for a remarkable cultural exchange. And this exchange hinges largely on Gandhi's nonviolence vocabulary. For some of us who, in the face of unbearable injustice and suffering, are searching for ways to put the full power of nonviolence into concrete, direct, and immediate action, the prospect of a vocabulary lesson may seem off-putting. When it comes to Gandhian nonviolence, however, absorbing the core meanings of a fairly wide range of particular words is necessary in order to understand the philosophy, psychology, and spirituality that grounded the life which grounded the action. For anyone really serious about putting nonviolence into practice, excavating the core meaning of such words is not an academic exercise.

Some of us will also be averse to the religious tenor of this vocabulary. By referencing the special role of religiously-based language in both the African American Freedom Movement and the Indian Freedom Movement I do not mean to imply that overtly religious language is a requirement for principled nonviolent struggle. It would appear, though, that a vocabulary of transformation—a vocabulary of "justice and righteousness"—is necessary. In our modern, pluralistic context, I think it may in fact prove important that this vocabulary is *not* overtly religious, as we build movement together. But, paradoxically, whatever language it is must reflect principles and motivations that inspire us to grow above and beyond that which we currently are. It must be a language that points to that *something more* which for many of us sparks what's best described as a religious impulse.

Okay then, enough preamble; here come nine gems from the Gandhian lexicon that are all about solid ground. Or you could say, in relation to the Gandhian Iceberg, that these words and phrases describe the ice itself. This is important. We need to have a good feel for the ice, for its essence, before we consider the different parts of the iceberg. There are lots of other important words for sure, some of which we'll no doubt be looking at together, but these nine are pretty much the All-Star Team.

AHIMSA

Here is the Sanskrit word we usually translate as nonviolence. According to Gandhi it is "the greatest and most active force in the world." Ahimsa is built from the root *himsa*, which denotes the desire to harm or kill, and the prefix *a*, which fully negates that root. While a strict translation might be "lacking the desire to harm or kill," in Sanskrit the term has a purely positive character reflecting an understanding and experience of the unity of all that is, and of the limitless power of love. I find it a bit confusing how some negative words manage such positivity, while others don't. Eknath Easwaran, a devoted student and interpreter of Gandhi's life and teaching, offers a helpful example: flawless. It's a great word with such a positive resonance. I wish some of that resonance would rub off on the word nonviolence, which I fear is forever fated to fall pretty flat.

Easwaran goes on to describe ahimsa like this:

> When all violence subsides in the human heart, the state that remains is love. It is not something we have to acquire; it is always present, and needs only to be uncovered. This is our real nature, not merely to love one person here, another there, but to be love itself.

According to Gandhi, ahimsa/nonviolence is based on the core assumption that "human nature, in its essence, responds to advances of love." It is "the highest expression of the soul," he says, and "the more you develop it in your being, the more infectious it becomes." Ahimsa/nonviolence is "mightier than the mightiest weapons of destruction devised by the ingenuity of man," Gandhi contends. What's more, and what turns the world as we know it completely upside down, it is "invincible" and "knows no defeat."

Let's let that sink in for a minute. Invincible. Knows no defeat.

If Gandhi's right on this point that would mean that all debate as to whether or not nonviolence "works" is academic, that all challenges, real and hypothetical, to its efficacy are ultimately hollow. This would mean that nonviolence from a Gandhian perspective is not the same thing as the nonviolence (or non-violence) that we generally think, read, and speak about in our U.S. community.

"You just don't see what's coming at you from another paradigm," says Michael Nagler, "even if it's right before your eyes." From the standpoint of our culture's dominant paradigm, true nonviolence—undefeated and undefeatable—comes at us from so far out of left field that few are even aware there is such a thing. Located within our love-in-action-starved society we're conditioned to go on defending or challenging nonviolence and its usefulness by our usual standards. Nonviolence in its customary box. We see it and speak of it as a tactical or strategic style that we may or may not choose to employ within a given set of circumstances. Even those of us who have made a conscientious choice to seek a nonviolent response under any and all circumstances tend to store our understanding of nonviolence in a box labeled Tactics and Strategies.

But to align ourselves with the Gandhian understanding, if we're determined to place nonviolence in a box we would do well to label it Unalterable Laws. In Gandhi's mind, ahimsa is a law in the same way that the law of gravity is a law. It's no accident, incidentally, that he called ahimsa "the law of love." Like gravity, ahimsa is something we can choose to work with, or not, but our choice has no impact on what it is, or what it does, and the question of whether or not it "works" reflects a fundamental misunderstanding in and of itself. As a spiritual law, working with nonviolence will feel and look differently than working with gravity, but the two share an unalterable nature. If we miss this part, we miss the whole thing.

HEART UNITY

It's difficult to determine the best order for these, as they're all nothing less than essential to the whole. Nevertheless, I'm wagering that heart unity should be as close as possible to the law of love, more or less an addendum to it.

Heart unity is the phrase Gandhi used to describe the spiritual connection—be it an individual-to-individual connection, or group-to-group connection—capable of overcoming bitter division. It's the mutual inner experience of unity and love that creates the space where misunderstanding, distrust, and separation can be transformed. The words brotherhood and sisterhood come to mind. Something Dr. King said in *Where Do We Go From Here?* does too:

The ultimate solution to the race problem lies in the willingness of men to obey the unenforceable… Desegregation will break down the legal barriers and bring men together physically, but something must touch the hearts and souls of men so that they will come together spiritually because it is natural and right. A vigorous enforcement of civil rights laws will bring an end to segregated public facilities which are barriers to a truly desegregated society, but it cannot bring an end to fears, prejudice, pride, and irrationality, which are the barriers to a truly integrated society. Those dark and demonic responses will be removed only as men are possessed by the invisible, inner law which etches on their hearts the conviction that all men are brothers and love is mankind's most potent weapon for personal and social transformation. True integration will be achieved by true neighbors who are willingly obedient to unenforceable obligations.

We'll be talking a lot more about heart unity in chapter three, because it's an especially salient component of Gandhi's Constructive Programme—characterizing roughly half of its items. Gandhi looked on the bitter communalism that poisoned relations between Muslims and Hindus, the deep-rooted prejudice and discrimination leveled by the Hindu majority against untouchables, the mistreatment and domination of women by men, the gross disparity between the wealth of the rich and the poverty of the poor, the marginalization of lepers and aborigines, the exploitation of farmers and laborers—and he concluded that each of these represented an opportunity to heal division and to weave outcasts back into the core fabric of India's national life and character.

In order to do this, though, Gandhi did not point to the realm of state-sanctioned laws and policies. Dr. King illuminated the distinction well. When confronted with such social evils, the authentic solution can only be forged in the human heart. Gandhi challenged the Indian people to look inward, at the prejudices in their own hearts, stating that "before they dare think of freedom they must be brave enough to love one another…and to trust one another." So love and trust, forged across lines of bitter division, is a prerequisite for freedom. Imagine. In our era of mass incarceration and Black Lives Matter—of mass deportation, unparalleled economic inequality, rampant human trafficking, and homelessness—this indispensable prerequisite puts the enormity of our task in sharpest relief.

It also provides a helpful context for one of this book's most central and recurring themes: atonement and reparations. Just as love and trust cannot be forged in situations of active abuse, they cannot be forged in situations where past wrongdoing and the need for restitution are continually swept under the rug. Few of us need to look any further than our own families for proof that unresolved or unacknowledged trauma due to abuse or other wrongdoing doesn't simply go away of its own accord. Trauma stays. And, whether it's at the surface or buried down deep, it ceaselessly calls the oppressor, the abuser, the plunderer, to grieve, to apologize, to request forgiveness, and to offer whatever restitution possible. In situations where crimes against humanity have not been so acknowledged, deep and abiding love and trust—even despite our best intentions—remain out of reach.

TRUTH

Most authors in the gandhiana genre, and Gandhi himself, would start here. But the truth is that I find Gandhi's *Truth* a bit opaque. His core assertion on the subject is well known:

> If it is possible for the human tongue to give the fullest description of God, I have come to the conclusion that God is Truth. Two years ago I went a step further and said that Truth is God... You will see the fine distinction between the two statements.

Or maybe you won't. When we turn next to satyagraha we'll begin to see how capital T Truth figures in with active nonviolent resistance. But first I want to dig into it from another angle, a more recent interpretation that I believe is completely harmonious with Gandhi's conception of Truth/God, but which I find to be much more empowering.

This interpretation is featured in *Fate and Destiny: The Two Agreements of the Soul*, a fascinating book by storyteller and mythologist Michael Meade. I found the most compelling part of the book to be Meade's autobiographical account of his life-changing—more like life-*defining*—experience of following his conscience to the brink of death. It's a mesmerizing real-life example of the archetypal "Hero's Journey."

At the age of twenty, Meade was drafted into the army. The war in Vietnam was in full swing. Unconvinced that U.S. warmaking in Vietnam made sense, Meade sought conscientious-objector status. He was denied. After weeks of inner deliberation Meade reluctantly opted to accept the army's "invitation" rather than face a prison sentence. There was a strong legacy of military service in his family.

It didn't take long, however, for Meade and all those around him to discover that he was an awful soldier.

> There was a basic problem—I didn't take orders well. I had always been headstrong and willful and inclined to go my own way. Now, people were ordering me all over the place. At a certain point, I couldn't go along with it, couldn't do it, wouldn't do it, and couldn't be made to do it.

Just a few months after his induction into the army, still in training at a U.S. base in Panama, Meade's daily military regimen had become so punctuated by his selective refusal of orders—those he found to be "foolish or mean-spirited or clearly ignorant"—that he was court-martialed and assigned a lawyer. At this point, Meade knew for certain that his decision to join the army had been "a crucial mistake." As he had done when he sought conscientious-objector status, Meade expressed his honest and level-headed argument that he found no moral basis to justify his forthcoming role in the killing and dying that was the Vietnam war. He was sentenced to six months in the stockade.

From the moment of conviction I began a descent, not just in entering the prison, but a turning inward and cycling down. Of course, I was singled-out for special attention in the prison and subject to an endless series of orders, threats, and humiliating treatments. When I refused all orders I wound up in solitary confinement and stayed there for many months. I had chosen to enter the army rather than go to prison; yet I had wound up in prison anyway. Somehow, the choices for me had narrowed down until something like fate took over.

As punishment led to greater punishment, Meade's "descent" eventually led him to stop eating and to throw his uniform and bedding out of his cell. Naked and fasting, he demonstrated that he "wasn't present in any normal sense," that his non-cooperation was total—a demonstration that would take him to death's door.

As much as I'd like to, I'm not going to give away the ending of Meade's story. I hope I've shared just enough of it to entice you to read it yourself. When I did, I was transfixed by Meade's take on the words fate and destiny. In short, he argues that destiny is where we end up if/when we faithfully follow the dictates of what Gandhi called "the inner voice"—our heart of hearts, our conscience, call it what you will. By "where we end up" I mean both inwardly and outwardly. And fate is what life throws at us, all that happens to us, the countless opportunities given to us to align our choices and responses with our soulsense.

What blows me away about Meade's saga is the way he becomes a willing slave to his own soul. As he "cycles down," his capacity for self-knowledge deepens, his spiritual attunement to the promptings of conscience becomes more refined, and his commitment to being faithful to conscience becomes gradually unshakable. The result is that eventually Meade becomes, in effect, choiceless. His life is a series of more and more immediate, intuitive, and integrated responses. His mind, his body, his spirit become instruments of conscience, or you might say, instruments of Truth. One outcome of this is that Meade magnetically attracts Truth toward himself. At a certain point, his transparency takes on the quality that people ascribe to gurus who in their God-centeredness act as mirrors to the spark of divinity in those who seek their blessing. In his Truth-centered state, residing in the embrace of full alignment with his conscience, Meade—naked and starving to death—heard the confessions of guards and other prison staff who wanted what he had, the peace that passeth all understanding, which settles on us when our lives are completely congruent.

The vision of such congruency, by way of Meade's personal narrative, was an epiphany for me. I saw for the first time that what Gandhi refers to as Truth has everything to do with honesty. It may seem a dull epiphany at first glance, silly even. But, by honesty I actually mean Honesty: a level of reckoning or union between self and reality that casts out all illusion, and which sets us on course to discover our true identity, our true destiny.

"If a man reaches the heart of his own religion," Gandhi said, "he has reached the heart of the others too." Though your destiny journey will differ from mine, our true destinies are never at odds with one another. That is to say, the assumption with Meade's "destiny" is the same as it is with Gandhi's "Truth": It's all good. We needn't worry that someone's heart of hearts will actually and sincerely subscribe to violence. The resort to violence is itself a resort to unTruth, a missing of the mark in our approach towards our true destiny.

Yes, of course this leads to all manner of abstract philosophical rabbit holes. The rebuttals about violence as an inherent part of the natural order, for example, within which human beings have their rightful place—or, say, level-headed arguments many make in favor of consuming animal products untainted by the factory farm industry.

In response, first off, it's a good time to remember the central Gandhian assumption that all life is one. The expression rings as cliché, for sure, but imagine if we actually lived as if "all life is one" were true. Is there any doubt that we'd come to see it as the most revolutionary concept of all? To understand Gandhi, we need to anchor ourselves to that revolutionary foundation.

From there, we can join Gandhi in acknowledging that, ultimately, Truth and nonviolence must remain aspirations, unreachable beacons that we nevertheless attempt to reach. "Perfect nonviolence whilst you are inhabiting the body is only a theory like Euclid's point or straight line," he wrote. "But we have to endeavor every moment of our lives." According to Gandhi, as human beings all we can do is approach absolute Truth in baby steps, by way of relative (lower case t) truth. One step, then another, then another. Just as perfect sighting and interpretation of destiny's smoke signals is not going to happen, perfect adherence to Truth and nonviolence is not going to happen. This is why—often despite appearances—strict dogmatism is unGandhian. That said, at the same time—and this is crucially important—discipline most definitely has its place.

> What is Truth? A difficult question; but I have solved it for myself by saying that it is what the voice within tells you. How then, you ask, different people think of different and contrary truths? It is because we have at the present moment everybody claiming the right of conscience without going through any discipline whatsoever that there is so much untruth being delivered to a bewildered world… If you would swim on the bosom of the ocean of Truth you must reduce yourself to zero.

This "reduce yourself to zero" rubs a lot of people the wrong way. In my experience, women especially tend to challenge this framing, in view of the degradation of self brought on ceaselessly by patriarchy and misogyny. But Gandhi means doing what Michael Meade did, becoming a transparent and choiceless instrument of Truth, love, nonviolence. It means an experience of Honesty that enables us to accurately read and follow our inner compass. Folks who have made good progress on this assignment reveal that as it approaches this zero the human personality, far from vanishing or degrading, actually flourishes and becomes wonderfully resplendent.

SATYAGRAHA

I bet Gandhi would have turned at least twenty ecstatic cartwheels if he ever learned of Michael Meade's one-person satyagraha. The word, which I referred to quite a bit in the introduction, is a Gandhi original, coined as a corrective for the label "passive resistance." As Louis Fischer notes: "There was nothing passive about Gandhi... [He needed] a better name for this new kind of mass-yet-individual opposition" that he had begun to experiment with in South Africa. *Satyagraha* did the trick. The word denotes active nonviolent resistance by combining *satya*, meaning truth or soul, and *graha*, to cling or grasp. Satyagraha (adherence to truth, soul force) links outward nonviolent resistance to the spiritual power that is its inner essence.

Fischer's phrase, "mass-yet-individual opposition," is almost definitive. Almost, because satyagraha is sometimes purely a one-person affair, as Meade so ably demonstrated for us. Nevertheless, Fischer's description underscores that satyagraha is always a bold expression of personal dignity, autonomy, and purpose. (Let's keep this in mind when we discuss swaraj later in this chapter.) Whether it's set in motion by a lone individual or by a group, if it's satyagraha we can rest assured that all those involved have prepared themselves to stand alone whenever necessary.

Gandhi's speech on September 11, 1906 (the other 9/11), which preceded the collective satyagraha pledge of nearly three thousand nonviolent resisters in South Africa, offers a stirring description of what such standing alone actually entails:

> There is only one course open to me...to die but not submit to the law [Britain's racist Asiatic Registration Act]. Even if the unlikely happened and everyone else flinched, leaving me to face the music alone, I am confident that I will never violate my pledge. Please do not misunderstand me. I am not saying this out of vanity. But I wish to put you, and especially the leaders on the platform, on your guard... If you have not the will or the ability to stand firm even when you are perfectly isolated you must

not...take the pledge... Although we are going to take the pledge in a body, no one may imagine that default on the part of one or of many can absolve the rest from their obligation. Every one must be true to his pledge even unto death, no matter what others do.

Clearly, the readiness and capacity of each satyagrahi to go it alone in such a way would lend great strength to a nonviolent battalion.

In *Stride Toward Freedom*, Dr. King notes six of satyagraha's most fundamental characteristics. In truncated form, nonviolent resistance (satyagraha):

1. is active and courageous, not passive and cowardly;
2. seeks reconciliation, not victory over;
3. distinguishes injustice from persons behaving unjustly;
4. requires the willingness to suffer without retaliating;
5. rejects physical and spiritual violence (hate, ill-will, humiliation, deceit, etc.); and,
6. is rooted in the conviction that the universe is on the side of justice and truth.

As an addendum to number six above, I will add that Gandhi's nonviolence philosophy was deeply impacted by his great optimism in human nature. Louis Fischer remarks that this quality "sometimes made Gandhi sound naïve"—a simple yet extremely important observation. There is something essential to Gandhi's overall attitude and orientation in that naïveté, or semblance thereof. Rather than writing him off when he begins to sound naïve, we'll do well to remember that Gandhi operates in an altogether different lane than any who would subscribe to the reigning winner/loser paradigm. Such recognition allows us to consider our own lives in relation to that paradigm, and to test whether or not we're giving it our undue allegiance.

Ironically, and as a further addendum, number six is also a place where I perceive that King and Gandhi play into our conventional success narrative in a subtle and seldom recognized way. I came to this conclusion when I discovered that a belief in number six was not essential to my nonviolence commitment. What I mean to say is that even if number six were not true, and the universe was either on the side of injustice or neutral on the matter (I don't have a hard time believing in such an impartial universe), I would still choose love. Why? Because the inner voice tells me that's how it is with me. That's who I am.

At the same time, I believe I have experienced something of the truth of number six. It's something like falling into an invisible stream or current which flows continuously in the direction of goodness and wholeness, a stream or current that is present and available to everyone at all times, whether or not we enter it. I believe I've dipped into it a handful of times in my life, usually on occasions when I've managed to get in sync with my true vocation. I think it's what Meade is describing in relation to destiny and congruence, and what Gandhi is referring to when he speaks of Truth and the inner voice. I can begin to get a handle on number six, I realize, when I see it as Meade's destiny or Gandhi's Truth writ large. (Very large.)

But, again, for me at least, the existence of such a stream or current does not necessarily signify that the universe as a whole is on the side of justice. I don't feel qualified to draw that conclusion. Nor does it signify to me that those of us who struggle for what's right are guaranteed a victory lap at the end of the game. All I know is that I want to enter that stream as much as possible and surrender myself to its current.

I nonetheless recognize and respect King's and Gandhi's rock bottom faith that ultimately the vast universe is on the side of justice, and I know that such faith represents the heart of the matter for a great many of us. It has sustained innumerable souls, sometimes through the fiercest of fires. "In spite of everything," one such soul, Anne Frank, wrote:

> I still believe that people are really good at heart. I simply can't build up my hopes on a foundation consisting of confusion, misery, and death. I see the world gradually being turned into a wilderness, I hear the

ever-approaching thunder, which will destroy us, too. I can feel the suffering of millions, and yet, if I look up into the heavens, I think that it will
all come right, that this cruelty will end, and that peace and tranquility
will return again.

A brief comment about number two as well (*Satyagraha seeks reconciliation, not
victory over*). The spirit of reconciliation and cooperation is not limited to the
end game. Throughout the struggle the satyagrahi is willing to be persuaded as
she attempts to persuade. This is a nod to our inherent limitations as holders
and interpreters of Truth. Gandhi was adamant that all parties to a conflict
hold at least a fragment of Truth and that, by its nature, the satyagraha
method invites forth such Truth fragments from each and every side. The
spirit of this conviction runs so counter to the vast majority of activism today
that its great significance is likely to evade us. "A nonviolent revolution is not
a program of seizure of power," Gandhi wrote. "It is a program of transformation of relationships, ending in a peaceful transfer of power." Conflict,
nonviolence insists, is an opportunity to restore relationship. This explains
why patience, humility, and respectfulness are the marks of a true satyagrahi.

Before leaving satyagraha I'll confess to a disappointment I have with
the way the word has come to be used. Gandhi argued that satyagraha was
by no means confined to the realm of politics or what we call activism. The
home setting was as good a theater as any for its practice. Gandhi's wife,
Kasturba, in fact, provided him with his first potent object lesson in the art
of satyagraha. The Gandhis' grandson, Arun, explains:

No one knew better than Kasturba that Mohandas' pursuit of perfection
could sometimes become hurtful to those whom he hoped to perfect. But
my sensible grandmother also knew by long experience how difficult it
was in such cases to find words that would convince her stubborn husband
he was being unwise or unjust. So Ba used her own behaviour, a quiet
form of persuasion by Satyagraha, to bring about a change in Bapu's
attitude. Indeed, it was she who first instructed him in these techniques.

"I learned the lesson of nonviolence from my wife," Mohandas once confided in an English friend… "Her determined resistance to my will on the one hand, and her quiet submission to the suffering my stupidity involved on the other hand, ultimately made me ashamed of myself and cured me of my stupidity."

The family home and other close quarters have been almost completely supplanted by bigger overtly political arenas as the inferred contexts for satyagraha. I fear that this has led to a good deal of misunderstanding about the true nature of soul force. I'm guilty of reinforcing it myself whenever I emphasize the public or politically-oriented facets of the tip of the iceberg, without mention of its close-to-home essence and origins. By flagging the way that might mislead, I hope to mitigate that at least a little.

We'll talk a whole bunch more about satyagraha in chapter 4. So, for now, let's move on to some simple but earthshaking math.

MEANS=ENDS

If we had to reduce Gandhi's nonviolence philosophy to its simplest form this would be it.

Nonviolent outcomes cannot flow from violent motivations, approaches, or tactics. If the ends sought are things like freedom, peace, reconciliation, justice, harmony, community, transparency, dignity, and respect, then the means must reflect the same tenor of those ideals. Revenge, secrecy, verbal and physical attacks, slander, insult, dishonesty, deception, exploitation, neglect—such as these can only lead to violent outcomes. "There is one thing about violence/nonviolence that is very simple and predictable," Michael Nagler says, "and it may be the only basic thing we have to know about it: somewhere, somehow, violence will always hurt, while somewhere, somehow, nonviolence will always heal." ‹

As we discussed in relation to Truth, this is not to suggest that one can approach any given situation or conflict with utterly pure and unadulterated nonviolence. But the law of means=ends insists that whatever you reap you sow. Very simple cause and effect: Nonviolence gives way to nonviolence; violence gives way to violence; a mix of the two gives way to a mix of the two. Gandhi held this theorem as absolute.

In terms of our daily lives this is where the rubber really hits the road. In our world, especially in the heart of the hyper-industrial, hyper-technological Empire, navigating the means=ends equation will humble us ceaselessly. Our chosen actions are so frequently a jumble of violence and nonviolence. Consider our diets, our clothing and transportation, the spaces in which we live. Consider our interpersonal relations and communication, our parenting, our work in the world. If awake to the means=ends reality, we become acrobats on a ropes course of constant moral dilemmas.

Like Michael Meade in the brig in Panama, we hope to be able and willing to heed the advice we receive from our inner voice. But that means we need to hear it. Which is where spiritual practice comes in. I'm not going to be able to rationally determine if it's morally superior to fly halfway across the world to serve on a peace team, or, rather, to refuse to do so out of love and respect for the biosphere. But an inner voice, or what a friend of mine calls "the more ancient place" inside us, can furnish the answer we seek—if we're able to access it. This takes practice and experimentation, which we'll be talking about in the next chapter when we explore self-purification.

These means/ends acrobatics point to another paradoxical twist. We want to take means=ends very seriously, the Gandhian schema quite literally hinges on it. And, we want to hold this simple equivalency lightly at the same time, honoring that we're imperfect, in process, and facing down a hydra with a thousand heads. If we succumb to perfectionism we're doomed to disappoint ourselves, and probably others, and to project a dour and dogmatic air that won't ingratiate a single soul to us, or to the nonviolence we espouse. But, if we strike a good seriousness/lightness balance, joy and integrity will get to strut their stuff arm in arm, and people will take notice. Not that getting noticed is the goal. Nevertheless and to our credit, we human beings are drawn by joy and integrity, and that's going to work to the Great Turning's advantage the further we walk the path of nonviolence.

One last comment on means=ends, of chief importance: Our human limitations deny us the ability to know the form or timing of outcomes. Most if not all of us are painfully aware of this already, but the reminder can be helpful. Rosa Parks did not and could not know that her choice to keep to her seat would spark more than a decade's worth of nonviolent struggle in a new, nation-changing chapter of the African American Freedom Movement. But it did. The politicos and physicists who forged the nuclear technology of the early to mid-1940s did not and could not know the extent of terror, suffering, and global insecurity their experimentation would set in motion. But it did.

DETACHMENT

And because our human limitations deny us the ability to know the form or timing of outcomes, Gandhi counseled detachment, the great principle he absorbed from his spiritual reference book, *The Bhagavad Gita*:

> By detachment I mean that you must not worry whether the desired result follows from your action or not, so long as your motive is pure, your means correct. Really, it means that things will come right in the end if you take care of the means and leave the rest to Him.

To the extent that our motives and means are pure we can trust that the outcome will be a good one, regardless of whether it's an outcome we can picture or which we actually desire. At its root, spiritual detachment accepts that only God (however we may understand ultimate reality, or *not* understand it) knows the best outcome. Our job is to keep the means in good order, and practice equanimity with whatever results may come.

Gandhi emphasized that we needn't only be on the lookout for the lows that come with apparent failure or setbacks, but also the elation that usually follows apparent victory or progress. Whether you're climbing up or down a ladder you're in a precarious position. Better to stand on the ground—steady, calm, and composed. According to Gandhi, that's what we're after if we're serious about long-haul struggle.

Easily said. But detachment represents some of our heaviest spiritual lifting. We're talking about giving everything we've got, then managing peaceful good cheer when all our hope and effort nuzzle into that handbasket and head promptly to hell. And we're not talking about getting a bad grade or missing a bus connection, we're talking about our best laid plans and best made actions to alleviate real life pain and suffering. To see such efforts go up in smoke and to know that the suffering persists or even worsens—no, this detachment thing is Herculean in such situations. Trusting that such outcomes are somehow all for the best from some disembodied divine perspective? That's a bitter pill when you're a witness to or recipient of brutalization or oppression, when your heart is burning with anger, grief, or fear.

And yet, that doesn't change the fact that this is what Gandhi taught, in keeping with countless other teachers from and beyond his religious tradition. Just because I can't or don't live up to it doesn't mean that's not exactly what he meant.

SWADESHI

I mentioned this one in the introduction when explaining why this book specifically addresses nonviolence practitioners in the U.S. A literal translation of swadeshi might read "of one's own country," but the modern terms "localization" and "localism" steer us much closer to Gandhi's way of thinking. Michael Nagler calls the principle of swadeshi "globalism in reverse."

Gandhi taught that our action in the world should begin with and for the benefit of those nearest and dearest to us, then extend outward from there. When, in 1936, Howard and Sue Thurman met with Gandhi and invited him to the United States to assist in the struggle for racial equality, Gandhi declined, saying that the best thing he could do for the U.S. struggle was to provide an "ocular [i.e., visible] demonstration" within his own context. His belief was that we can be most effective, and are called to be most effective where we're physically based. The implications in his context were especially powerful in terms of eradicating untouchability, building heart unity between Hindus and Muslims, liberating women, revitalizing village industries, promoting and modeling educational reform, advocating sober living, and many other projects that needed to be embraced at the village level in order to really take root. As Michael Nagler astutely observes, at the time of the Thurmans' visit to India, Martin Luther King Jr. was a precocious and sometimes naughty seven year-old. Consider the impact Gandhi's "ocular demonstration" would eventually come to have on the soon to be Rev. Dr. King and, in turn, on the phase of the African American Freedom Movement for which he would serve as chief spokesperson.

Swadeshi is a powerful proposition, perhaps most cogently captured by Gandhi's simple, but supremely revolutionary assertion that "a man's first duty is to his neighbor." "If every one of us duly performed his duty to his neighbor," Gandhi argued, "no one in the world who needed assistance would be left unattended. Therefore, one who serves his neighbor serves all the world." Gandhi's high dream for India was a return to the social structure experienced by his ancestors: a constellation of autonomous, self-sufficient, mutually beneficial and cooperative villages. He was bold enough to confess his hope that the state would eventually wither away altogether. If everyone tended to his or her neighbor, Gandhi the anarchist concluded, society would find itself functioning on a human scale that would render the monolithic state obsolete.

In the United States, you can't get much more countercultural than this. To illuminate swadeshi in concrete terms Gandhi once used the example of a barber. If luck would have it that you live in a village with a barber whose skills leave something to be desired, Gandhi explained, the thing to do is *not* to up and travel to a neighboring village where an expert awaits with curlers and mousse at the ready. The swadeshi response would be, rather, to frequent and support your local barber so s/he can hone the needed skills. Makes sense, right? But this is so utterly antithetical to the capitalist compact, which has made certain that few if any would wear a bad haircut as a badge of honor the way Gandhi would. But that's the call.

Even more countercultural is the way swadeshi forces us to go without altogether. Gandhi's take on the matter is characteristically plainspoken and, to me, particularly inspiring. When asked about the "innumerable machine-made things" that were beginning to be imported to India, or in some cases manufactured there, Gandhi said: "My answer can be only one. What did India do before these articles were introduced? Precisely the same should be done today." Gandhi was talking about a shift that represents a complete reorientation for those of us in the U.S., even those of us trying to live more "sustainably" or trying to reduce our "ecological footprint." Rather than seeking ways to manipulate things externally so we can continue to have what we want—low-flush toilets, electric cars, fair trade chocolate, etc.—the call is to change things internally so we want something different. Gandhi's answer, to choose to do things the way they used to be done, puts in sharp relief how lazy, spoiled, and atrophied most of us have become in the age of high tech. Fighting words, I know.

It's important to note the obvious and paradoxical fact that Gandhi, swadeshi's great proponent, obviously ventured far beyond the village sphere. His work took him not only across the length and breadth of his own motherland, but as far afield as the British Empire's home base in London, and its prized colony, South Africa. Apparently, Gandhi discerned that there were valid exceptions to the rule of swadeshi, occasions when one's dharma, or spiritual path, led an individual into wider orbits. Similar contradictions and inconsistencies dapple Gandhi's statements on a variety of topics, some of which we'll discuss in the pages to come. With regards to swadeshi, however, whether or not we allow for the occasional exception, the principle sets our default invisible boundaries close to home, providing a means for re-fashioning a profoundly neighbor-centered society.

Before leaving the principle of swadeshi I'd like to point out that it has had a major impact on the inner structure of this book, which I hope will help rein us in whenever we begin to wander too far ahead of ourselves. The book's primary concerns move outward in concentric circles, swadeshi-style. The principal concern of the book is the individual who feels or will feel led to be part of a U.S.-based integral nonviolence submovement. Moving outward from that starting point, the book's secondary concern is the integral nonviolence submovement itself. And moving outward still, the book's third, outermost concern is the wider national movement of movements that the integral nonviolence submovement aims to serve. Clearly this is plenty of terrain for us to cover. We can leave our critical exploration of wider international movement alliances, and of the overarching global movement of movements itself, for another, not too distant time.

SWARAJ

My personal favorite. Again a powerful linguistic-spiritual coupling, with the prefix *swa* (same as in swadeshi) meaning self, and *raj* denoting rule. The usual translations are self-rule or home-rule, both of which are conventionally interpreted to mean political liberty. But Gandhi used this term comprehensively. Leadership theoretician, James MacGregor Burns, explains:

> In Gandhi's reformulation of the concept, swaraj stood above all for freedom, both political and spiritual. While he accepted Western liberties of thought and speech, true freedom meant 'disciplined rule from within.' Swaraj fused independence from racial or colonial oppression with inward liberation, a transformation of both society and self; indeed, the 'swaraj of a people,' he said, was the 'sum total' of the swaraj of individuals.

The beginning place is personal self-rule. On the surface this means self-reliance and self-sufficiency. But underneath that is the true engine of swaraj: the personal experience of one's own dignity, integrity, and worth.

King nails it again:

> The tendency to ignore the Negro's contribution to American life and to strip him of his personhood is as old as the earliest history books and as contemporary as the morning's newspaper. To upset this cultural homicide, the Negro must rise up with an affirmation of his own Olympian manhood. Any movement for the Negro's freedom that overlooks this necessity is only waiting to be buried. As long as the mind is enslaved, the body can never be free. Psychological freedom, a firm sense of self-esteem, is the most powerful weapon against the long night of physical slavery. No Lincolnian emancipation proclamation or Johnsonian civil rights bill can totally bring this kind of freedom. The Negro will only be free when he reaches down to the inner depths of his own being and signs with the pen and ink of assertive manhood his own emancipation proclamation. And, with a spirit straining toward true self-esteem, the Negro must boldly throw off the manacles of self-abnegation and say to himself and to the world, "I am somebody. I am a person. I am a man with dignity and honor. I have a rich and noble history. How painful and exploited that history has been. Yes, I was a slave through my foreparents and I am not ashamed of that. I'm ashamed of the people who were so sinful to make me a slave." Yes, we must stand up and say, "I'm black and I'm beautiful," and this self-affirmation is the black man's need, made compelling by the white man's crimes against him.

Let's forgive Dr. King the sexist focus on manhood and harvest this as an amazing description of the personal side of the coin that is swaraj.

As we do, we move close to the heart of King's nonviolence philosophy—and Gandhi's too. Both held that the human personality, uniquely embodied in every individual, is of inestimable worth and significance. As Michael Nagler argues, this belief is inherent to nonviolence itself: "For every nonviolence advocate throughout time, it has been axiomatic that life is sacred… While the sum total of all life is in a way more precious than that of a given individual, in a way it is not. Infinity equals infinity." The assertion cuts to the core of swaraj. "A shift in emphasis from the lower to higher self of the human individual," M.P. Mathai explains, "was the point of departure for Gandhi in his pursuit of a new social order…The individual is the key figure in all transactions…the measure of all things and the supreme consideration."

This philosophical premise, which goes by the name personalism, places the preservation of personal human dignity at the center of all things Gandhian—and Kingian. When reading Gandhi you'll want to keep a lookout for personal dignity by other names too. He just as often referred to it as self-respect or honor. If the word *honor* rings a bit Marine-esque to you, I doubt Gandhi would flinch. For him, honor was our most precious birthright, something worth battling for with all one's might, something to lay down one's life for, if necessary. Gandhi didn't shy away from words that invoked a call to sacrificial battle, trusting that people were quite capable of interpreting martial-sounding metaphors.

As self-evident as the importance of personalism may appear, it's really important to name and own it. The personalist conviction, after all, is not only the basis of Gandhian swaraj, it's the basis of our love of enemy stance, of our preferential option for reconciliatory closure, of our satyagrahic belief that all parties to a conflict have some piece of the truth to bring to bear. At bottom, this personalism stuff is at the heart of our nonviolence, the ice of the iceberg.

Gandhi the personalist dreamed of an independent India comprised of individuals who experienced swaraj in their own hearts, just like King described above, and in the outward living of their daily lives. He longed to see the individuals who comprised the national community experience their full and beautiful stature as human beings. In order to understand Gandhi's work, this reformulation of swaraj is absolutely essential. It allows us to see the yardstick with which he measured India's readiness for action and her progress on the road to restoration. "This was Gandhi's refrain," Louis Fischer summarizes, "dignity, discipline, and restraint would bring Indians self-respect, therefore respect, therefore freedom."

For quite some time now I've carried a vague but persistent hunch that in the present U.S. context this word swaraj and Gandhi's way of using it to turn political liberty inside out is of special and major importance. I think those of us who recognize our own occupied status and our collusion with the forces of Empire, should do what we can to fully grasp and embody swaraj, and to see the Great Turning itself as a swaraj movement. Perhaps it's because of our society's extreme individualism that I feel this way—that only the integrated transformation of self and society can bring us an abiding experience of something truly worthy of the word freedom.

Lastly, let's be clear that Gandhi's insistence that political freedom was bound up with personal inward freedom was never meant to perpetuate a spirituality disconnected from concrete, outward expression. Political independence rested on the Indian people's reclamation of their sense of personal dignity, as evidenced not by adherence to a given set of spiritual disciplines devoid of concrete social significance, but by principled daily conduct that gave outward expression to true self-discipline, and which represented the greater society's strides toward liberation. While this work of reclaiming one's full stature as a human being was essentially spiritual, its mark was transformed patterns and behaviors in daily life.

SARVODAYA

As mentioned in the introduction, sarvodaya means "the uplift of all beings." Gandhi used the term to reference the new, just social order he envisaged—a social order that would serve the greatest good of all life. Independence from Britain was important, terribly important. But Gandhian nonviolence does not shy away from the highest of dreams. With sarvodaya we see Gandhi's grand vision for India, and by extension the whole world, which places the struggle for independence from the British Empire in its proper context and under its appropriate heading.

Grounded in the core belief in the oneness of everything, sentient and non-sentient, and in the principles of nonviolence, sarvodaya means equal opportunity for all people to develop all dimensions of their personhood, within a world teeming also with nonhuman life. Gandhi explored frameworks for the building up of a sarvodaya order in the realms of the social, the economic, the political, and the educational.

In our own context today, I see the Great Turning as an excellent analogue for sarvodaya and hope that it will be the banner we gather under as we carry out our work together. In their book, *Coming Back to Life*, Joanna Macy and Molly Brown describe the Great Turning like this:

> If there is to be a livable world for those who come after us, it will be because we have managed to make the transition from the Industrial Growth Society* to a Life-Sustaining Society. When people of the future look back at this historical moment, they will see more clearly than we can now, how revolutionary our actions were. Perhaps they'll call it the time of the Great Turning… They will recognize it as epochal. While the agricultural revolution took centuries and the industrial revolution took generations, [the Great Turning] has to happen within a matter of years. It also has to be conscious—involving not only the political economy, but the habits, values and understandings that foster it.

Macy and Brown present a vision of movement—they sometimes use the word revolution—that is intrinsically holistic and deeply inclusive. At the foundation of the Great Turning is the core understanding of the inter-connectedness of manifold forms of oppression and degradation: from environmental destruction to war to mass incarceration; from homelessness to economic inequality to hunger; from racism to sexism to religious intoler-ance; from assembly line education to genetic engineering to animal cruelty.

---

* The phrase "Industrial Growth Society," coined by eco-philosopher Sigmund Kvaloy, includes but expands on "capitalism." This is because state-controlled industrial economies are just as likely to be dependent on extraction and consumption as those economies we usually associate with the word "capitalism."

In the face of all of these and more, the Great Turning is an ever-expansive umbrella for our every prayer and action in defense of life and justice on Earth.

I believe that our continued existence—and that of countless other species—will largely depend on the extent to which our as yet disparate movements identify and embrace one integrated, transcendent, and unifying vision. We can no longer afford to pursue our individual efforts in isolation from one another, or worse, to have them work at cross-purposes. We need to truly and mutually support one another and draw collective inspiration from our shared attempt to usher in the new epoch, here, as we are, at the eleventh hour.

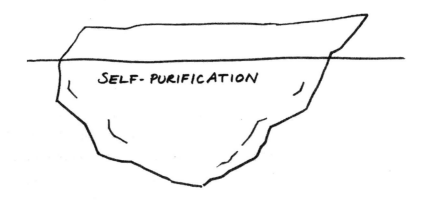

2.
UNDER WATER

I'M NOT ENLIGHTENED. Nor do I ever expect to be. Mine is not the voice of an Eckart Tolle, or Ammachi, or Dalai Lama speaking from the other side of that mysterious borderline. I come at this thing as a baffled and broken seeker.

It is true that for many years I've studied the role self-purification plays in the Gandhian schema, and that I've conducted a great many experiments with it in the laboratory of my life. It is also true that, as I write these words, the inscrutable chemicals of my pharmaceutical antidepressant of choice are coursing through my body, that I'm estranged from my nearest and dearest friend, and that I'm aware of my acute fear of what I might witness when I return to Palestine next month, and of a certain marrow-deep loneliness that I desperately hope isn't awaiting me there. Whatever authority I may have to talk about Gandhian self-purification, I assure you, doesn't come from that distant country called Illumination. If anything, it comes from the school of hard knocks. The school of keep trying.

I'm happy to report, nevertheless, that I've learned a handful of unmistakably golden things at that illustrious institution. For example: Not being enlightened doesn't mean I can't be ready for what's coming.

———

A few months following my interview with Ruby Sales, I had the rare privilege of interviewing Harry Belafonte. Yes, Harry Belafonte, the world famous singer and actor. But more to the point, Harry Belafonte the visionary freedom fighter. Indeed, the "King of Calypso" was and remains a deeply influential member of the African American Freedom Movement, and he was a close friend and confidant of Dr. King. Belafonte and King were born just two years apart—Belafonte being the older of the two—and their perspectives on life and movement were deeply resonant. Because Belafonte held himself completely apart from the church and the black preacher circles that King usually moved in, their friendship represented a place of repose for Dr. King, a place where he could relax, sometimes vent, and simply be.

At one point during the interview, to my surprise, Belafonte told me that Dr. King had a tic, a subtle hiccup-like gulp that would come and go. The tic's existence was far from common knowledge. Only those close to King observed it. "Sometimes it was more severe than others," Belafonte said,

> then it would go away. But it was always constantly in the neighborhood. And then he came to a point when it just wasn't around anymore. I didn't see it. And I remember saying to him, "Martin, I notice you don't have that tic. Is it still around?" And he said, "No, it's gone." I said, "Wow, how did that happen?" And he said, "I made my peace with death." I said, "You made your peace with death?" He said, "Yeah. It no longer preoccupies me. It doesn't threaten me." In the very deep sense. He said, "I'm concerned about leading others to their death, but not about my own."

———

ALIGNING PRINCIPLE AND PRACTICE

Gandhi's aim was to personify a purified and liberated India, and he called on any who would listen to join him in the pursuit. "Apply everything to yourself," he wrote to his cousin, Maganlal, for example. "Nobility of soul consists in realizing that you are yourself India. In your emancipation is the emancipation of India. All else is make believe."

As I alluded to in the introduction, for a lot of people the phrase self-purification conjures up some pretty repellant images of things like hairshirts and sackcloth. For others, meditation and fasting come immediately to mind. And yes, such spiritual practices (the latter two at least) were part of Gandhi's regimen.

But Gandhian self-purification is a comprehensive and holistic process that expands far beyond what are commonly thought of as spiritual disciplines. Gandhi sought to enact swaraj in his own life—and to openly display the interwoven nature of its inner and outer dimensions. Self-purification, as Gandhi taught it, is the personal side of the swaraj equation. As such, it is never separate from the social sphere, nor is it about achieving a certain spiritual state for one's own personal aggrandizement. Self-purification, rather, is about tuning the instruments that we are, readying the individuals that we are, so we can represent in our own lives and persons the world we seek to build and inhabit, and so we're ready to serve. In other words, our efforts in the realm of self-purification are deliberately made to clear the way for constructive program and satyagraha. Throngs of well-meaning folks make great strides in inner work—spiritual, psychological, and emotional—undertaken, for many, over the course of years or even decades. But far too few of us go the next crucial Gandhian steps and offer ourselves fully to radical service and sacrificial nonviolent resistance.

It's an all-encompassing process that requires an immense amount of courage—or what Gandhi spoke of just as often, fearlessness, which was one of the eleven vows and observances at both of the ashrams he established. This courage/fearlessness was not only needed in order to face death, it was needed in order to face life and to live it with full integrity.

Self-purification from a Gandhian standpoint is obviously a vast and expansive arena. I've nevertheless found it helpful to work with a concise definition. Here's the best one I've managed so far:

> *Gandhian self-purification is the work of getting real about our core principles and commitments, and bringing our behavior into alignment with them.*

In other words, self-purification is all about aligning principle and practice. Close observer of Gandhi that he was, Louis Fischer came to understand this process of alignment, and its necessity, exceptionally well:

> Millions had read Ruskin and Thoreau, and agreed with them. Many Hindus had read them and agreed with them. But Gandhi took words and ideas seriously, and when he accepted an idea in principle he felt that not to practice it was dishonest. How can you believe in a moral or religious precept and not live it?...The gulf between word and belief is untruth. The dissonance between creed and deed is the root of innumerable wrongs in our civilization; it is the weakness of all churches, states, parties, and persons. It gives institutions and people split personalities.

So, at its root, Honesty is the alpha and omega of Gandhian self-purification. And it takes more than courage alone to practice it. The aspirant, Gandhi argues, also needs one-pointedness—a laser-like and resilient focus of attention, intention, and energy.

Courage and one-pointedness fuel self-purification; self-purification generates courage and one-pointedness. When given the chance to roll this can be an incredibly powerful cycle.

And, in case you're wondering, it's a cycle that needn't be experienced as drudgery or self-flagellation. When asked whether he could encapsulate his approach to life in three words, Gandhi didn't hesitate: "Renounce and enjoy," he said. Eknath Easwaran translates those first three words of the Isha Upanishad even better: "Renounce and rejoice." Either way, the takeaway is the same. According to Gandhi, a full 50 percent of the assignment has everything to do with joy.

Can we take words like congruency, integrity, discipline, one-pointedness, principle, and commitment, patiently hold them in our hearts, and recognize their promise of deep joy? In the end, self-purification is nothing more or less than our journey into authenticity, our journey into an experience of who and what we truly are. It is the discovery of our vocation. The root of the word comes from the Latin *vocatio*, meaning "a call" or "a summons." Self-purification aims to unmuffle our ears, so that we can each receive our own unique summons—the call which inaugurates our own Hero's Journey, and which beckons us out of "the wasteland." The call that gives answer to our deep longing to respond to whatever it is that most breaks our heart and whatever it is that brings us most fully alive. This is *enjoy* in its truest sense. An *enjoy* that has nothing to do with superficiality.

And yes, of course, this is an *enjoy* suffused with play, delight, laughter, rest, and celebration. As we make our way, if we're not experiencing the stuff of self-purification as an even mix, more or less, of letting go and loving it, we should probably re-evaluate how we're going about it.

Confession: My homespun definition of self-purification points to a problem with the iceberg model. I'm sorry to say it but our glacier has a major flaw. I already talked about the fact that the iceberg is one integrated chunk of ice, and I told you how the fluctuating waterline can indicate that the three parts of the model blend and cohere in a number of ways. But, even with those disclaimers, the awkward truth remains that limiting self-purification to one section of the illustration is just plain problematic. It's not enough to say that self-purification overlaps with, or prepares us for, or clears the way to, constructive program and satyagraha. From the Gandhian standpoint, constructive program and satyagraha *are* self-purification. Both are, after all, intrinsically self-purifying—that is, they're all about aligning principle and practice.

To illustrate, with regards to the connection between self-purification and the concrete experiments in social uplift that comprised India's Constructive Programme, at times Gandhi actually referred to them interchangeably:

> The measure of our purification seems hardly equal to the prize to be won. We have not yet consciously, and on a national scale, got rid of the curse of untouchability... Great though the awakening has been among the rich, they have not yet made common cause with the poor... Though much progress has been made in the case of drink and drugs, much more yet remains to be done... We have not shed the desire for foreign cloth and fineries, nor have the cloth merchants fully realized the magnitude of the wrong they have done to the nation by their trade... These and several other evils that can be easily recalled show how much still remains to be done in the matter of self-purification. And so, it is little wonder if we do not find the atmosphere of *Purna Swaraj* [complete self-rule] pervading us.

As for the self-purification/satyagraha connection, African American freedom fighter CT Vivian put it succinctly: "It is through action that we come to know who we are."

And Dr. King elaborates:

> For more than a century of slavery and another century of segregation Negroes did not find mass unity nor could they mount mass actions. The American brand of servitude tore them apart and held them in paralyzed solitude. But in the last decade Negroes united and marched. And out of the new unity and action vast monuments of dignity were shaped, courage was forged and hope took concrete form... For the first time in his history the Negro did not have to use subterfuge as a defense,

or solicit pity. His endurance was not employed for compromise with evil but to supply the strength to crush it… He came out of his struggle integrated only slightly in the external society but powerfully integrated within. This was the victory that had to precede all other gains.

Nevertheless and alas, I've yet to find a way to fully capture self-purification's all-encompassing nature in a visual, without it becoming unwieldy and ugly. I will say of the iceberg illustration, in its defense, that it conveys self-purification's role as the biggest, weightiest, most foundational part of the structure. "Without self-purification the observance of the law of ahimsa [nonviolence] must remain an empty dream," Gandhi wrote, a fact that is arguably our biggest collective blind spot when it comes to understanding the man and what he was up to. Thomas Merton, Trappist monk and Gandhi interpreter extraordinaire, observed this with precision. The italics are his:

In Gandhi's mind, nonviolence was not simply a political tactic which was supremely useful and efficacious in liberating his people from foreign rule, in order that India might then concentrate on realizing its own national identity. On the contrary, the spirit of nonviolence sprang from *an inner realization of spiritual unity in himself.* The whole Gandhian concept of nonviolent action and satyagraha is incomprehensible if it is thought to be a means of achieving unity rather than as *the fruit of inner unity already achieved.*

———

Key Concepts Review: Pop Quiz 1

What was Gandhi's favorite mathematical formula?

a) $a^2 + b^2 = c^2$

b) $e = mc^2$

c) $f(x) = a_0 + \sum_{n=1}^{\infty}(a_n \cos \frac{n\pi x}{L} + b_n \sin \frac{n\pi x}{L})$

d) *means=ends*

Gandhi's aim to personify a purified and liberated India exemplifies this, his most prized equation. If the ends are pre-existent in the means and the most basic tool for social transformation is the human individual, then as closely as possible the lives of those seeking change should reflect the change sought. Therein lies the simple logic behind the most famous of all Gandhi-isms: Be the change you wish to see in the world. (Nevermind that there's no evidence whatsoever that Gandhi ever uttered or wrote that statement.)

What he did say, and which is my all-time favorite Gandhi quote, is this: "I can indicate no royal road for bringing about the social revolution, except that we should represent it in every detail of our lives." That packs a Gandhian punch. And, like "Be the Change," it places the responsibility squarely where it ought to be, on our own able shoulders.

But hold on here. *Every* detail of our lives?

Now there's a monster assignment. And I don't know about you, but I often feel that I'm running a fool's errand trying to represent a Gandhian revolution in the details of my life. One small for instance: How could it possibly make a difference, in the grand scheme of things, that I'm writing these words longhand, on buses, in libraries, parks, at my daughter's piano

POP QUIZ 1 ANSWER KEY: A smiley face stamp if you went with d.

lessons, and at my favorite laundromat, rather than punching away at a keyboard in front of the eerie glow of a computer screen? It definitely feels more Gandhian this way—no arguing that. But there's something ridiculous about it too. At this very moment the woman seated to my right, here at the laundromat (yes, I know Gandhi didn't use washing machines), is communing with her iphone or some such gadget, and the flatscreen tv above the change machine is flashing shiny stuff, and shiny faces.

Yes, there's something ridiculous going on here, my writing like this, knowing that my Gandhian scrupulosity creates hardly the tiniest ripple in the social or ecological fabric.

And yet, ridiculous or not, I'm aware, deep in, that it matters to me. I know this book will turn out better this way. The same way I know that I have better conversations and think better thoughts by candlelight than I did when I still lit my home with electric light.

But it's really tricky stuff, and all the trickier the more directly we participate in the mainstream. What I've discovered is that "every detail" is like ahimsa. It's an aspiration. Gandhi's own self-deprecation might come in handy here:

> I must not flatter myself with the belief, nor allow friends like you to entertain the belief that I have exhibited any heroic or demonstrable nonviolence in myself. All I can claim is that I am sailing in that direction without a moment's stop.

"Sailing in that direction without a moment's stop"; answering the aspiration; edging closer, then closer still. And, I'd add: trusting that the ridiculous has its place in the Great Turning.

———

Several recurring and interconnected themes more or less define Gandhi's journey with self-purification. Let's explore some of these now, beginning where he did.

PRAYER

For Gandhi, prayer is to self-purification as self-purification is to the whole iceberg. The foundation. Priority one.

As food is necessary for the body, prayer is necessary for the soul.

Prayer is the greatest binding force, making for the solidarity and oneness of the human family.

I have not the shadow of a doubt that the strife and quarrels with which our atmosphere is so full today are due to the absence of the spirit of true prayer.

Prayer is the first and last lesson in learning the noble and brave art of sacrificing self...in the defense of one's nation's liberty and honor.

Prayer 'is the key of the morning and the bolt of the evening.'

Interfaith communal prayer was indeed held each morning and evening at Gandhi's ashram communities. In addition, an hour of hand-spinning cotton at the spinning wheel, which he also viewed and experienced as a form of prayer, and which he called a "sacrament," was a daily expectation for all ashramites. Gandhi was also a devoted practitioner of ramanama—repetition of the mantra. His mantra, Rama—one of the hundreds of deities in the Hindu pantheon—was gifted to him as a boy by his wetnurse, Rambha. He found that repeating the name of Rama was a matchless tool for fending off his childhood fears of thieves, serpents, and ghosts. His childhood practice of turning to his mantra apparently went dormant during his adolescence, but it returned in earnest during his adult years. Gandhi called this form of prayer his "staff of life."

Fasting played an important role in Gandhi's self-purification regimen as well. "What the eyes are for the outer world," he said, "fasts are for the inner." Even for an Indian Hindu, Gandhi turned to fasting with unusual frequency and vigor. This is because, at its core, for Gandhi, fasting represented the essence of prayer:

> There is no prayer without fasting, taking fasting in its widest sense. A complete fast is a complete and literal denial of self. It is the truest prayer. "Take my life and let it be, always only all for thee," is not, should not be, a mere lip or figurative expression. It has to be a reckless and joyous giving without the least reservation. Abstention from food and even water is but the mere beginning, the least part of the surrender.

Gandhi advised and employed prayerful fasts for a great variety of physical and emotional ailments, from headaches to "fretting and foaming" (we've all been there), from indigestion to depression. It is also well known that Gandhi used fasting, even with a willingness to give his life, as a potent and controversial form of political and social witness. Given its place at the heart of his spiritual practice, it should come as no surprise that Gandhi would reserve fasting, the "truest prayer," as the "last weapon of a Satyagrahi...the last duty which it is open to him to perform."

For Gandhi, in a word, the purpose of all these forms of prayer was God-centeredness. It also happened to be the purpose of his life, the one of his one-pointedness. But it is equally true that Gandhi's God-centeredness existed within the context of his avid universalism. He held in reverence the great plurality of religious paths, and he did his best to instill this ethic in his ashram communities—which were always interfaith—by including "equality of religions" as one of their guiding vows and observances.

As we consider how it relates to our own lives and practices, I encourage us to take Gandhi's lead and let God-centeredness be its fully expansive self.

"Far be it from me to suggest that you should believe in the God that I believe in," he said, "but your belief...must be your ultimate mainstay." Anyone, according to Gandhi, including atheists, could hold the inner commitment to Truth requisite for satyagraha. It follows that self-purification doesn't need to be framed in overtly religious terms.

But language is tricky. If it's going to be self-purification along Gandhian lines, it's going to be a deep dive, a profound letting go, a stripping down experience of faith or something akin to faith, which, as we've already discussed, is tethered to *something more*. In the end, Gandhi's vision of Truth presupposed that all persons have the final say on the nature of their beliefs, and if/how/when to speak of them. If the word or concept of God doesn't work for you, I hope you'll be able to lean into this conversation by way of your "ultimate mainstay," however you may conceive of it. In our beautifully pluralistic age, it would appear that heart unity requires us to become adept at such translation and decoding, so that we might come in contact with the true and full meaning behind our limited, imperfect words.

The Summer Day

Who made the world?
Who made the swan, and the black bear?
Who made the grasshopper?
This grasshopper, I mean—
the one who has flung herself out of the grass,
the one who is eating sugar out of my hand,
who is moving her jaws back and forth instead of up and down—
who is gazing around with her enormous and complicated eyes.
Now she lifts her pale forearms and thoroughly washes her face.
Now she snaps her wings open, and floats away.

I don't know exactly what a prayer is.
I do know how to pay attention,
how to fall down into the grass,
how to kneel down in the grass,
how to be idle and blessed,
how to stroll through the fields,
which is what I have been doing all day.
Tell me, what else should I have done?
Doesn't everything die at last, and too soon?
Tell me, what is it you plan to do with your one wild and precious life?

—Mary Oliver

What constitutes a prayer? If indeed we are each autonomous (though also joined one to another) in the realm of the spirit, then the field must be open and unbounded.

In 1931 Gandhi wrote:

> I am not a man of learning but I humbly claim to be a man of prayer. I am indifferent as to the form. Every one is a law unto himself in that respect. But there are some well-marked roads, and it is safe to walk along the beaten tracks trod by the ancient teachers.

True that, and not to be discounted. We are each a law unto ourselves *and* invaluable wisdom has been gifted to us by the ancients. But it's critical to recognize that the well-marked roads Gandhi had in mind here were mapped within his particular religious and cultural context, and that the spiritual traditions he was drawing on were largely beholden (and remain largely beholden) to patriarchy. Most of the ancient teachers Gandhi is referring to here were certainly men.

And, of course, Gandhi's statement about the form of prayer not being important, when viewed in context, was a statement made about prayer as Gandhi understood and practiced it. The key to Gandhi's morning and the bolt of his evening revolved around seated, silent meditation—an undisputed treasure in the self-purifier's toolbox. But it's important to inquire whether and why we may associate such meditation with prayer or spiritual discipline more than, say, ecstatic dance, or singing (which Gandhi was pretty into himself), or gardening (he liked that too). We have been taught and conditioned that "prayer" looks, sounds, and feels a certain way, when clearly people make use of innumerable paths to self-surrender and communion with Life-God-Truth-Love. Prayer has everything to do with intention. That's the point Gandhi was getting at when he encouraged us not to fret over form.

My mention of singing just now brings to mind a powerful case in point. Let's listen to Marshall Frady describe one of his experiences as a white journalist following the black freedom struggle into the Deep South:

> One smouldering night in a little Alabama town, I found myself standing in the back of a shoebox tabernacle crammed with a congregation of black maids, janitors, beauticians, schoolteachers—all the windows open to the hot ripe night outside and cardboard fans advertising *Peoples Funeral Association* fluttering over the packed ranks of glistening faces—as a local preacher, a heavy, sweat-washed man just released from jail that afternoon, led them through one of those mightily swooping hymns of the movement: *O freedom! O freedom! O freedom over me, over me...* I stepped outside to stand for a moment in the dark under a chinaberry tree, suddenly a bit woozy, and lighted a cigarette with trembling fingers. And with those voices in the church surging on in the night—*And before I'll be a slave, I'll be buried in my grave, and go home to my Lord and be free*—I still distinctly remember the prickling that shivered over my hide, and blurting out, "Good God." Such moments were a kind of Damascus Road experience in the lives of more reporters than me.

The nonviolent activists who did the heaviest lifting during the freedom movement were motivated by a profound spiritual commitment—a commitment that included the willingness to suffer, and for some the willingness to die, for the cause. This kind of spirituality brought an unshakable quality to the movement. It was the embodiment of personal swaraj, and it lent an air of inevitability to the national struggle, a sense that it was only a matter of time before freedom would be secured. This inevitable quality saturated the music that was the living soundtrack of the movement. Mass meetings culminating with the full-voiced and harmonized assertion that "We Shall Overcome" ushered forth into marches punctuated by the shouted call and response, "How long? Not long! How long? Not long!" These were the sounds of a people grounded in a spirituality of impatient yearning—a yearning for justice both long overdue and on its way.

Movement scholar Clayborne Carson's landmark book, *In Struggle*, details the history and enormous impact of the Student Non-Violent Coordinating Committee (SNCC), the student-led movement organization that spearheaded such critical movement campaigns as the sit-ins, the Freedom Rides, and Freedom Summer. Carson shines a light on the essential role music played in the movement, recounting the statements of two freedom fighters, about their experience of raising their voices in the context of a mass meeting:

> As Bernice Reagon, one of the Albany student activists [and future founder of Sweet Honey in the Rock], recalled: "When I opened my mouth and began to sing, there was a force and power within myself I had never heard before. Somehow this music…released a kind of power and required a level of concentrated energy I did not know I had." Goldie Jackson, a black woman who had lost her job after allowing SNCC workers to stay in her house, remembered praying and singing in the church for the rest of the night: "Two things we knew held us together: prayer of something good to come and song that tells from the depth of the heart how we feel about our fellow man."

One clear mark of the Great Turning is a heightened awareness of Life-God-Truth-Love's wonderfully accessible, immanent nature. Another clear mark is a heightened awareness that the centuries-long, sweeping, and forcible suppression of the sacred feminine has carried incalculable costs for us as individuals and as a civilization. The opportunity to open ourselves to other well-marked or not so well-marked spiritual roads, which have seemed or have been deemed off-limits in our patriarchal society, gives us a significant advantage over Gandhi and most of his contemporaries. As we step into the process of self-purification, we get to embrace the reality that prayer can be expressed in countless ways: meditation, dance, hiking, music, yoga, tai chi, tantra, gardening, spiritual reading, and, lest we forget, stargazing.

This latter practice is one of my personal favorites. Lifting my eyes to the heavens usually gets me out of my own way, by reminding me where I actually am, and of the unfathomable, quiet mystery of existence itself. Rabbi Michael Lerner, co-founder of the Network of Spiritual Progressives, asserts that our capacity for deep-rooted personal and collective transformation is intimately linked to "our capacity to respond to others as embodiments of the sacred and to the universe with awe, wonder, and radical amazement." In the age of climate change, Lerner argues, a new consciousness inclined toward such awe—inclined toward justice and generosity too—"is not some utopian ideal—it is the survival necessity for human life on this planet."

In the end, whatever forms of prayer we might employ, along whatever self-purification path we might trod, it is the quality of connection with Life-God-Truth-Love, and the progress we make in aligning creed and deed, that will be the determinant measures of the strength of our practice.

INNER EXCAVATION

Gandhi pursued his goal of personifying a purified and liberated India by attempting to reduce himself to zero. Let's remember, though, that when it comes to this kind of self-surrender we're not talking about a negative or destructive breaking down of what we are. We're talking about a letting go of the concepts, stories, and habits that we have come to identify with, but which actually block us from an authentic experience of what we truly are, and which separate us from a direct encounter with the unity and wholeness of life, and with our own unique and precious aliveness.

For Gandhi, the desire to let his life, his self, become a transparent channel of love, Truth, or God—the words he usually used to identify the *something more* we're talking about—is definitive. If we want to practice Gandhian non-violence we don't get to leave that aspiration out, and we don't get to finagle things so room remains for our personal ambitions and self-driven agendas.

> Not until we have reduced ourselves to nothingness can we conquer the evil in us. God demands nothing less than complete self-surrender as the price for the only real freedom that is worth having. And when man thus loses himself, he immediately finds himself in the service of all that lives. It becomes his delight and his recreation. He is a new man, never weary of spending himself in the service of God's creation.

Conquer the *what* in us? Yes, "evil" is another word to which many of us are allergic. But let's read this as a reminder, a characteristically strident Gandhian reminder, that the Domination System is not separate from us. We participate in it, both in the outward living of our lives and in the interior workings of our minds and hearts. King's observation comes to mind, that nothing external to us can bring us to that spiritual place where we are able to sign with the pen and ink of our own assertive personhood an inner emancipation proclamation. It is strangely paradoxical, this juxtaposition of assertion and surrender, but we've been on the path long enough to know something about how it works. Cycling down, God willing, brings us into an innermost room where our self-centeredness, cowardice, jealousy, and malice await us. In that innermost room we get to greet such as these, perhaps even embrace them, for they have no doubt been carrying a heavy burden on our behalf, ask them for their stories, deeply listen, then kindly invite them to go.

It's not as easy as that sounds, of course. At least it hasn't been for me. In the introduction I remarked that the realm of self-purification is fundamentally positive and empowering. You'll notice that I didn't say it was fundamentally comfortable. When I consider the level of inner excavation it requires, in fact, the first word that comes to mind is *excruciating*.

It brings me back to something Harry Belafonte shared with me during our interview, when I asked him when and how he saw Dr. King pursue self-purification. While I was expecting him to talk to me about the depth of Dr. King's prayer practice, the way he plumbed the scriptures, or something else along those lines, Mr. Belafonte went someplace altogether different:

> I saw it in his anxiety. When he came upon a moment and all of a sudden was severely challenged by it. "What right do I have to do this? What right do I have to say that I approve or I agree that the children should be brought into the Birmingham fray, at this tender age, violating mothers and fathers and families? In all this fear and mayhem? What right do I have to do that? Who am I to do this? Give me the sign." You know? It's almost biblical. "What right do I have to bridge this gap between Vietnam and the struggle here?"—that was so evident once he did it. It transcended the mortality of politics. It was immortal what he did. And every time he had to do this, he either got a tic, or he got some preoccupation, or he went into melancholy. And then he emerged.

Hearing the Voice

"Give me the sign."

Gandhi referred to the giver of signs as the "Inner Voice," and his accounts of hearing it, which often bear a great likeness to Belafonte's description of Dr. King's anxiety, are instructive:

The hearing of the Voice was preceded by a terrific struggle within me. Suddenly the Voice came upon me. I listened, made certain it was the Voice, and the struggle ceased. I was calm. The determination was made accordingly, the date and the hour of the fast were fixed.... The Voice was more real than my own existence. It has never failed me, or for that matter, anyone else. And everyone who wills can hear the Voice. It is within everyone. But like everything else, it requires previous and definite preparation.

It was only after making "a ceaseless effort to attain self-purification," Gandhi said, that he "developed some little capacity to hear correctly and clearly the 'still small voice within.'" Whether or to whatever extent our inner experience might resemble Gandhi's, in our quest for Honesty we need to learn how to access ways of knowing that lie beyond thought. What's more, most if not all of us need to do some profound work to resolve or integrate psychological and emotional traumas, and to overcome our inner blocks. While the strategies we might employ today will differ from his, in its essence I believe such inner work is what Gandhi was pointing to when he said that hearing the Voice requires "previous and definite preparation."

It's another paradox, from a certain vantage point, but the type of self-surrender that Gandhi is talking about almost always appears to require a high level of self-knowledge, as it does emotional maturity. Until we know ourselves, we are unable to surrender ourselves. For many if not most of us there is so much accumulated and unresolved pain, injury, and confusion in our minds, spirits, and bodies, that in order to clear the way to that place where we can bridge principle and practice—to that place of sheer Honesty—our prayer life must be imbued with or complemented by serious inner inquiry and healing. Thankfully, since Gandhi's time, enormous strides have been made in all manner of counseling, therapy, and spiritual direction, very much including the aforementioned areas of resolving and integrating trauma and removing inner obstacles.

The folks that have inspired me most in this realm of inner excavation are the steadfast ones I've seen busting out their well-worn toolboxes time and again, and making use of whatever gets the job done. And I've noticed that breakthroughs and settling ins happen for these folks in a great variety of ways, often, maybe even usually, at points where different modalities and ways of experiencing and understanding intersect. Like Gandhi, we're each responsible for conducting our own made-to-order "experiments with Truth" in the laboratories of our unique lives, with the help of our unique tool collections.

This latter point hits a nerve for me, I realize. I carry the frustration—which is shared by many—that adequate guidance and accompaniment with the psychological and emotional pieces of this work oftentimes lands out of reach for those of us without access to a good amount of money. Thankfully, though, the architects of the Great Turning—both within our integral nonviolence submovement and the wider movement of movements—are beginning to surmount this challenge. We have many in our midst with the needed wisdom, skills, and experience to lead us through this work. The more widespread gift economics becomes, which we'll be discussing in the next chapter, the more their expertise will be freed up for the sharing, by way of grassroots networks of mental/emotional health workers. Some of the folks who are part of this emerging network are professional therapists of one form or another, while others hold no formal accreditation. Obviously beware of imposters from either category; our psychological and emotional selves have been through enough already.

Feeling the Body

Whichever tools and modalities we employ, as we dig down we may discover that the lessons and emotional charges embedded in the deep are more powerfully and directly accessed physically than they are mentally or verbally. The testimony of a growing number of changemakers committed to inner work reveals that emotional-somatic expression, in need or want of no conceptual counterpart whatsoever, often leads to release, integration, or progress on the path of self-knowledge and self-surrender that no amount of talk therapy, spiritual reading, dreamwork, or journaling could ever catalyze.

It's important to acknowledge that this somatic dimension of our inner work marks a significant divergence from Gandhi's own self-purification understanding and regimen. It's a divergence that's well worth discussing.

Though some will certainly resonate with his views on the matter, most of us in our day and age are going to need to have something of a nonviolent throwdown with Gandhi when it comes to the body. Much to his credit, Gandhi argued that only an India that was physically healthy could attain swaraj. But his teaching on the subject of health usually approaches the human body in strictly utilitarian terms, likening it to an almost mechanical instrument designed for service and service alone. And underneath this teaching lies Gandhi's deep and general negativity toward the body because of its capacity as an instrument not of service but of sensual temptation and degradation. Nonetheless, for those of us who choose to enter a spat with Gandhi about the body, we should do so with the humility befitting a visitor in a foreign land. His views in this area, after all, were no less shaped by his history and culture than our views are shaped by our own.

As it relates to prayer, some of us have discovered that the goal or practice of forgetting, leaving, or escaping the body, or of achieving a bodiless stillness or unknowing, is not necessarily as valuable as a coming into or being present with the body and with the immediacy of life *living* our body. Some of us walk a path that includes both of these types of experiences—sometimes leaving the body, sometimes coming into it. In my own experience these two can happen at the same time. I'm thinking, for example, of times when my own experience of making music has brought me into communion with *something more*. My arms, hands, fingers, working the strings and fretboard, my voice reaching for, lifting up, my ears absorbing miraculous waves of sound, my spirit moving somehow both in and beyond my physical form. There have also been times when I've been submerged underwater, or soaring through the wilderness downhill skiing, and my body has been on fire with life while my consciousness dips into some whispered hint of that which is eternal. Then there's making love, that singular embodied connection, power, and vulnerability that reveals something more so dependably, so mysteriously, for me and my lover alike. The marriage of body and prayer.

The body obviously plays a huge role on both sides of the self-purification scale: renounce *and* enjoy. And, tragically, many of us too often downplay the second part, forgetting that self-purification isn't just a wrestling match with shadows and demons. Similarly, many of us too often under-appreciate the physicality of the enjoy side of the equation. How we are emancipated in the receiving and embracing of profound delight, those joy-filled often sensual encounters with the wilderness, with the ocean, with music, art, and food; with gratitude and awe; with deep sleep and replenishing leisure; with play. With each other. We are sexual, creative beings. We are drawn to and made for touch, connection, and expression. We know from our own treasured experience that tears of joy and laughter are as purifying as tears of sorrow and regret. We're built for fun and physicality. Some of us are athletes. A great many of us are artists. And let's face it, Gandhi wasn't into that stuff as much as most of us are. He might rebuff the conclusion, but we know intuitively and experientially that such delight—not the shallow pleasures of distracted indulgence, but the real deal—does not work at cross-purposes to our journey into one-pointedness and congruence. On the contrary.

The Sky's Sheets

When he touches me I clutch the sky's sheets,
the way other
lovers
do.

The earth's weave
of clay.

Any real ecstasy is a sign
you are moving
in the right
direction,

don't let any prude tell
you otherwise.

—St. Teresa of Avila (1515-1582)

Amen.

And, before we get too cozy in the winner's circle, it's only fair to hear and show up when Gandhi calls us back to the mat for our quarrel about the body. When it comes to our atrophied limbs and spirits due to our modern technology dependencies, for example, or to our reliance on the pharmaceutical-industrial complex for health care, or to all the pseudo-food that many of us still indulge in—all of which we'll be discussing shortly— he's definitely got a thing or two to teach us.

For now, though, let's get back to going in.

Overcoming Blocks

The recent writings of Brené Brown offer excellent guidance on the stuff of inner excavation. Our unwillingness and inability to surrender to vulnerability, and to speak our shame out loud, Brown contends, represent the biggest barriers on our journey toward inner congruency, authenticity, and the fullness of life. Embracing vulnerability and learning to expose to the light of day whatever shame we carry, she argues, frees us from fear. So freed we develop the courage to be imperfect and the courage to love ourselves as we are. In turn, this courage and love free us from risk aversion—from that fear of the unknown, the unpredictable, the guaranteeless, which keeps us from Honesty. Which keeps us from a true reckoning with our highest dreams. Which keeps us from hearing our unique summons and pursuing our real vocation.

Committed nonviolence practitioners at the Possibility Alliance, in La Plata, Missouri, have found Brené Brown's analysis to be right on the mark. Over the course of nearly a decade, the Possibility Alliance, arguably the most inspiring collective experiment in integral nonviolence in the U.S., has hosted thousands of earnest pilgrims searching for a way of life rooted in service, nonviolence, and authenticity. Core members of the community report that fear unquestionably represents the greatest block for would-be Gandhians. This fear, they confirm, is consistently anchored by the kind of vulnerability-avoidance and unspoken shame described by Brown. And, they've observed that it typically takes the form of three particular psychological blocks. Any of these ring a bell?:

- The disbelief that I am really and truly capable of embodying the kind of love Gandhi is pointing to when he speaks of ahimsa, satyagraha, and heart unity.
- The doubt that I can actually hold the practice of such love as my highest life priority—above such things as safety, comfort, and control.
- The refusal to embrace the fact that *now* is the only moment to live out my heart's truest, deepest longing—that no matter what my circumstances or situation, *now* is the moment to embody truth and love.

Overcoming such blocks is personal transformation of the highest magnitude. And, unfortunately, there's no foolproof cookie cutter recipe that I or anyone else has to disseminate. In the end, while we'll likely bump into each other along the way, each of us travels our own singular path of self-purification.

But much has been learned. Key milestones and core practices for inner freedom have been identified. In addition to Brené Brown's work, a great many other resources represent coherent and powerful companions for us as we continue in search of the fullness of life. Three such examples are *Spinning Threads of Radical Aliveness*, by Miki Kashtan, *A New Earth* by Eckart Tolle, and *The Presence Process* by Michael Brown.

In my own case, in addition to written resources like these, I'm aware that three strands of my journey have proven especially significant. Perhaps one or the other of them will speak to your own experience. The first has been those handful of occasions in my life when I've crossed paths with women and men who have overcome the three aforementioned blocks. It's impossible to measure the value of my hearing the stories of such individuals, of grabbing hold of the threads in those stories that most pierced my heart, of giving those threads a tug and watching where they led me.

The second strand that comes immediately to mind is the experience of lowering my bucket into the wells of forgiveness. Forgiveness, that is, of myself and of others; as forgiver and forgiven. In my life, it is probably this piece that has best exemplified Brené Brown's key insight that vulnerability is at the heart of our journey to freedom. Forgiveness is the great liberator. It sets free captive hearts, imaginations, families, friendships, life force. And— there's no way around it—forgiveness requires immense vulnerability and courage. To be forgiven requires us to open ourselves to the grief and regret attached to our wrongdoings, to speak our shame out loud, and to ask for deliverance. To forgive, in a great many cases, also requires the willingness to grieve, and it demands a generosity of spirit and trust which allows those who have wronged us to mourn, to offer restitution, and to reach, with us, for reconciliation, for a new start.

The third strand I want to acknowledge is completely intertwined with my experience as a white, heterosexual, able-bodied, and formally educated male in our U.S. society. One of the most formidable blocks to radical witness and revolutionary nonviolence that I've faced, and that I've seen a great many other privileged potential satyagrahis face, is an unwillingness to dig into one place, one vision, one direction for an extended period. I and so many others I know have frequently succumbed to the well-intentioned but slippery inclination to "check things out," to "wander," or, as I've heard others (always white folks) sometimes refer to it, to "follow my bliss." Over the years this tendency has stolen me away from my vocation on a good many occasions, for various stretches of time. And, I dare say, I believe I've watched it steal some amazing potential satyagrahis away for good.

It takes presence and consistency to build relationships and to lay the foundation for transformation (our own and that of our community). The abundance of time and the luxury of mobility afforded those of us with such unearned privilege enables us to travel with great regularity, if not leave altogether. It enables us to attend workshops, conferences, retreats, and festivals galore. But when we bring brutal, self-purifying Honesty to bear on this tendency, do we actually find that following our "bliss" in such ways brings us an experience of true bliss? Or, is it the case that we allow our genuine need for self-care, respite, and learning to serve as a front for escape and indulgence? A consistent and abiding experience of life lived with full integrity is the bliss the Gandhian Iceberg points to. Since privilege can be so wily and seductive, in order to faithfully steward our wiggle room we need to keep a vigilant lookout for our favorite and best rehearsed excuses.

The path we've been walking these past several pages—from prayer to inner excavation to unearned privilege—brings us now to a place on the iceberg where the waterline laps up from self-purification into the realm of constructive program. We'll see as we move forward that, if we want it to, it will also splash up and over the tip of the iceberg to include the stuff of satyagraha. For now, though, let's keep our attention more or less here, under water, on the level of the individual and the personal, as we consider what I believe to be one of the Great Turning's most essential and humbling demands.

Atonement and Reparations (pt. 1)

When Ta-Nehisi Coates' seminal essay "The Case for Reparations" came out, I skimmed it. I was pretty sure I knew what he was going to say, and I was pretty sure I was going to agree with him. The luxury of halfhearted intellectual agreement, devoid of sincere probing or any move toward real action, is one of the many insidious privileges afforded white people in our society. I was sympathetic to the call for reparations for the victims of white supremacy, I understood its rationale, I hoped that someday it might happen. So I chose to skim.

When I went to Palestine for the first time a year later, something shifted. Something which opened me up to my own process of inner atonement, and to the recognition that reparations—if they are to be real, if they are to truly matter—must always go hand in hand with such atonement.

I, like so many firsthand and distant observers of the Israeli occupation, watched in horror as fundamentalist Jewish Israelis—with the open approval and concrete support of their government and its armed forces—defied international law and common decency by stealing land and homes out from under Palestinian families. Such theft is part of Israel's grand strategy of gradual takeover—a strategy built on the pillars of raw military firepower, U.S. collusion, and the ceaseless collective punishment and mass intimidation of the Palestinian people. While it is deployed, this strategy destroys any possibility of a negotiated peace.

I was astonished and sickened to witness such blatant injustice, and to hear and read Israeli settlers justify their actions, over and over again, by way of their claim to entitlement—that is, by way of their ancient and deeply defective ideology of chosenness. In Palestine, in a stance of righteous indignation, all my Gandhian preparation notwithstanding, I found my core commitment to not "otherize" my fellow human beings turning to ash. I quickly came to view these Israeli settlers as qualitatively different from me, and to hold them apart from myself psychologically, in order to maintain my own cherished sense of identity as a just and loving human being.

Then, at a very specific moment, something shifted in my consciousness.

I was watching a father—an Israeli settler, assault rifle slung over his shoulder—escorting his young son along the Prayer Road in Hebron, en route to the synagogue for Sabbath prayers. At that moment it occurred to me: That one there, that little boy—that's me.

Though several more generations distanced me from the original crime committed by my forbears, and from our collective memory of it, I too was born into an unlawfully, immorally, and shamefully stolen settlement. I too knew no other place as my home.

And I too was the inheritor of an ideology of chosenness—call it Manifest Destiny or white supremacy—which came with all the affixed rationalizations which explained why it was somehow okay under these circumstances, in relation to these others, for it to be this way.

Looking at that boy, I considered the odds. What chance did this little one have against such a narrative? What chance did he have of breaking free of the indoctrination that began at the moment of his birth, growing up in that story and in that stolen land as the only home he'd ever known?

That's privilege, true. But it's also curse. To be divorced from one's own best human instincts, to have one's moral compass eclipsed from the day of birth, by a myth of exceptionalism, by a lie enforced by callousness and brutality. And by the words or silence of those charged with teaching and modeling what it means to be a human being, to be a part of the human family.

What are the chances for a child born to such a curse? However will he manage to get out from under that?

For those of us who are white in the U.S. (that's who I'm going to address for the next few paragraphs), such questions, if we let them, bring us to the threshold. To that place where we encounter the possibility of finally and unequivocally reckoning with the true nature of our own inheritance. To that place where we see that part of what's been handed down to us is the luxury to ignore the simple and profound justice that reparations would represent, and the level-headed arguments that the progeny that inherit the spoils of plunder do indeed bear responsibility, no matter when the initial crime was committed. That the passing on and the receiving of such an inheritance—the unearned wealth, the rationalizations, the luxury of not needing to sweat over the matter whatsoever—is its own crime. Our crime.

At the threshold we're invited to acknowledge those of our ancestors who first came into possession of our immoral surplus. In their blindness and brokenness they established the cycle of white dominance that continues to so greatly pervade and define our national experience. They passed down to us stolen property and the profits of suffering and labor that was not their own, a surplus of collective material wealth and innumerable other unfair advantages. Along with it, they passed down the grievous and suppressed memory of their crimes. I'm speaking, of course, of those of our ancestors who carried out systematic genocide against Native Americans. Deep in the recesses of our ancestral memory we know that there were ten million people in this land, now called the United States, when European explorers first arrived here in the fifteenth century. We know too that only 300,000 of those ten million remained at the turn of the twentieth century.

I'm speaking, of course, of those of our ancestors who, as Ta-Nehisi Coates reminds us, chose to establish a nation "predicated on the torture of black fathers, on the rape of black mothers, on the sale of black children." That is, those who participated in the enslavement of upwards of four million Africans, the destruction of their families, and the systematic crucifixion of the surviving vestiges of their personal autonomy and culture.

I'm speaking also, of course, of the ones who stood passively by, watching or looking the other way, and those who, in subsequent generations, including our own, resurrected those inaugural crimes and the narratives that justified them, dressing them up in new guise befitting the day.

In the context of our nation's tortured racial history, the treasure of authentic forgiveness and reconciliation can only be forged through a powerful interracial expression of the kind of courage and vulnerability we've been talking about. But those of us who are white—and especially, in my opinion, those of us who are white and claim to be committed to integral nonviolence—bear the greater responsibility to move this process forward. But to do so, to actually begin to authentically atone and concretely enact reparations, we have to see clearly and feel deeply the necessity of it. We have to be convinced, on the most personal level, that our personal integrity requires this of us.

Such a reckoning is not merely for our own deep good as individuals. It is no doubt a necessary precondition for the Great Turning itself.

ADDICTION, SOBRIETY, and HARNESSING LIFE FORCE

I stepped on a BART train in San Francisco recently and had a surreal flash of an opium den. Almost every single soul was utterly riveted on their handheld contraption or laptop. It's scary what's happened, and how quickly. I wonder if it would change people's perception of such behavior if wires from the devices plugged straight into our foreheads. I try to stay open-minded about it, but it's hard when you know something about where those gadgets come from, and where they go when they fall apart or aren't fast enough anymore. It's hard when you feel what this society-wide, increasingly worldwide, addiction is doing to our collective soul. This addiction so few are talking about.

Among all the others. The variety of monkeys leaping for our backs in this day and age is overwhelming, as is their tenacity. From sugar to pot, booze to texting, gossip to porn, we all have our dependencies, indulgences, and self-medication go-tos. My purpose in pointing this out is not to encourage self-flagellation as penance for our addictive sinfulness. Where the core value of this discussion really lies, I believe, is in recognizing about ourselves what Gandhi recognized about the people of India: Our vitality, self-respect, and capacity for service are seriously hampered by addiction. We can't pretend to be taking self-purification seriously without addressing this head-on.

Gandhi believed that emotions and sense desires were expansive reservoirs of spiritual vitality and life force. By gaining mastery over them, he taught, an individual could harness that vitality and force and direct it in service to their highest purpose. This belief is not a Gandhi original of course. It's common to certain strands of his and many other religious traditions, and is expressed in various ways in monastic communities the world over.

A good friend of mine—choosing to take Gandhi at his word—recently undertook a strict fast from cars. News of this brought back memories of my own such fast years ago. When we connected about it my friend and I arrived at what I think is an important insight. Every one of us draws our own unique behavior boundaries within the mess that is ours today—boundaries which are largely shaped by how much we choose to and feel called to interact with the mainstream. For all of us, though, it can be a powerful thing to undergo lengthy enough and specific enough fasts to break some of our fundamental dependencies. I believe that has been true for me in the case of cars. I had two years of almost pure independence from the automobile. (Yes, I ate food that was transported in vehicles, went to concerts of bands that toured in them, hosted guests who arrived in them etc. etc.) It drove my family crazy, as is quite likely the case with my friend's family right now. And while I will now on occasion accept a ride or borrow a friend's truck, I do so from an experience of inner freedom.

This principle does not apply universally. When it comes to overcoming certain addictions it would appear that a "lengthy enough fast" must be nothing less than complete and perpetual abstention. But my point is that such dependency-breaking fasting as my friend is currently engaged in is a potent strategy that can be applied widely.

In short, the manifold dependencies we face are serious barriers to the one-pointedness that self-purification and nonviolence require of us. We scapegoat particular substances with the "addictive" label, but swaraj, as a call to freedom both inward and outward, calls us to expand our definition of addiction and to take seriously the work of supporting one another in achieving genuine sobriety, that is, freedom from unhealthy dependency itself. We need to seek remedies for our hurt, confusion, fatigue, despair, and lack of direction that are not at odds with our most cherished convictions and commitments. And as we do so, we need to acknowledge that addiction is not only psychological or spiritual. Addiction has a physical dimension too—usually a powerful one—and our dependencies often have serious impacts on our physical health. Like Gandhi, we should write up our self-purification recipe with an eye not only to harnessing mental and spiritual power. We're also looking to experience and maintain optimal physical vitality and well-being. Remember, we're striving for congruency on as many levels as we can muster.

Toward that end, within the realm of harnessing life force three particular areas drew Gandhi's special interest and concern: brahmacharya (celibacy), control of the palate, and the sublimation of anger. Admittedly, to many of us these are areas where Gandhi's teaching betrays serious limitations.* We proceed, nonetheless, recognizing that harnessing life force is a crucial element of self-purification, and trusting that there's good wheat here amidst whatever we might experience as chaff.

Brahmacharya

While the word brahmacharya denotes a much more inclusive and holistic process of training the senses and achieving self-control, which Gandhi certainly advocated, he used the word almost exclusively to denote celibacy. Gandhi's views on sex and his own sexuality are a veritable hornet's nest. And while I'm a bit reluctant to give that nest a swift kick, it's important to do so. Regardless of whether a person feels called to celibacy, I feel that Gandhi as a teacher leaves much to be desired on the subject, especially from our collective vantage point now. This is not because Gandhi advocated and practiced celibacy himself, per se, but because his rationale, in its entirety, betrays what

---

*   In the introduction, pages 19-21, we discussed other questionable or suspect areas of Gandhi's teaching and/or modeling. See also the note corresponding to this page (102) in the Notes section, which features commentary on Gandhi as parent and husband.

I and many others perceive to be Gandhi's own unresolved psychological trauma and a general lack of experience, maturity, and open-mindedness in the sexual realm.

I'm not going to go into the gory details. If you're interested, they're not difficult to track down. From Gandhi's childhood marriage and early sex-related traumatic experiences, to his denigrating comments about sex, to his homoerotic correspondence (and who knows what else) with his close friend and nonviolence co-conspirator Hermann Kallenbach, to his ill-fated experiments of sleeping naked with naked young women in order to test his resolve as a brahmacharyi—the dirt is there to dig up, if you want to. For my part, beyond those suggestive headlines, I'll simply point you to Erik Erikson's treatment of the subject. Way back in 1969, in clear, openhearted language, Erikson addressed Gandhi directly in the form of a letter—yes, a letter written twenty-plus years after Gandhi's death—explaining, in effect, the critical distinction between self-discipline and psychological repression. Erikson's letter to Gandhi underscores that as we acknowledge Gandhi as a great teacher and model, it's crucial that we also acknowledge that he was not so for everything. Here's just a small sampling of Erikson's analysis. "Your precocious sexual life," he says to Mahatmaji,

> combined with your moral scrupulosity, could not contain and, in fact, aggravated a sense of sadism in your sexuality... It makes supreme sense that you should have resolved your sexual conflicts by making it a matter of will, sealed by a vow, that as you would not attack an inimical person with weapons, you would not attack a loved one with phallic desire.

> ...[But] not once, in all of your writings, do you grant that a sexual relationship could be characterized by what we call "mutuality." This is by no means a capacity easily developed or sustained without self-control and sacrifice, but as an approximation and a goal, it describes the only kind of sexual relationship in which the other person does not become a mere object either of sexual or aggressive desire... The point is that

mutual consent and artful interplay truly disarm what debasement and what violence there is in merely taking sexual possession of one another.

With mutuality and artful interplay, in other words, there is most definitely room in the Great Turning for sex and sex positivity. Thank you, Professor Erikson.

For some of us, though—the above conclusion notwithstanding—the quarrel with Gandhi about sex, which is clearly inseparable from our quarrel with him about the body, revolves around a much more basic premise than the one Erikson deals with in his letter. Gandhi's baseline argument is that acting on sexual desire, in and of itself, saps a person's physical and spiritual vitality and that, therefore, doing so for any reason other than procreation is a moral degradation. Each and every part of this premise is open to debate. Many of us—to our delight—have found the opposite to be true.

The bottom line remains: Each of us is tasked with getting real about our core principles and commitments, and with bringing our behavior into alignment with them. As we discern for ourselves in the area of sex and sexuality, as is the case with so many other areas, we certainly need to be on the lookout for unhealthy dependencies, be they physical, emotional, psychological, or any combination thereof. That said, as we chart our course in the wonderful world of sex let's not feel unduly restrained by Gandhi's apparent ignorance of the possibilities.

Control of the Palate

If you've read his autobiography you know that Gandhi was obsessed with all things dietary, and that his experiments with various food combinations and renunciations take up more pages than any other subject. This sharp focus on diet is a testament to Gandhi's means=ends foundation, and, when it comes to the matter of harnessing energy, it's perfectly fitting. Next to the sexual impulse, Gandhi believed that the palate was the most difficult and important source of sensual energy to control, harness, and redirect. In short, his advice was to eat only when hungry, and to view food as one would view medicine. That is, we should appreciate food, select it, and consume it for its utilitarian value alone. The best food, according to Gandhi, was that which provided the optimal nutrition for the body in its capacity as an instrument of service. The tongue's preferences for sweet or spicy pleasure were nothing but the mind's not-so-whimsical way of testing our self-purificatory resolve.

As with the realm of sex, while Gandhi is definitely on to something of great importance in aspiring to harness physical and spiritual vitality by reining in the palate, getting with him on general principle doesn't necessarily mean we're with him on his chosen strategies. I want my whole self to be optimally primed for service, and my body as an instrument of service, in my experience, is not separate from my body as an instrument of sensuality. In opposition to Gandhi, I believe that depriving myself of delight carries a significant cost, and so for me the strictly utilitarian value of food does not stand alone.

Here again, in saying this I don't mean to suggest that I get to ignore the ever-present danger of unhealthy dependencies related to food. Nor do I get to ignore certain moral claims that reach far beyond my own body and my own potential delight. If I seek to live with integrity such moral claims must have their say. In terms of the palate, my first question can certainly be: Is this food, which I'm privileged to receive, healthy for my body? And the second: Is this food enjoyable to eat? But then come such as these: What are the true costs associated with this food? Have those who worked to bring this food to my table been treated fairly? Has this food come at the cost of unconscionable suffering to animals? Has this food come at the cost of unconscionable exploitation of the earth?

And because such questions, with only the slightest adjustment, can be applied to any number of aspects of our day to day lives, the necessity of material simplicity, in all its forms, begins to come into focus. The major takeaway from Gandhi's "control of the palate" dictum, I believe, is that congruency insofar as our relationship with food is concerned represents a major step—a step that will make a lot of other steps look like a piece of cake (homemade, locally-sourced, and naturally sweetened).

Before departing the palate, a quick word on Gandhi and vegetarianism. Gandhi was born into a vegetarian family, but he wasn't philosophically converted to vegetarianism until his student years in London. His commitment to vegetarianism was rooted in his foundational belief in the unity of all life, in his desire to reduce suffering, and in his supposition that there were no nutritional requirements that a plant-based diet could not meet for human beings. That said, Gandhi admitted that he did not discover an alternative which he found adequately comparable to the bone-strengthening nutrition of goat milk, which was a basic staple for him. While Gandhi regarded his vegetarianism as a natural expression of his comprehensive approach to nonviolence, he remarked that he had meat-eating friends who were better nonviolence practitioners than many of his vegetarian friends.

Needless to say, were Gandhi to witness the industrial farming of our day and age, with its heinous brutality to animals and the earth, he would be beyond horrified. Doubtless he would sternly advise all—vegan, vegetarian, and meat-eater alike—to utterly renounce and resist it.

The Sublimation of Anger

Here's what Gandhi had to say about it in September 1920:

> I have learnt through bitter experience the one supreme lesson to conserve my anger, and as heat conserved is transmuted into energy, even so our anger controlled can be transmuted into a power which can move the world.

Seven or so years later, in July 1927, he said this:

> Anger wells up in my breast when I see or hear about what I consider

to be misdeeds. All I can humbly claim for myself is that I can keep these passions and moods under fair subjection, and prevent them from gaining mastery over me.

And then, in May 1935:

It is not that I do not get angry. I don't give vent to my anger. I cultivate the quality of patience as angerlessness, and generally speaking, I succeed.

Gandhi's self-evaluation notwithstanding, Judith Brown concludes that he had a ways to go in the anger department, at least in his later years:

Although the aging Mahatma seemed to the public a tranquil spirit, he was often moody and experienced a turbulent anger with himself, his family and his close colleagues. He admitted that this was a besetting problem, and at times it disrupted his closest relationships and life in the new ashram he was forming at Sevagram.

Brown goes on to clarify that Gandhi, "a visionary haunted by his own inadequacies," most definitely reserved his harshest judgment and vehemence for himself. Unfortunately, aside from her mention of silence as a helpful antidote—"He found that one of the benefits of his frequent silences was that it seemed to eat up his anger"—and Gandhi's previously mentioned recommendation of fasting for "fretting and foaming," I have uncovered no additional concrete guidance from him when it comes to the rubber hits the road process of conserving and transmuting the energy of anger and redirecting it. In fact, in one of his more unhelpful remarks he all but dismisses those of us who might inquire:

How I find it possible to control [my anger] would be a useless question, for it is a habit that everyone must cultivate and must succeed in forming by constant practice.

One is left to wonder what Gandhi actually knew about working with anger, which he sometimes referred to as "a short madness." His few comments on the subject suggest that his relationship with it was likely governed by the same repressive-suppressive tendency that marked his relationship with all things sexual. Modalities that encourage the open and safe expression of anger, and our embrace and integration of anger as an invaluable aspect of ourselves and as a magnificent inner messenger, have proven immensely liberating and empowering for many nonviolent changemakers.

Despite Gandhi's reticence on the matter, his (and Dr. King's) insistence that our nonviolence must attack unjust systems and conditions, rather than human beings, leads us in the same crucial direction. Our commitment to reserve our compassion for individuals, while directing our righteous indignation at unjust conditions, enables us to invite anger to the party much more freely. In this way, and—it would appear—in this way only, can anger bear its essential gifts. As is so often the case, Gandhi comes at it with different language. Ironically, it's sometimes language that itself bears fiery hints of his insistent and crucially important anger:

> The standard of purity that I want...is not to have such passions [e.g., anger] at all and yet to hate the wrong. When I feel that I have become incapable even of thinking evil, and I hold it to be possible for every God-fearing man to attain that state, I shall wait for no man's advice, and even at the risk of being called the maddest of men, I shall not hesitate to knock at the Viceregal gate or go wherever God leads me, and demand what is due to this country which is being ground to dust today.

MATERIAL SIMPLICITY

We've already noted that courage and one-pointedness are both *fuels for* and *fruits of* self-purification. Two additional elements fulfill the same dual function. The first is heart unity, which we've already been introduced to, and which we'll be looking at more closely in the next chapter. The second, which we couldn't help but hint at and is now requesting our full attention, is material simplicity.

Up front, let's underscore that for Gandhi material simplicity was inseparable from solidarity with the materially poor, and that solidarity with the materially poor was basically everything. In his quest "to see God face to face" Gandhi saw his relationship with and service to the poor as his dharma, his spiritual path:

> If I could persuade myself that I should find [God] in a Himalayan cave I would proceed there immediately. But I know that I cannot find Him apart from humanity.

> It is an obsession...with me that we are all living at the expense of the toiling semi-starved masses.

> I cannot imagine better worship of God than that, in His name, I should labor for the poor.

Gandhi believed that those of us with excess are called to simplify not merely to unencumber ourselves in a physical sense. We simplify in order to be in right relationship with our fellow human beings, and with the planet too, which unencumbers us spiritually.

When it comes to integral nonviolence, it's critical to acknowledge that the call to this particular form of solidarity can only apply to those of us who don't qualify as materially poor. Gandhi, by the way, born as he was into a family situation where he not only never went without his basic necessities, but was educated abroad in England, took a job in South Africa, etc., did not qualify as such, by any stretch, in his Indian milieu. (At the peak of Gandhi's career, life expectancy in India was twenty-seven years old.)

But, easy as it may be to conclude that someone like me or Gandhi isn't poor, it begs the question, who is? And therein lies our bridge to the philo-sophical and spiritual basis for Gandhi's steadfast commitment to downward mobility.

Asteya

St. Basil put it plainly: "You with a second coat in your closet, it does not belong to you. You have stolen it from the poor one who is shivering in the cold." According to the principle of asteya, non-stealing, anything we acquire beyond what we need has been stolen. No matter how it may have come into our possession, if it's more than our basic needs require, we lifted it.

Gandhi believed this literally—"Divine law gives to man from day to day his daily bread and no more"; "the earth has enough to satisfy everyone's legitimate needs but not anyone's greed"—and he maintained that the observance of asteya was essential to the pursuit of a nonviolent life. Boiled down, the observance—which Gandhi instituted as a vow at his ashrams—says to the adherent: If you have more than you need, someone somewhere is going without. And, if you have more than you need, there's room to simplify. John Dominic Crossan's soulful rendering of Jesus' beatitudes suggests that Gandhi was in some pretty impressive company with this view:

> Only the destitute
> are innocent

> Only those who have no bread
> have no fault

Whether or not we agree with Gandhi that this formula (excess for one=lack for another) is a scientific absolute, we have to admit that if it were used as a universal rule of thumb the Domination System wouldn't stand a chance.

Clothing, Housing, Transportation, and Health Care

The method to Gandhi's inspiring madness in the material world begins to take shape, as does the call to a radically simplified lifestyle—a lifestyle that the planet can live with, and that our souls crave with all their silent might. But let's keep going. It will be helpful to consider Gandhi's trajectory in relation to some of the nitty gritty day to day choices we all have to wrestle with.

As a law student in Britain in his early twenties, mimicking his idealized version of a British gentleman, Gandhi could be seen wearing an expensive evening suit and nothing less than a top hat. In contrast, from 1921 until his death in 1948, the loincloth had become his principal garment. While enjoying a lucrative law practice in South Africa, prior to establishing his first land-based community, Gandhi rented "an English villa at the beach a few doors down from the Attorney-General's home." In contrast, at Sevagram Ashram, during the last chapter of his life's journey, Gandhi lived in a mud hut which mirrored the habitations of the Indian peasantry. As for trans-portation, throughout his career Gandhi's preference was to ride third-class rail, in solidarity with the poor masses. Louis Fischer remarks that by 1925 Gandhi mourned that he was no longer able to travel "like a poor man" as "his co-workers made him travel in a second-class compartment" so he could attend to his voluminous correspondence and other writing projects, as well as his need for rest. As for the field of health care, though Gandhi took obvious pride in calling himself a "crank" with "quack" remedies, his core arguments represented, and continue to represent, a compelling challenge to the health and healing status quo. Gandhi was extremely suspicious of Western medicine and the trend toward its acceptance in India, and he was a staunch pioneer of and advocate for *nature cure*, a healing modality still practiced in India.

Nature cure places far more faith in prevention than in cure. As an avid nature curist, Gandhi consistently prescribed "the judicious use of earth, sun, ether, light, and water" as principal healing agents for "body, mind and soul." Steady repetition of the mantra (ramanama), which Gandhi called the "sovereign remedy," was also among his favorite prescriptions. As was walking: "In my opinion," he said, "a brisk walk in the open is the best form of exercise." Many a walking companion testified that it was a serious challenge to keep up with Gandhi on his regular evening strolls.

The sentiment provides an apt segue, as we head now to what may be our biggest lifestyle conundrum of all.

Technology

It's a massive topic, and a wholly appropriate one to close out our exploration under water with self-purification. But before I cut to the quick let me confess the sharp irony that I'm writing this section on an airplane. Yes, I'm penning this section on technology and nonviolence while soaring thirty-five thousand feet above the earth in the most carbon-emitting monstrosity of them all. (My friend Zac calls such plane trips "time travel".) I'm coming back to the states from Palestine, via Tel Aviv, after serving a stint as a volunteer with Christian Peacemaker Teams (CPT) in Hebron. We'll visit CPT briefly in chapter four. It's only fitting to get the props in place—airplane, embarrassment, and all—before launching into a nitty-gritty and necessarily messy talk about tech.

We've already spoken to the personal and collective addiction-factor in relation to all our current gadgetry, but here I want to speak plainly about Gandhi's wide angle views on technology. As we listen to him, let's bear in mind that Gandhi wasn't only one of the premier proponents of love-based nonviolence in human history. He was also a keen firsthand observer of the Industrial Revolution.

As difficult as it may be for us to accept, the headline, friends, reads as follows:

THE GANDHIAN REVOLUTION WILL NOT BE COMPUTERIZED!

A funny thing to include in a book that will be edited, designed, and printed with lots of help from computers. The paradoxes abound—which I generally take as a sign that we're on to something important. To clarify the above headline, by "will not be computerized" I actually mean to implicate the whole tech jumble. I've gotten in the habit of scapegoating the computer because I see it as the current ringleader in the hierarchy of high tech, but that shouldn't overshadow the fact that today the whole tech panoply deserves to stand trial.

Be that as it may, as a helpful test case let's consider some of the environmental impacts of the computer. And, as we do so, let's invite the means=ends principle to look on. The entire process of manufacturing a desktop computer and its monitor, from raw materials to the shelf at the big box store, takes five hundred pounds of fossil fuels, forty-seven pounds of chemicals, and one and a half tons of water. Altogether, that's the equivalent weight of your average rhinoceros. (Imagine lugging him home from Best Buy.) Said computer is made up of about seven hundred different materials and chemicals sourced from somewhere between twenty-five and fifty countries, and it requires up to 200,000 miles of transport. (That's a trip to the moon.) And of course the process of disposing and "recycling" it, which will most likely land it in a mountainous heap somewhere in Southeast Asia, China, India, or Pakistan, will usher in its own shockingly destructive environmental consequences. (In

2014, the combined weight of all those mountainous heaps of e-waste was just shy of forty-two million metric tons.)

If we wanted to use a wider-angled lens, we could also explore the plethora of negative impacts computers are having on the greater ecology, inclusive of our social, emotional, psychological, and physical selves. For now though, it's enough to say that despite all touting, habit, and hard-wired denial, the computer represents an environmental, human health, and human rights nightmare, and that it stands as a symbol for the entire exponential onslaught of modern gadgetry that currently holds our society spellbound.

If indeed the computer is the reigning champ of today's high tech hierarchy, Buddhist author Clark Strand makes a compelling and entrancing case that it and all the rest of our digital contraptions stand on the shoulders of the good old incandescent light bulb:

The time we once knew was marked off in shades of darkness and light. It was in the position of the sun or of the shadows on the ground. We may still have glimpses of that time today. They are commemorated by those quaint words *dawn* and *dusk*, which mean so little to us now when either can be obliterated at the flick of a switch.

To turn out the lights is to turn *over* the human mind—to overthrow it, as it were, so that we can get some perspective on what we truly want and need, so that we can realize that human consciousness…perceives only the narrowest bandwidth and the smallest part of what is.

Darkness is the one remaining revolutionary act. Changing the political order does not matter. Economies are all more or less alike. Governments and cultures rise and fall. The person who chooses to turn off the lights and lie awake in darkness embraces the truth of a life before and beyond all of these…

Others argue that the telephone, automobile, or tv represent the banana peel at the top of our technological slippery slope. Whatever the case, it should come as no surprise that Gandhian nonviolence has always been and remains diametrically opposed to the craze for technological advancements such as these.

Gandhi offers us a profound invitation to face into what we've lost in our surrender to the lure of tech, and what we stand to gain by pulling the plug on it. A century ago, he denounced many common beliefs that are still associated with technology (he spoke of it as "machinery" back then). Two of them, which remain ultra-salient today, were these: that technology somehow has the capacity to save us; and, that there's no turning back—that is, that high tech is here to stay so we might as well accept it, if not dive headlong into the frenzy. The poor were Gandhi's primary concern and consideration, as usual, but he worried too over the spiritual alienation and physical stagnation that new machinery and industrialization signaled for the whole of India and for all the world. If Gandhi were living today there can be no doubt that he would also be appalled and verbose about high tech's egregious environmental consequences.

I refuse to be dazzled by the seeming triumph of machinery... I would not weep over [its] disappearance or consider it a calamity.

What I object to is the 'craze' for...what they call labour-saving machinery. Men go on 'saving labour' till thousands are without work and thrown on the open streets to die of starvation. I want to save time and labour, not for a fraction of mankind, but for all; I want concentration of wealth not in the hands of a few, but in the hands of all. Today machinery merely helps a few to ride on the back of millions.

Whilst this machine age aims at converting men into machines, I am aiming at reinstating man turned machine into his original state.

God forbid that India should ever take to industrialization after the manner of the west. The economic imperialism of a single tiny island kingdom [Great Britain] is today keeping the world in chains. If an entire nation of three hundred million took to similar economic exploitation, it would strip the world bare like locusts.

A time is coming when those who are in the mad rush today of multiplying their wants, vainly thinking that they add to the real substance, real knowledge of the world, will retrace their steps and say: "What have we done?"

Today there is such an onslaught on India of Western machinery that for India to withstand it successfully would be nothing short of a miracle.

You cannot build nonviolence on a factory civilization... If India became the slave of the machine, then, I say, heaven save the world.

Such views on technology may seem extreme to most people today, as they did to most of Gandhi's contemporaries. The man called it like he saw it, and, as it turns out, Gandhi pegged quite accurately where the Industrial Revolution was heading. Our current situation gives more than ample evidence that high tech creates more problems than it solves, at least for those of us committed to living in an equitable, peaceful, and environmentally stable world. This is not to discount that high tech does at times help us solve deeply significant problems, and does at times serve as a powerful tool for good. We can give an appreciative bow to Edward Snowden and Chelsea Manning, for example, for the ways their use of tech has exposed and challenged the inhumanity of the Domination System. We can observe with deep gratitude and awe the benefits that human-made technology has made possible for the disabled community. We can acknowledge great advances in medicine and surgery. But only time, and a Great Turning, will tell if we as a species are capable of achieving such positive modern advances without simultaneously setting unfettered consumption, violence, and destruction in motion. Insofar as the future development of appropriate technology is concerned, the Gandhian insistence that the earth provides for everyone's basic needs, but no more, will likely prove to be our most decisive litmus test.

For now, though, it's critical that we accept that high tech negatives grossly outweigh high tech positives. And, in our state of addiction to the contraptions and practices our tech age holds as essential, we have become utterly alienated from Gandhi's basic admonition that we not only can go back to a simpler way, but that we most definitely should.

For this reason, Gandhi included *bread labor* as one of the eleven vows and observances at his ashrams. He borrowed the phrase from Tolstoy (who borrowed it from the Russian peasant-philosopher-author Timofej Bondarev), to signify the discipline of manual labor towards one's own sustenance and self-reliance. Gandhi saw bread labor as an absolutely essential component of personal and national swaraj. Bread labor would not only promote self-sufficiency, Gandhi believed, it would provide the only reliable foundation for a just economy. It would also act as a spiritual leveler of all classes and clans, giving Indians of every stripe a personal experience of the inherent dignity of the physical labor customarily consigned to the poor and the poor alone.

Lanza del Vasto, founder of the Community of the Ark—one of the most longstanding and powerful Gandhian experiments worldwide—understood the revolutionary significance and potential of bread labor perfectly:

> Work with your hands. Don't force others to work for you. Don't make others into slaves, even if you call them paid workers. Find the shortest, simplest way between the earth, the hands, and the mouth. Don't put anything in between—no money, no heavy machinery. Then you know at once what are the true needs and what are fantasies. When you have to sweat to satisfy your needs, you soon know whether or not it's worth your while. But if it's someone else's sweat, there is no end to our needs. We need cigarettes, cars, soft drinks, appliances, electronic devices, and

on and on. Why not go the other way instead? If we want a more fraternal and just world, let's do it! Let's not wait until others do it. Do it yourself. Show that it is possible to live this way... Learn to do without... Learn how to celebrate... Prepare the feast from what your hands have grown and let it be magnificent.

Though all the world may write this off as utopian hogwash, we can feel in our gut that Lanza del Vasto is preaching unadulterated truth here. We know that this is what nonviolence looks like. Remember Gandhi's answer when asked what he proposed people should do in the absence of all the stuff that modern industry and machinery was making possible? In a nutshell, it was this: With respect to daily living, we should do as our ancestors before us did. As it turns out, I'm afraid, this was simply more than his contemporaries were willing to take. As it is for most of us. Our tech age is itself incontrovertible proof that the means=ends core of Gandhi's teaching was and remains relegated to the fringe.

Reaching for whatever loophole might save us (says the man on the jet plane), we join the fictional interviewer in Gandhi's definitive *Hind Swaraj*, who asks Gandhi how, in view of his strict denunciation of big industry's expansion, he could justify using a high tech printing press to publish his writings. Gandhi's response—which, if we want it to, can let us off the hook— was that sometimes a poison is needed to neutralize another poison. In other words: Sometimes the ends justify the means.

Wait. He said that?

The hypocrite!

Indeed. Judith Brown notes Gandhi's similar moral inconsistency with regard to trains. She lends emphasis, though, to his self-awareness about the matter. "Every time he used a train," she writes, "he would realize he was violating his sense of what was most deeply right, but this would have to be endured." She cites Gandhi's own admission: "The theory is there," he said, "our practice will have to approach it as much as possible. Living in the midst of the rush, we may not be able to shake ourselves free from all taint."

The key difference between Gandhi's tech use and the current tech use of just about everyone currently associated with social change efforts is that Gandhi's inconsistencies existed within the context of his clearly articulated and ceaseless quest to steer his nation toward the simpler, village and swadeshi-based way of life that characterized ancient India. Today, unlike Gandhi, the vast majority of us do not use technology in order to work against it. Even those of us who are in philosophical agreement with Gandhi on the subject of high tech tend to be as enamored with it and as devoted to it as anybody.

Gandhi definitely saw the writing on the wall. But there's no way he could have imagined what it's like now, how far we've fallen, how alienated and sedentary we've become.

But these are the cards we hold. This is the situation from which, in which, we must move. Gandhi's printing press and train quandaries give us a little to work with, but as with so much else it's left to us to improvise in defense of truth. So let's not worry overly whether or not Gandhi deserves a pass for his tech inconsistencies—or, for that matter, any other inconsistencies. The question is, the question always is: Given *our* situation, what are *we* going to do?

Seated as I am on this Boeing 747, it's helpful for me to remember and name that I made my decision to fly from San Francisco to Tel Aviv, and back again, within the above conceptual framework. In the end, God only knows if it was the right thing to do. Obviously, my best guess is that it was. I think Christian Peacemaker Teams holds an important piece that will fit snugly into the puzzle of the Great Turning, and this round-trip flight enabled me to play a small part in that.

When I consult the "more ancient place" inside me, the place beyond thought, what I notice is a subtle and wonderful feeling of anticipation. And I've come to believe that it's an act of self-purification, in and of itself, just to picture it: the moment when the last of all such flights touches down, because the Great Turning has finally carried the day. The moment when we come back to Earth.

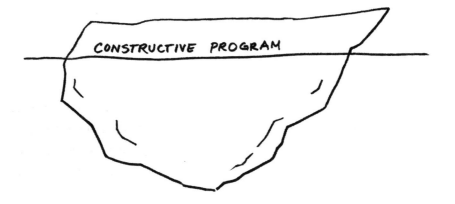

3.
ABOVE WATER

GANDHI WAS ON THE ROAD A LOT. And from 1919 onward, hordes of people would turn out for his gigs. We're talking multitudes. It's not difficult to ascertain that in early and mid-twentieth century India the microphones and loudspeakers on hand had to have been a poor match for the sprawling crowds. Carrying his message throughout the nation, Gandhi needed a strategy for clear communication. His hand raised with fingers outstretched, he spoke into a microphone for those ears near enough to hear. "These must be our priorities," he'd say, indicating five revolutionary social assignments, one per finger. This was Gandhi's condensed prescription for national regeneration—the road to freedom. "Hindu-Muslim unity," he'd say, grabbing his thumb. "The end of untouchability," grabbing his index finger. "Khadi," his middle finger. "The uplift of women," the ring finger. "Sobriety," the little finger. Then, to finish the illustration Gandhi would grab hold of his wrist. "And the trunk of the tree is nonviolence."

It was a memorable, repeatable demonstration. Those within range of the loudspeakers would memorize the formula as Gandhi repeated it to them. They would then turn to those behind them and pass on what they had learned, finger by finger, phrase by phrase, finishing with the stability of the wrist: nonviolence. Then row by row the message would roll like a wave through the crowd. Eventually even those at the fringes of the gathering were readied to return home bearing the message. "This is what Bapu said we need to do. These are the things he said will lead to India's freedom."

———

```
          Key Concepts Review: Pop Quiz 2

    Read each sentence. Choose the phrase that best
replaces the word in italics.

    (1) I just love the way our farmer's market embodies
the spirit of swadeshi!

        (a) hardcore competition
        (b) thrilling adventure
        (c) self-reliant localism
        (d) none of the above

    (2) Struggling for swaraj is hard work, but it sure
is worth it.

        (a) home-rule (based on a transformation of
        self and society)
        (b) the sake of my ego and image
        (c) exquisitely manicured shrubbery
        (d) none of the above
```

POP QUIZ 2 ANSWER KEY: Another smiley face stamp if you answered c and a. (In that order!)

Recalling the primacy of the individual in Gandhi's thought, it's a short climb to understand his fundamental suspicion of the state. This suspicion throws a good amount of light on the meaning and place of constructive program in Gandhi's comprehensive philosophy. The individual, as Gandhi's prime consideration and measure, is not the one typically venerated by the West, competitive and personally ambitious. Gandhi's individual is the universe made small, infinitely unique, unimaginably precious, and wholly connected to all else.

It was because of his love for this individual that Gandhi hoped the state would eventually wither away, to be replaced by "an enlightened anarchy." An enlightened anarchy, that is, where "the sovereignty of the people [would be] based on pure moral authority."

It bears repeating: Political independence was a necessary and important facet of swaraj, but it was only a facet. Gandhi knew that elite Indians were just as capable of hijacking freedom as elite Britons. "Real swaraj will come," he said, "not by the acquisition of authority by a few, but by the acquisition by all of the capacity to resist authority when it is abused…No government on earth can make men who have reclaimed freedom in their hearts salute against their will." The ultimate goal was to be free of government control, be it foreign or national. And social reform, if it was undertaken voluntarily, would simultaneously prepare India for such freedom and concretely enact it. This is what Gandhi was getting at when he said, "The postponement of social reform till after the attainment of swaraj is not to know the meaning of swaraj."

It all goes back to the original hypothesis: Home-rule/self-rule required the Indian people to reclaim the sense of personal dignity and self-respect they had forfeited to their British occupiers. And Gandhi concluded that the hands-on, constructive work of establishing the new, nonviolent society was an indispensable part of this process. It's the exact same conclusion he drew about self-purification. Except that with constructive program it was nation-purification. Once again the logic exemplifies the means=ends premise that Gandhi loved so much: As soon as the Indian people collectively embodied the goals of self-sufficiency and freedom, the political reality would come to reflect that transformation.

To understand constructive program, Gene Sharp suggests we picture a person living in an unsafe, run-down house with a shattered foundation. If he or she is wise enough, rather than retreating to sleep outside in the bitter cold, this person will lay the foundation for a new house while the old one still exists. After all, while far from ideal, the old house still provides relative security and warmth. "As the new structure rises, and is ready for occupation," Sharp explains, "it is possible to withdraw from section after section of the old one, which finally stands deserted and unneeded." Old house, to a combination of old house and new house, to new house—that's the trajectory of constructive program.

Because the outcome desired in Gandhi's India was Indian self-sufficiency and the sense of self-respect that would come from it, the Constructive Programme that Gandhi proposed and promoted, as Sharp's "new house" illustration demonstrates, was especially geared for the work of building up rather than tearing down. Sharp's description also underscores that the Constructive Programme was trained inwardly. "Our contribution to the progress of the world," Gandhi said, "must consist in setting our own house in order." The task, therefore, was autonomous nation-building focused on the self-improvement of local communities and the healing of internal social rifts. In the face of British imperialism, Constructive Programme, in effect, ignored the British—a strategic turn with powerful effects. The program was not dependent on a British response. Its integrity would hold regardless of how the Empire might choose to react.

———

In the U.S., it's helpful to recognize that constructive program usually goes by its alias, community organizing. There's not always a one-to-one correspondence between the two, but the terms are uniquely kindred. Legendary SNCC field worker, Bob Moses, summarizes the community organizing that imbued the civil rights chapter of the freedom struggle: "It [community organizing] doesn't make good copy, but it made the movement. It was the tissue and bones, the inner structure of the movement."

Case in point: In the fall of 1963, Bob Moses' fellow SNCC organizer, Charlie Cobb, began to envision a radical grassroots educational initiative—Freedom Schools. Cobb pictured community-based learning programs that would give poor blacks "an educational experience...[that would] make it possible for them to challenge the myths of our society, to perceive more clearly its realities, and to find alternatives—ultimately new directions for action." Less than a year later, during the Mississippi Freedom Summer of 1964, forty-one Freedom Schools were launched. Located in a total of twenty Mississippi communities, typical enrollment at the schools ranged from twenty-five to one hundred students. Legendary historian Howard Zinn helped design the curriculum, expressing his hope that it would facilitate the Freedom Schools' efforts to find "solutions for poverty, for injustice, for race and national hatred." The curriculum, according to Charlie Cobb, "included normal academic subjects, contemporary issues, cultural expression, and leadership development, [which included] the history of the black liberation movement and the study of political skills."

Meanwhile, organizer-educators Septima Clark, Dorothy Cotton, Bernice Robinson, and Andrew Young were heading up a similar and complementary project, the Citizen Education Program, under the auspices of the Southern Christian Leadership Conference (SCLC), Dr. King's organizational base. The program initially established a grassroots Citizenship School program at the legendary Highlander Folk School in Tennessee, but eventually grew to spawn schools in community centers in hundreds of cities and towns throughout the South. The Citizenship Education Program trained thousands of blacks in literacy, planned parenthood, and civic participation, as well as in the advanced social change arts of community organizing and direct action.

Self-propelled, and not answering to the oppressive regime, the Freedom Schools and Citizenship Schools were the stuff of constructive program through and through. The schools, established as they were in the heart of the South, were deeply significant spaces where blacks could gather to teach, learn, and organize together with a large measure of autonomy. In the ultra-racist context of the Jim Crow South, such spaces were rare and precious. Two other examples were the historic black colleges and the black church. These were everyday spaces, as well as subversive constructive program spaces. We can think of them as behind-the-scenes greenhouses where the seeds of the movement were sown, watered, and tended.

Constructive program is always and everywhere a grassroots affair. And when constructive program happens within a unified and coherent movement its impacts can be profound and lasting. In such a context, the on-the-ground, person-to-person work of constructive program not only serves to meet the day-to-day needs and aspirations of the people, it works as a kind of glue, binding the people to one another in shared struggle and shared development. This is what Bob Moses was getting at when he said that community organizing was the "tissue and bones" of the movement. The Freedom and Citizenship Schools exemplified this. The schools' empowerment of poor, rurally-based blacks to more fully pursue their personal and collective potential, and to more fully struggle for and exercise their citizenship rights wasn't going to draw the newspaper reporters and tv cameras—it didn't "make good copy," as Moses said—but that doesn't change the fact that the schools epitomized the foundational constructive program work that makes movement possible.

Throughout the Southern Freedom Struggle, a healthy and sometimes messy tension was at play between the proponents of community organizing (read "constructive program") and the proponents of mass mobilization (read "satyagraha"). It's a generalization but the first is usually associated with community organizing mentor extraordinaire Ella Baker, and SNCC, and the latter with Dr. King and SCLC. (Ironically, and quite fittingly with regards to the tension in question, Ella Baker was officially an SCLC organizer.) Thankfully, in the end, the movement fairly consistently managed to strike a potent balance between these two elements, recognizing, in effect, that they were mutually reinforcing and interdependent. The most effective movement campaigns reached the national spotlight through mass mobilization, but were always grounded by local leadership and local initiative. While thousands of supporters were drawn from afar into several of the movement's powerful epicenters, such as Birmingham and Selma, the campaigns in such locales always sought support for concrete change at the local level. The precedent for this local change orientation was indelibly established by Rosa Parks, when she sparked the movement's inaugural campaign in Montgomery, Alabama. While heading home to her family, Ms. Parks refused to move her body off of a specific seat on a specific bus in a specific city in the Jim Crow South. Her protest was as localized as it gets, and there was nothing abstract about it. And, as we all know, the year-long bus boycott Parks' one-person localized act of conscience catalyzed ended up having inconceivably immense implications nationally.

This observation recalls the foundational Gandhian commitment to swadeshi, the localism principle at the heart of constructive program. James Lawson, nonviolence trainer for the student leaders who spearheaded the Nashville sit-in movement, and so very much more, highlights its significance:

Gandhi insisted, and I completely agree, that nonviolence has to be rooted in the local scene—in reshaping people and the environment in which the people live... Nonviolent theory is that you root the work in your own environment and place, with your own people and time. And that if you work diligently there, other people in other places will find sympathy with this because their environment is the same.

I've zeroed in on the Freedom and Citizenship Schools in order to highlight the resonance between constructive program and community organizing. But grassroots education was just one of a great many constructive program areas that the movement explored and developed during that phase of the struggle. Arguably, the most significant of them all was grassroots voter registration. But I'm not going to go into that here. Nor to the tenant union organizing, farm cooperatives, business development initiatives, tutoring programs, or credit unions. Nor to SCLC's Operation Breadbasket, or the Freedom Singers, or the Free Southern Theater.

The takeaway stands: The tissue was healthy, the bones were strong.

Gandhi's Constructive Programme evolved over the course of roughly forty years. Its genesis can be traced to Phoenix Settlement and Tolstoy Farm, the two land-based communities Gandhi established during his formative South Africa years. After his return to India in 1915, the program steadily developed and coalesced. By the mid-1920s three particular Constructive Programme priorities had emerged as definitive pillars of the swaraj movement—khadi (promotion of hand-spun, hand-woven cloth), Hindu-Muslim unity, and ending untouchability. As noted at the beginning of this chapter, in my description of Gandhi's hand demonstration, priority-wise, sobriety and the uplift of women were next in line.

Surprisingly, as central as the Constructive Programme was to the movement and to Gandhi's holistic nonviolence philosophy, he didn't publish a complete and systematic description of it until 1941. At that point, having identified and adequately tested what he believed to be the most essential projects of social reform, Gandhi drew up a master plan for India's "new house" and presented it to the nation. The Constructive Programme consisted of the following nineteen projects, to be undertaken across India. In addition, and with a respectful nod to the principle of swadeshi, Gandhi encouraged others to add to the list depending on the needs and circumstances of their own particular contexts:

1. Communal unity (i.e., Hindu-Muslim unity; heart unity across religious lines)
2. The removal of untouchability
3. Sobriety/prohibition of alcoholic drinks and drugs
4. *Khadi* (promotion of hand-spun, hand-woven cloth)
5. Other village industries
6. Village sanitation
7. New or basic education (for children)
8. Adult education
9. Uplift or liberation of women
10. Education in health and hygiene
11. Promotion of provincial languages
12. Promotion of Hindi as national language
13. Economic equality
14. Service of *kisans* (farmers)
15. Organizing laborers
16. Service of the *Adivasis* (aborigines)
17. Service of lepers
18. Service of students
19. Improvement of cattle

The items in the program fall into four broad categories: heart unity, swadeshi, health, and education. As with just about everything we're discussing, though, these groupings are by no means mutually exclusive.

Arguably the most prominent area of the program is heart unity, where we would most likely locate Hindu-Muslim unity, ending untouchability, the uplift of women, economic equality, organizing laborers, and the service of kisans, Adivasis, lepers, and students.

Swadeshi is strongly pronounced as well, through the inclusion of khadi, other village industries, and village sanitation, but also because the program in its entirety was meant to be operationalized at the village level.

In terms of health, both personal and communal, we can note the inclusion, again, of village sanitation, and its interconnection with education in health and hygiene, and sobriety/prohibition.

The realm of education is also of central importance, as evidenced by the inclusion of new or basic education, adult education, education in health and hygiene, service of students, the promotion of provincial languages, and the promotion of Hindi as national language. It's important to observe that these latter provincial and national language components existed within the context of the dignity and culture-sapping encroachment of English, the occupiers' language. Reclaiming India's rich plurality of regional tongues and elevating Hindi to the throne as the unifying national language was another pure embodiment of swaraj, both inward and outward, personal and collective.

Improvement of cattle, a late addition to the Constructive Programme put forward in Gandhi's revised 1946 edition, is in something of its own category. This point on the program was principally motivated by the Hindu tenet that reverence for and protection of the cow enjoins humanity to all that lives. But it is also true that in addition to shoring up the nation in a moral sense, the improvement of cattle would also bolster its rural economy. As such, this final addition to the program was intimately linked to khadi and the other village industries that heralded the return to the human-scaled village-based economic model that Gandhi championed.

Now that we have a general feel for the whole program, let's dig in and see if we can get a firmer grasp of its true depth and reach—and a clearer sense for what it has to teach us about our own work today. To do so let's return to Gandhi's hand demonstration and take a closer look at his Constructive Programme top five.

KHADI

From Louis Fischer's account of his visit with Gandhi in 1946:

> I went to Gandhi's room and found him spinning. I said I thought he had abandoned spinning. "No, how could I?" he asked. "There are four hundred million Indians. Subtract one hundred million children, waifs, and others; if the remaining three hundred million would spin an hour each day we would have Swaraj."
>
> "Because of the economic or spiritual effect?" I asked.
>
> "Both," he said. "If three hundred million people did the same thing once a day not because a Hitler ordered it but because they were inspired by the same ideal we would have enough unity of purpose to achieve independence."
>
> "When you stop spinning to talk to me you are delaying Swaraj."
>
> "Yes," he agreed, "you have postponed Swaraj by six yards."

Like salt, khadi (homespun cotton) is not the kind of thing one would usually associate with revolution. But Gandhi reports: "God whispered into my ear: 'If you want to work through nonviolence, you have to proceed with small things." Michael Nagler treats khadi excellently in *The Search for a Nonviolent Future*, a gold mine for students of Gandhi. The Constructive Programme, Michael explains, had "an overall design, which was extremely simple and could be visualized in a single, oft-repeated image: Constructive Programme was a 'solar system,' Gandhi would often say, and charkha (the spinning wheel) was the 'sun.'" The khadi campaign, symbolized and actualized by the spinning wheel, was the epitome of swadeshi. "Khadi connotes the beginning of economic freedom in all of the country," Gandhi said. "It means a wholesale Swadeshi mentality, a determination to find all the necessaries of life in India and that too through the labour and intellect of the villagers." There were stretches in Gandhi's career when his ceaseless campaigning for the khadi movement was nothing less than obsessive. From village to village he argued that the ancient spinning industry, which had been surrendered to the foreign occupier (Britain's monopoly on the textile industry was as fixed as it was with salt), represented the purest means of attaining the inner attitudinal shift toward self-reliance that would clear the path to political liberty. Gandhi also knew that there would be no better way to promote and galvanize the swaraj movement than to have India's peasantry donning the home-spun clothing that represented the movement's moral force.

Furthermore, the social impact of khadi was not limited to the poor. Wealthy Indians participated in the campaign as well, and in wearing the finished product, the informal homespun uniform of the movement, they experienced a new, powerful sense of national pride and solidarity with their fellows. Again Michael Nagler explains: "Wearing their beliefs on their bodies, many well-off Indians found out firsthand that brotherhood is more satisfying than status." I'm reminded of the India segment of the documentary film, *A Force More Powerful*. I'm honestly not a big fan, because of the way the film reinforces an icebergless Gandhi. But the imagery of the khadi-clad resisters is incredibly inspiring. What a deep joy it would be to suit up with a team like that, at a moment like that.

As we've already discussed, following khadi, Gandhi placed "other village industries" in his Constructive Programme recipe. The spinning wheel was the gateway to revitalizing India's entire village economy, which Gandhi believed to be the surest foundation for the nation's economic future. Other lost or dwindling industries needed to be revived along with khadi, in the same spirit of swadeshi, and with the same payoff—meaningful labor, necessary goods, and the personal and collective self-esteem that was swaraj in the making.

A good friend of mine makes regular use of a question that cuts to the quick of the spinning wheel's significance: "What are they holding over us?" (I take the "they" in this case to refer to the Domination System, of which we're a part.) The spinning wheel helps me recognize the extent to which my own life, my own living, is constricted by the hydra of capitalism, one of the Domination System's favorite tools. And of course capitalism's impacts are far, far more debilitating for the majority of humanity than they are for me. The Domination System holds capitalism and its insistence that there will be winners and losers, over all of us. And far too often we offer capitalism our unwavering, if unwitting, allegiance. The commodification of things like food, housing, health care, education, entertainment, and recreation are so accepted, so routine, so everyday that we forget that it doesn't need to be set up like this. The spinning wheel reminds us that there is another way—the one Lanza del Vasto described in the previous chapter—and that despite appearances we have the power to choose it.

The conversation is ongoing as to what should shine, or is shining, as the sun in our own constructive program solar system. I've heard compelling arguments that local healthy food, by way of permaculture, represents our best counterpart to the charka (spinning wheel). The bicycle—spinning wheels indeed—makes for a strong contestant too. Both definitely exemplify the positive, proactive essence of constructive program, its near-universal accessibility, and its power of peaceful subversion. Local food and bikes thumb their noses at extraction-based, spirit-deadening capitalism in dozens of ways. Just a few examples: They enact a withdrawal of support from and dependence on some of the biggest and most destructive industries—factory farming, automobiles, and fossil fuels. They support physical health and well-being. And they encourage face-to-face fellowship with other members of our communities.

Until very recently, the question of what our counterpart to the charka should be hasn't concerned me much. I wasn't easily persuaded that we needed a centerpiece on our banquet table. Then I read *Waking Up to the Dark*.

As funny a juxtaposition as it is, Clark Strand's extraordinary book has persuaded me that the sun shining at the center of our constructive program solar system should be darkness. My own experience living without electric light convinces me that Strand is spot on when he argues that restoring ourselves to the natural rhythms of day and night and season to season is a truly revolutionary shift. As things stand today I've come to believe that no single lifestyle choice holds the same potential for transforming our personal and collective consciousness to the degree needed to turn the Great Turning. I know many avid permaculturists, local food crusaders, and car-free cyclists who have not shaken free of their personal status quo enough to boldly step away from the consuming/extracting mainstream. Were they to cash in their bulbs for candles, I'd be willing to bet that most of them would.

I suggest we let candlelight and darkness, what Strand calls "the Dark Revolt," be the transformative slippery slope that sends us headlong into the Great Turning:

> The last true revolutionary act left to human beings in the twenty-first century is to turn out the lights. Other acts are possible—acts we may *call* revolutionary—but they do not meet the criteria of the word as it must necessarily be interpreted today. Nothing short of turning out the lights will lead to an overturning of the endgame global system that now has is in its thrall...

> Turn out the lights—and leave them off—and we will experience a consciousness our minds have never known but our bodies still remember. Leave them on, and it scarcely matters what else we do or leave undone. We will not significantly alter our path through time. Nor will we alter the path of our species, which has taken a collective detour leading nowhere but oblivion and extinction. We persist perpetually in making all of this seem more complicated than it is...

> Let there be darkness.

Whatever our centerpiece may turn out to be, if in fact we end up with one, it's crucial to recognize that nonviolence needs to be made new in each movement, each culture, each epoch. While we certainly want to integrate and incorporate lessons from the past, imitating what's been done before isn't going to generate the nonviolent force needed in the here and now. Our predecessors didn't figure it all out, and their circumstances were different than ours. We honor them best by fully expressing our own wisdom and creativity.

And, at the end of the day, let's remain clear that the most important thing is that we're working shoulder to shoulder on a robust, personally and socially transformative constructive program—and not spending an inordinate amount of time talking about it.

SOBRIETY (revisited)

This is a great example of a place on the iceberg where the water rises and falls and the dividing line between two aspects of the Gandhian approach becomes indecipherable. Therefore, though we already discussed sobriety at length when we were under water with self-purification, it's equally important to look at it here, above water with constructive program.

In Gandhi's case, while there is zero evidence to suggest that he ever personally suffered from it, the impacts of alcoholism drew his special and profound concern. Gandhi was deeply pained looking on as the mental, spiritual, and physical vitality of a great many of his fellow Indians was being destroyed by alcohol dependency and abuse. And, Gandhi observed, right along with that vitality went their self-respect and capacity for service. To add further insult to injury, guess who had a monopoly (a la salt, a la textiles) on the alcohol industry? Yes, surprise surprise, Britain was making money and subduing the people with one fell alcohol-induced stroke.

Gandhi was likewise deeply troubled by India's rampant addiction to opium and other intoxicants.

But again, the specifics of Gandhi's time and place are not our chief concern here. Our chief concern is the fact that our own vitality, self-respect, and capacity for service are just as hampered for us as they were for those in Gandhi's India. And, while I would certainly argue that alcohol use is a huge barrier to swaraj in our own context, we've already established that we need to chart a course to well-being in the face of a much greater spectrum of dependencies, and we need to envision structures and practices that will enable us to offer sturdy, ongoing support to one another as we do so. Here again we are fortunate to have tools in our toolbelt that Gandhi and his contemporaries never had access to. In the century that's passed since Gandhi called for prohibition of alcohol and drugs in India, we've learned an enormous amount about the nature of addiction and sobriety.

How can serious nonviolence practitioners best engage with one another about the dependencies that are tripping us up, and about dependency itself? 12-step programs have cropped up in dozens of flavors, of course, enabling people to hone in on their particular addictions. But I'm curious to know if certain principles and modes of support can be applied in a more holistic fashion, so we nonviolence practitioners can share sobriety fellowship across the great spectrum of our struggles.

Some friends and I experimented for several months with a 12-step inspired group we called First World Lifestyles Anonymous. It may sound funny, but we were dead serious about this thing. It was our attempt to create a space for talking through our struggles and our breakthroughs as members of our extraction and consumption-driven society. It was a worthy experiment, and more such experiments may help us discover what it really and truly means to be sober, how to get there, and how to stay there.

Recalling our First World Lifestyles Anonymous experiment I'd be remiss if I didn't give a solemn bow in honor of Alcoholics Anonymous (AA), the 12-step flagship. I'm unable to think of a more far-reaching example of constructive program on the planet. When my dad first got sober, my big brother and I tagged along with him to AA meetings every now and then. As a thirteen year-old, listening to the raw, confessional honesty of the folks in those rooms, my first and lasting impression (as a kid who'd been raised as a dutiful, if not altogether faithful, churchgoer) was that I had finally experienced what the word *church* was actually meant to signify. People talking about their lives, their struggles and accomplishments, their faith, their pain, their strength and hope. And all sorts of people too. What a sight to see, and not an uncommon one in those rooms: the staunchest Republican businessman sitting next to the hippy with tats and dreds, and each of them drawing strength and wisdom from one another in their shared effort to go another day without a drink.

I honestly can't remember a time when I heard AA referred to as a social movement. But that's how I see it, a constructive program social movement. No signs or banners, no marches, vigils, or speeches—but a movement of enormous power. I know AA/12-step isn't a cure all, or a fit for every addict. And I am of course aware that AA/12-step doesn't call into question the treacherous systems of oppression that Gandhian nonviolence demands we wrestle with. The narrowness of AA/12-step's mission—to help people attain and keep their sobriety—is a great strength, but also a great limitation. Be that as it may, the amount of fellowship and sobriety that particular structure has engendered is mind-boggling. There's a lot we can learn from it.

HEART UNITY (pt. 1)

The remaining three fingers on Gandhi's Constructive Programme hand—Hindu-Muslim unity, the uplift of women, and ending untouchability—all fall in this domain, so I'm opting to gather them together. You'll remember heart unity as one of the nine nonviolence All-Stars discussed in chapter 1. In short, it signifies the establishment of human connection and justice across lines of bitter, often violent division. As Gandhi envisioned a purified and liberated India, the work of healing internal social division and of freeing marginalized groups from their second-class status was at the forefront of his consciousness. One could argue, in fact, with little difficulty, that his entire personal-social-political platform was based on this fundamental heart unity aspiration.

A fascinating fault line in the Indian politics of Gandhi's time shows the true nature of the equality he sought. This fault line was the recurring question of the makeup of the Indian legislative assemblies that were overseen by the British. On more than one occasion Gandhi's quest for heart unity-based equality rubbed up against the vehement desire of India's minority groups, so called, such as Muslims, untouchables, Parsis, Anglo-Indians, Christians, and Laborites, to have separate electorates, which would guarantee their representation in the legislative assemblies. Gandhi bitterly opposed separate electorates. In one case, regarding the possibility of separate electoral seats for Untouchables, he was so forcefully opposed that he undertook a fast unto death. It nearly went that far. Gandhi's rationale and passion on the subject befuddled many, supporters and detractors alike, some of whom decided that he was basically out of his mind. Why, they strained to understand, would the mahatma, who claimed to be giving everything for the poor and under-represented, balk at a guarantee that marginalized groups would have a say in the political deliberations that would impact their lives and destinies? But Gandhi's answer was simple and, well, very Gandhian: In the India of his dreams, heart unity would render separate electorates utterly unnecessary. Indians would vote as Indians for their fellow Indians on the basis of their character and qualifications. And leaders deputized by an electorate would serve in the best interests of all. This is definitely the naïve-sounding Gandhi again—the same Gandhi audacious enough to aim for the uplift of all beings and a face to face encounter with God. To him, the institutionalization of division by way of separate electorates, or any other form of segregation, bore the signature of divide and rule imperialism. He wanted nothing of it, and he desperately wanted his nation to want nothing of it too.

The controversy surrounding Gandhi's stance on the question of separate electorates has been newly revived due to the recent re-release of B.R. Ambedkar's *Annihilation of Caste*. Ambedkar, a contemporary and frequent sparring partner of Gandhi's, is indisputably the most lauded Dalit (formerly "untouchable") leader and hero in modern history, and *Annihilation of Caste* is his most scathing attack on both caste and the Hindu religion that birthed it. The new edition of the book features an in-depth introduction, *The Doctor and the Saint*, written by the remarkable Arundhati Roy. Over the course of the introduction's 150 some odd pages Roy more or less bludgeons Gandhi for his views and actions (and inaction) related to the caste system.

To Roy's and Ambedkar's credit, despite Gandhi's incessant struggle for the end of untouchability, he clearly needed to be schooled on the fundamental and treacherous injustice of the caste system as a whole. Ambedkar was well suited to the task, as is plainly evident in *Annihilation of Caste*. Even by the standards of his day, Gandhi's belief that, in principle, caste represented a meritorious system of social organization was antiquated and deeply flawed. Yet, what is equally clear is that the true nature and reach of Gandhi's heart unity commitment and rationale escaped Ambedkar, as it did so many of Gandhi's contemporaries, and that it continues to elude people today, including, apparently, Arundhati Roy.

"If I could tear [my heart] open, you would discover there are no compartments in it," Gandhi wrote in 1921. But don't mistake the comment as evidence of what we in the U.S. today refer to as "colorblindness," the shortsighted and counterproductive belief that not seeing racial or ethnic difference, or somehow seeing beyond such difference, represents a virtuous social goal. On the contrary, Gandhi recognized and reveled in the unparalleled and outrageously complex diversity of his motherland, and he refused to ignore or minimize the deep effects of the longstanding abuses leveled against untouchables and many other marginalized communities. The reason that Gandhi's heart unity commitment and rationale baffled and incensed so many of his fellow Indians, including Ambedkar, (and why I believe it lands similarly for many today) is that they made the mistake of assuming that Gandhi was operating in the paradigm with which they were most familiar, and that his primary motives, therefore, must have been political. They weren't. Gandhi's primary impulse was spiritual. To those who thought he had lost his mind, as many did (and still do) on the electorates question, Gandhi's reply was characteristically forthright: "I hug the belief that I may not be insane and may be truly religious."

In *The New Jim Crow*, Michelle Alexander presents a powerful contemporary analogue to Gandhi's stance on separate electorates. Her commentary on affirmative action and "racial bribes" echoes Gandhi's prophetic warning that we run a great risk of trading in the possibility of deep-rooted transformation and authentic reparations when we jump at guarantees of short-term and structurally superficial reform, however well-intentioned they may appear to be.

As with Gandhi's fight against the "rank irreligion" and "segregation gone mad" of the institution of untouchability, heart unity was also the defining motivation for his struggle on behalf of Hindu-Muslim friendship, "the firm rock on which [he] hoped to build a united, free India." Heart unity also fueled his struggle against the legal and customary repression and oppression of Indian women and girls, by men, through barring access to education and the vote, through forced marriages, child marriage, forced widowhood, the dowry system, and purdah, with its various forms of segregation and seclusion. In all three of these social crusades we see that Gandhi's refusal to brook the institutionalization of inequality, and the outright bigotry that so often accompanied it, was a defining mark of his nonviolence. He saw with stark clarity that polarization and hatred based on race, gender, and religion had infected the collective psyche of his nation—and his world—and that heart unity represented the only trustworthy antidote.

We needn't delve more deeply into the particularities of these three of Gandhi's Constructive Programme top five. Unsurprisingly, my hope in gathering them under the heading of heart unity is not that our attention will fall on the details pertaining to the social curses of Gandhi's time and place, but to the question of what social curses are analogous for us in our own context. The crucial work for us, after all, is to identify our own heart unity assignments, already undertaken and still to undertake.

It wasn't until a few short years ago that I felt the core significance and concrete relevance of heart unity actually come home to me. It arrived by way of particular leaders, all formerly incarcerated folks, of the movement to end mass incarceration. Witnessing the spirit and great strength of their social change organizing and their process together, a simple and counter-intuitive realization was given to me. I suddenly saw that my work within the movement to end mass incarceration was the most potent contribution I could make to the movement to counter climate change.

Come again?

While my surface level thinking on this has changed since reading *This Changes Everything*, the essence remains. My realization was twofold.

First: We definitely find ourselves in an "all hands on deck" situation. The team we need to assemble to turn the Great Turning must include people who are currently incarcerated or currently under the boot of the prison industrial complex in some other form. The same applies to those impacted by the system's twin, mass deportation, not to mention its cousins, U.S. homelessness, human trafficking et al. Understandably and necessarily, because of the structural violence folks in those situations are facing down, the nitty-gritty climate change work that Naomi Klein and co. are talking about rarely finds its way onto their radar. Basic needs must be met and a modicum of freedom must be attained before a person can contemplate taking on the machinery of Empire.

In this same light it's critical to observe that the soon-to-be majority of folks in our country will not be descendants of the Manifest Destined and the plantation owners. They will be the descendants of slaves. They will be the descendants of immigrants both "legal" and "illegal." They will be people of color. And the changemakers within our communities of color, and in poor white communities too, have always carried out the lion's share of their constructive program / community organizing efforts around issues related to basic human needs and survival. I'm generalizing, for sure, but it's an accurate enough observation, and an incredibly important one: Folks without privilege in our society have never had the luxury of choosing their cause. Their cause, their social struggle, has been scripted for them in advance, and delivered right to their door. When, that is, the boot of Empire kicks it in, bearing poverty, incarceration, deportation, unemployment, and social contempt to a degree white America could never imagine.

Second: At the most basic moral level, the ground floor of means=ends, do we really think we get to pull off a Turning worthy of the adjective Great while two-plus million of our family members are locked in cages? While hundreds of thousands of the world's twenty-one million trafficked human beings are living and suffering among us—the majority being women and girls trapped in the sex trade? While an average of 350,000 are being deported every year? While well over half a million are living on the streets? In short, in the U.S. today mass incarceration, human trafficking, mass deportation, and homelessness are analogues for Indian untouchability during Gandhi's lifetime. Of which he said:

> Swaraj is a meaningless term if we desire to keep a fifth of India under perpetual subjection.... Inhuman ourselves, we may not plead before the Throne for deliverance from the inhumanity of others... I would far rather Hinduism died than that untouchability lived.

Heart unity was a deal-breaker for Gandhi, a mandatory prerequisite for freedom. Hearkening back to chapter 1, he put it plainly when speaking of his fellow Indians: "Before they dare think of freedom they must be brave enough to love one another...and to trust one another." For us, in our context, loving and trusting one another means an end to the social ills noted above, along with a slew of other blatantly oppressive and dehumanizing systems and conditions. What's more, some of our most committed and inspiring nonviolence practitioners are teaching us to embrace the realization that the selfsame experience of heart unity calls us and moves us to extend the reach of our compassion and thirst for justice to include all non-human life and the totality of the earth and biosphere. Gandhi, the devout Hindu, would no doubt smile on this extension of the heart unity doctrine, capturing as it does the essence of our oneness with the whole of creation. In the age of the Great Turning I'm not sure it's possible to overemphasize the importance of this shift.

One more observation before transitioning to heart unity from a different angle. I mentioned before that Gandhi's focus and passion veered into the obsessive with the khadi campaign. The same can definitely be said of Hindu-Muslim unity and the removal of untouchability. For Gandhi, these represented something of a magical trio. "To paraphrase a Biblical verse, if it is no profanation," he wrote in 1924, "'Seek you first Hindu-Moslem unity, removal of untouchability, and Khaddar [homespun], and everything will be added unto you.'" Gandhi knew his nation. And while he insisted that all of the social reforms of the Constructive Programme were necessary, he concluded that these three, if achieved, would yield the key to swaraj. It was the kind of incisive strategic-spiritual calculation that typified Gandhi's leadership.

HEART UNITY (pt. 2)

We can step away from Gandhi's constructive program top five now. But we'd be remiss to not tarry a bit longer with heart unity, which I contend is the highest wall our U.S. society—and perhaps the entire human community—needs to climb together. It happens to be the same wall Gandhi's India needed, and unfortunately failed, to climb.

Economic Equality

Of this sweeping, amorphous and holy grail of the Constructive Programme, Gandhi wrote:

> By the nonviolent method, we seek not to destroy the capitalist, we seek to destroy capitalism... An economics that inculcates Mammon worship, that enables the strong to amass wealth at the expense of the weak, is a false and dismal science. True economics...stands for social justice.

And the people said *Amen!*

So Gandhi went on preaching. The return to the human-scaled village-based economic model of India's yesteryear was the remedy, he said,
where each and every village would be a republic unto itself, independent
and happily, voluntarily interdependent with its surrounding villages. Khadi
and the "other village industries" identified in the Constructive Programme,
Gandhi hoped, would give India its start, by clearing the path to self-sufficiency for the peasantry and laborers.

But all too easily the framing of such radical societal transformation in
economic terms can distract us from the fact that, at its root, the economic
equality point on Gandhi's Constructive Programme was the stuff of heart
unity through and through. No chasm was (or remains) greater in the Indian
context than the chasm between rich and poor, and Gandhi knew that swaraj
would remain out of reach until that chasm was bridged.

In addition to preaching the gospel of simplicity, khadi, and swadeshi,
Gandhi gave a few more teeth to the economic equality point of the
Constructive Programme by calling on the rich of the land to adopt the
practice of "trusteeship," a bold summons to those with wealth to voluntarily
redistribute it. A direct extension of asteya (non-stealing), trusteeship was
based on the belief that any possession that comes into our keeping is not
"ours" but has been entrusted to us by God, to be used and stewarded for
the well-being of all. According to Gandhi:

> The contrast between the palaces of New Delhi and the miserable hovels
> of the poor laboring class nearby cannot last a day in a free India in which
> the poor will enjoy the same power as the richest in the land. A violent
> and bloody revolution is a certainty one day unless there is a voluntary
> abdication of riches and the power that riches give, and sharing them
> for the common good...

> Trusteeship provides a means of transforming the present capitalist order
> of society into an egalitarian one. It gives no quarter to capitalism, but

gives the present owning class a chance of reforming itself. It is based on the faith that human nature is never beyond redemption.

For those of us in the U.S., Dr. King situates the goal of economic equality with his usual clarity and power. In November 1966, King admitted to his SCLC staff the limitations of the movement's accomplishments over the preceding decade of struggle, which included the movement's most lauded legislative gains, the Civil Rights Act and the Voting Rights Act:

> Even though we gained legislative and judicial victories during this period, that rectified long-standing evils [and] caste structures...these victories did very little to penetrate the lower depths of Negro deprivation… However difficult it is for us to admit this, we must admit it: the changes that came about during this period were at best surface changes.

Dr. King then proceeded to describe for his co-workers how the new demands the movement was beginning to press were in an altogether different category than what had come before. The movement was now aiming for true equality and power-sharing, which meant that it was going to hit at the core of the racist establishment in a way and to a degree never before seen. This, King and his colleagues knew all to well, had everything to do with economics. Unlike the acquisition of voting rights and desegregation statutes, King explained, advances toward authentic economic equality would actually "cost the nation something":

> You can't talk about solving the economic problem of the Negro without talking about billions of dollars. You can't talk about ending slums without first saying profit must be taken out of slums. You're really tampering and getting on dangerous ground because you are messing with folk then. You are messing with the captains of industry… Now this means we are treading in very difficult waters, because it really means that we are saying that something is wrong with the economic system of our

nation… It means that something is wrong with capitalism.

King knew, of course, that the redistribution of wealth he was proposing—which would take the form of things like full employment legislation, a guaranteed annual income for all, a national health care system, a revamped and equitable tax system, and an end to slums—would not merely mess with the captains of industry. What he was proposing would level a blow to the white status quo altogether, because it would, by necessity, rein in the standard of living of the privileged. In comparison, removing "Whites Only" signs and giving blacks the vote hadn't cost white folks and the rest of the nation a dime. (Not to discount the fact that a lot of egos and racist psyches took a serious hit when such changes were enacted.)

Obviously the cost King identified in 1966 was never paid, and the redistribution of wealth he envisioned was never actualized. (I believe King's assassination in 1968 was a significant part of the reason why.) And today, such redistribution would "cost the nation" a great deal more.

To take matters a critical step further, we recognize that the prospect of such wealth redistribution within the United States—where the wealth of the mostly white hoarding class would be deliberately shared with the rest of the nation—serves as a sobering microcosmic picture of the United States' relationship with the rest of the world. Today we of the United States make up less than 5 percent of the world's population and we use approximately 25 percent of the world's resources. Just as the wealth gap within the United States guarantees us social hostility, instability, and violence, who could rationally argue that until we as a nation give up this shamefully unfair 5 percent / 25 percent scheme the world can be anything but war-ridden and climate catastrophe-bound? With such an egregiously unjust baseline intact, no economic or social theory, no technological fix, smoke, or mirrors can finagle a way out of such consequences.

The Great Turning, in no uncertain terms, requires us to give up such consumption, hoarding, and inequality, both domestically and globally. It will be a profound and unsettling upheaval for nearly all of us. But the force of the shock will most likely come in direct proportion to the amount of unearned and spiritually deadening privilege each of us has been enjoying.

Gift Economics

Arguably, our most powerful tool for this piece of the work is our closest contemporary corollary to Gandhian trusteeship: gift economics. The gift economy turns market capitalism on its head. In this model, the bi-directional transaction that defines the consumerist marketplace—where you give me money and I give you a product or service in return—is replaced by the uni-directional offering of a gift, no charge. In effect, with gift economics we renounce the practice of putting a price on that which is priceless. (Isn't everything priceless, in the truest sense?) We give, therefore; we do not sell.

It's an economic model that dates back quite a while. Ever since the Big Bang the whole of creation has functioned on the constant giving and receiving of energy.

For life on Earth it all begins with the sun:

The Sun Never Says

Even
After
All this time
The sun never says to the earth,

"You owe
Me."

Look
What happens
With a love like that,
It lights the
Whole
Sky.

—Hafiz

Seen over the expanse of our sojourn on Earth, humanity's separation from this practice and spirit of exchange is only a recent phenomenon. If we rewind, just a little, we recall that our ancestors were nature-based people who functioned within the gift. That is, they functioned within the natural give and take—with each other and with the earth—which is modeled by all living creatures and ecosystems.

And now, thanks to the dictates of justice, the call to forge economic equality is pointing us back in the direction of the gift.

Instead of relying on fees and price tags, the gift economy is anchored by a trust that the bearer of gifts—that is, whomever is providing the community with needed goods and services out of generosity—will be cared for in return. This is not because the recipient, whether an individual or a collective, owes the gift-giver, but because that individual or collective is moved and able to give their own gift in return. If the recipient doesn't wish to or is unable to give a gift in return, the gift economy leans even more deeply into its trust, keeping faith that if in fact the gift giver's offering is truly needed in service to the community, provision will come from somewhere else and the gift giver's needs will be met.

As unrealistic as it may sound, as it turns out, such trust in the innate generosity and other-centeredness of the human being is having amazing results in places where folks have taken the leap of faith required by the gift economy. Not least among these results: People with skills and visions that are not typically assigned much if any market value are breaking free from wage dependency in order to practice their true vocation. Goods and services that are usually only available to those with money are becoming accessible to those without it. Attitudes of compassion and generosity are being fostered. Deep-rooted fear and anxiety attached to all things money-related are being overcome. And human beings are re-learning a true and just economics, as modeled by nature herself—the greatest gift giver of all—and as written in our hearts.

It is also true that in the U.S. today the practice of gift economics and its potential societal impact have only barely begun to be felt. Despite its immeasurably ancient origins, from a certain perspective the concept is new. And given how deeply countercultural it is, it's a pretty tough sell.

As far as I can tell, though, the main reason gift economics hasn't taken off yet, and can't, is that two other intertwined and utterly essential heart unity ingredients are, for all intents and purposes, nowhere to be found.

Atonement and Reparations (pt. 2)

> What I'm talking about is more than recompense for past injustices—more than a handout, a payoff, hush money, or a reluctant bribe. What I'm talking about is a national reckoning that would lead to spiritual renewal... Reparations would mean a revolution of American conscious-ness, a reconciling of our self-image as the great democratizer with the facts of our history.
>
> —Ta-Nehisi Coates, "The Case for Reparations"

Nowhere is white privilege more pronounced than in the realm of economics. As difficult as it may be for some of us to admit, the gift economy, for all its moral virtue, makes for a prime example. Like "simple living" and "vol-untary poverty," the gift economy, generally speaking, is made much more readily attractive and plausible to white folks than it is to people of color.

This is due to the simple fact that white folks have white connections, and are therefore far more likely to enjoy familial financial security and privileged access to things like quality education, employment, and inheritance. Gift economics—as well-intentioned and important as it is—remains incomplete and aspirational because it represents only one side of the coin of economic justice. Operationalizing a sweeping national atonement and reparations campaign, I believe, is the indispensable other side of that coin.

As we touched on in chapter 2, white America has in no way, shape, or form collectively atoned for its racially-based wrongdoing, both past and present. What's more, only the smallest fraction of those of us who are white have begun to wake up to the insidiousness and bankruptcy of the "white savior complex" to which many of us have succumbed. Yes, it's past time to admit that a good number of us pride ourselves in being part of the rescue crew, without reckoning with the fact that we're the ones who set the house on fire in the first place, and who still unwittingly fan the flames.

Nothing, perhaps, exposes this dynamic better than the intersection of U.S. white supremacy and the climate change crisis. Ta-Nehisi Coates speaks directly to this in his era-defining *Between the World and Me*, while calling the American Dream by its true name:

> Plunder has matured into habit and addiction; the people who could author the mechanized death of our ghettos, the mass rape of private prisons, then engineer their own forgetting, must inevitably plunder much more... Once, the Dream's parameters were caged by technology and by the limits of horsepower and wind. But the Dreamers have improved themselves, and the damming of seas for voltage, the extraction of coal, the transmuting of oil into food, have enabled an expansion in plunder with no known precedent. And this revolution has freed the Dreamers to plunder not just the bodies of humans but the body of the earth itself... The two phenomena are known to each other. It was the cotton that passed through our chained hands that inaugurated this age.

Dr. King, in that same 1966 speech cited previously, retraced the Dreamers' plunder to a still earlier epoch. Over the course of human history, he pointed out, conquesting groups have typically assimilated with the indigenous populations of the territories they seize. "But this wasn't so in America," King said. "The white man literally sought to annihilate the Indian." In *Where Do We Go From Here?* he elaborated further:

> The common phrase, "The only good Indian is a dead Indian," was virtually elevated to national policy. Thus the poisoning of the American mind was accomplished not only by acts of discrimination and exploitation but by the exaltation of murder as an expression of the courage and initiative of the pioneer.

Like Dr. King, Naomi Klein rewinds to white America's original crimes against indigenous people in order to better understand how we ended up in our current civilizational dead-end. Like Coates, she connects the dots between the plunder of human bodies and the plunder of the earth itself. For all its research, commentary, and analysis, Klein's *This Changes Everything* boils down to a simple story of the collision of two basic and fundamentally opposed worldviews. One worldview is based on the domination of both people and land; the other is based on human interdependence and the conviction that land is not a thing to be owned or exploited. At the heart of this simple story is the recognition that all over the world a great many of the epicenters of the current climate justice struggle are headed up by indigenous people seeking to protect the land from relentless corporate encroachment. In other words, at the heart of the story is the full-circle coming around of the original clash between *take* and *steward*.

In many of the climate action epicenters that Klein describes, inspiring cases of reconciliation are underway between indigenous folks and non-Native folks, as they team up—often across bitter lines of division and racism—to struggle for environmental and social justice. Her observations remind me of some of my own in relation to the movement to end mass incarceration, another struggle where the full-circle coming around of unchecked racism and unacknowledged wrongdoing is opening up invaluable opportunities for connection, reconciliation, and unified action across lines of deep distrust and misunderstanding.

These are hopeful and deeply instructive examples. And, here again, we need to be humble enough and summon strength enough to be brutally honest. Taken to scale, we as a national community haven't yet begun to understand, let alone practice, the stuff of heart unity and beloved community. And how could we, unless and until those of us who are white choose stewardship over theft? Which is to say: How could we until we atone, deeply and sincerely, and repair whatever is reparable?

As a white American, I can only hope that our forbear pioneers of white allyship, people like Anne Braden, Bob and Dottie Zellner, Stan Levison, Andrew Goodman, Mickey Schwerner and Rita Schwerner Bender, Jonathan Daniels, Jim Zwerg, Viola Liuzzo, James Reeb, and many others, along with subsequent generations of committed and integrous white allies, will afford folks of color a measure of faith that there are those among the white community who know that the Great Turning will not be and cannot be a white-led undertaking, and that there are those among us who recognize that the Great Turning requires sincere and transparent expressions of atonement and reparations on our part—expressions which represent a lived commitment, not merely a professed commitment, to full equality, economically and allwise.

Those of us who have come to recognize this, at least a solid core of us, have begun to descend into the truth, and the grief, that almost everything that's been taken can never be restored. We know not what to do with this, but to grieve it, to prepare ourselves to be of service to the struggle, and to repay what we can.

Before now, most of us deemed any suggestion of honest reparations as little more than naïve fantasy. The hypothetical form and magnitude such restitution would need to take simply boggled our minds—if, that is, we allowed them to wander that far.

But we're in a different place now, at least a small but earnest number of us. And we're listening, with contrite hearts, ashamed to have taken so long.

And here are two examples of the type of things we're hearing: the first related to the economics of slavery in the U.S., and the second to the conquest of the land that now comprises the U.S.:

- Leaving aside that which can never be repaired—the kidnapping, the Middle Passage, the murder and rape, the destroyed families, the cultural crucifixion—if we merely take into account the matter of financial compensation for the forced labor of U.S. slaves, we determine that their unpaid wages for the period of 1620 to 1840 would today equal somewhere between $6.5 to $10 trillion.
- Again owning the painful truth that no form of restitution could ever hope to even approach ameliorating our ancestors' crimes against Native Americans, if we only take into account the conquest of land, we acknowledge that a vast and beautiful expanse of an overwhelming 1.5 billion acres was stolen from Native Americans and settled by white conquerors between the years 1776 and 1887.

We acknowledge also the words of Daniel Wildcat, a Yuchi member of the Muscogee Nation and professor at Haskell Indian Nations University in Lawrence, Kansas. Wildcat reminds us, in no uncertain terms, that true restitution requires us to decouple the word "reparations" from its generally accepted and horribly insufficient meaning, as strictly financial compensation:

Reparations are ill-suited to address the harm and damage experienced by people who understand themselves, in a very practical and moral sense, as members of communities that include nonhuman life. For many Native Americans, our land (including the air, water, and biological life on which we depend) is a natural relative, not a natural resource. And our justice traditions require the restoration of our land relationship, not monetary reparations.

Within this call to such a deeper level of restoration, the question quietly looms: How can we ever hope to provide an even partially dignified answer for such wrongdoing? We are both convicted and renewed when we face the facts and when we allow the question to begin its work on us. While we don't yet know the answer, we have struck on its beginning: We'll make a start.

Ta-Nehisi Coates suggests that the passage of congressional bill HR40, which calls for a government-commissioned study of slavery and its lingering effects, as well as recommendations for "appropriate remedies," would represent a good first step. Though his suggestion doesn't speak to Native American genocide and the white conquest of Native land, or to other communities of color who have also been victims of white supremacy, perhaps such a commission will have a part to play in initiating an important national process. From a Gandhian perspective, however, entrusting something this important to the U.S. government makes little sense. Taking our cue from Gandhi's Constructive Programme, and his call for trusteeship, a self-propelled citizen-led initiative would seem a much better fit. We needn't wait, after all, to study and recommend. We needn't wait to act.

Fully embracing the immediate need for atonement and reparations, I believe, brings us face to face with the radical heart of the Great Turning's call, and with the sheer enormity and mysteriousness of the task in front of us. There are two principal reasons I say this. The first is that white atonement and reparations in the United States must be carried out within the wider context of our nation's exploitation, past and present, across the globe. While the vast majority of that exploitation has definitely been white-orchestrated and white-driven, our unconscionable 5 percent / 25 percent baseline is now very much a multiracial fixture (multicultural, multifaith, and multigenerational too). Because white folks don't hold an exclusive monopoly on materialism and over-consumption, those of us who are white need the leadership and support of communities of color to help us understand how we can best steward the unearned and surplus wealth in the wider white community, if not in our own households. (Is it possible to responsibly steward the spoils of plunder? Surplus that never should have existed? Surplus reaped through unadulterated capitalism and conquest?) Clearly real reparations won't be as simple as cutting a check, no matter how fat it might be. Real reparations will mean an honest reckoning with the original clash between *take* and *steward*, and the legacy of capitalism that we've all inherited from it, that we've all been tainted by. If indeed we choose to place reparations at the heart of our own constructive program, it would appear that Gandhi's insistence that "the earth has enough to satisfy everyone's legitimate needs but not anyone's greed" must again serve as a definitive litmus test. Perhaps the redistribution of white wealth will be enough to see that everyone in the United States can have their basic needs met, beginning with the victims of white supremacy, that the action phase of the Great Turning can be funded, and—simultaneously—that we as a nation comprising 5 percent of the world's population can simplify enough to begin living on our commensurate fair share of the world's beautiful bounty.

The second reason that the prospect of atonement and reparations brings the radical core of the Great Turning's call and the immensity of our assignment into sharp focus is that—as any staff member at a domestic violence shelter will tell you—cases of behavioral and moral conversion on the part of batterers are exceedingly rare. What's more, these same people will remind us that restitution and reconciliation, as unlikely as they are under the best of circumstances, are utterly impossible until the cycle of violence and abuse has stopped.

Given the red alert climate emergency, it's either the case that we simply don't have enough time—which is not the premise I've chosen to build this book upon—or that we have another topnotch paradox on our hands. Consider its various layers: We need to build a heart unity movement capable of dismantling the Domination System to a large enough extent that our global climate does not reach an irreversible and catastrophic tipping point; there would appear to be no pathway to such a level of heart unity that does not include major expressions of white atonement and reparations for the victims of white supremacy; and, the abuses fueled by capitalism and white supremacy continue unabated.

Because of the unforgiving timeline forced on us by our quickly heating planet I believe those of us who are ready and willing to work to build a just and life-sustaining society are now faced with the kind of fated and graced choicelessness modeled for us by Michael Meade in chapter 1. On one hand, this is a bitter pill to swallow. We don't get to wait for mass incarceration, mass deportation, human trafficking and the like to come to an end before we upend the forces of extraction and consumption—forces that are fueling those gravely unjust systems, while threatening our very existence at the same time.

On the other hand, I believe this understanding, in a strange and paradoxical way, may hold the key that unlocks the Great Turning. Remember Ta-Nehisi Coates' insight?: "The two phenomena are known to each other. It was the cotton that passed through our chained hands that inaugurated this age." My friend Katy Chandler, co-creator of the Be the Change Project in Reno, extrapolates prophetically: "What if the captives cannot be set be free until the earth is restored? What if the earth cannot be restored until the captives are set free?"

As with the Gandhian Iceberg, it would appear that we're called to somehow do it all, and that we're called to somehow do it all *right now*.

Therefore, at the risk of giving away too much of this book's finale, I join with a growing number of changemakers in asserting that our interdependence and heart unity needs to be forged and claimed in a crucible of bold, unified, and immediate action, and that this action must simultaneously attack the entrenched structures and mindsets that uphold environmental plunder *and* white supremacy. This crucible of bold, unified, and immediate action will represent, in fact, the repudiation of the illusion that environmental plunder and white supremacy are separate. We will come to recognize fully that these are, and have always been, an interwoven fabric—and we will move accordingly.

It will be a come as you are party. With and in our imperfections, the various social justice, peace, and ecological movements will need to jump into this crucible together, and get busy like never before.

CONSTRUCTIVE PROGRAMME REALITY

Awkward though it may be, it's time to acknowledge the rose-colored glasses. Depending on who you read you're going to get widely divergent pictures of the on-the-ground reach and results of Gandhi's Constructive Programme. Based on my own review of the literature, and my own visit to India in 2005, I venture to guess that it was by and large the stuff of holy failure. At the height of the struggle, the association in charge of promoting the khadi campaign—the Constructive Programme project with the largest reach—boasted that spinning had taken hold in a total of five thousand Indian villages. Not too shabby, one might think. But we're talking about an India with a total of 700,000 villages. Do the math and you discover that spinning penetrated a fraction of one percent of Gandhi's target audience. Gandhi's emphasis on the Constructive Programme, it turns out, was met with a good deal of resistance, and the khadi campaign, specifically, often attracted outright ridicule.

The literature reveals that Gandhi's call to economic equality by way of trusteeship, the voluntary redistribution of wealth by the wealthy, was even more of a flop. The rich simply ignored the summons. "The response was nil," says Louis Fischer. It brings to mind Frederick Douglass' famous claim: "Power concedes nothing without a demand; it never has and it never will." Dr. King mirrored the sentiment just as famously: "Never forget that freedom is not something that is voluntarily given by the oppressor. It is something that must be demanded by the oppressed."

Historian and Gandhi biographer Joseph Lelyveld concludes that the

Constructive Programme, while frequently paid lip service by the Indian National Congress and other of Gandhi's contemporaries, was basically left undone. The reasons he cites are telling:

> All the Gandhian organizations [spearheading Constructive Programme efforts] shared a common defect: a reliance, in theory, on selfless village interns—in Gandhi's terms, satyagrahis—and the absence of any sure method for discovering, recruiting, training, or sustaining such a vast army of inspired, literate workers uninhibited by inherited restraints of caste.

Ouch. It hits close to home. An absence of movement workers, and an absence of a sure method of finding, preparing, and keeping movement workers, within a society that restrains certain folks on the basis of caste.

In the epilogue to *Gandhi: Prisoner of Hope*, Judith Brown also describes the yawning gulf between Constructive Programme vision and Constructive Programme reality. Brown quite fittingly uses present-day India—at the time of her writing that meant 1989—as one of the yardsticks by which she measures the impact, or really lack thereof, of Gandhi's social reform crusade. She describes an India teeming with Gandhi statues, and with roads and institutions named after him, which nevertheless presents barely a whiff of evidence that such a thing as Constructive Programme ever existed. As I've said, my own visit to India fifteen years later corroborates Brown's unfortunate conclusion.

Of course there are inspiring examples of modern day constructive program in India, as there are throughout the world. But taken to scale, it is painfully clear that the Indian nation of Gandhi's dreams has never come close to being built. Truth is, swaraj never made it out of the research and development phase.

But here's the thing: None of this negates the viability of Gandhi's prescription for India's uplift and regeneration. Gandhi spoke to this dynamic frequently with regards to nonviolence in general, when people would point to specific cases where the apparent results were less than impressive. Such results weren't due to a deficiency in nonviolence, Gandhi would remind his peers. "Millions like me may fail to prove the truth in their own lives," he said. "That would be their failure, never of the eternal law." Remember: According to Gandhi nonviolence is an unalterable law that is not subject to defeat. Poor results are due to our own shoddy implementation.

The discrepancy shouldn't surprise us and, if our eyes are open wide enough, we can see that it's intimately connected to the pedestalization of prophets and the misappropriation of their teaching and accomplishments. We've been here plenty of times before. Gandhi is simultaneously revered and ignored by modern India, just as Dr. King is simultaneously revered and ignored by the modern U.S., just as Jesus is simultaneously revered and ignored by modern Christendom. Yes, and more to the point, the reflex to marginalize these and other such martyrs, along with their prophetic visions, was alive and well when they were alive and well.

Authors M.P. Mathai and Michael Nagler, among others, present a constructive program picture that contradicts Lelyveld and Brown to varying degrees. But my point is that, in the end, it doesn't actually matter. Wherever the truth lies in terms of concrete outcomes in India, Constructive Programme was a brilliant idea, and the possibility that India couldn't or didn't pull it off during Gandhi's day doesn't mean that we shouldn't try to pull it off now. We should certainly learn what there is to learn from India's experience, but, whether Gandhian constructive program is an untested theory or a tried and true model—or, most likely, somewhere in between—our assignment remains.

When I facilitate workshops on Gandhi's approach to nonviolence I invite participants to consider the signs of our time, and to imagine what a constructive program might look like for us today. I place a stack of paper and crayons in the center of the circle and instruct folks to trace their hand and mimic Gandhi by identifying five constructive program priorities.

Generally, the exercise takes all of ten minutes for folks to complete. Here's a sample hot off the press:

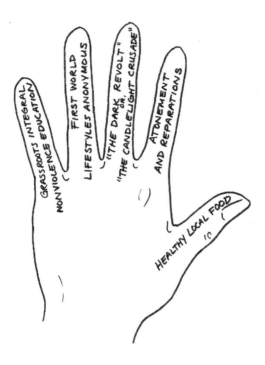

Each time I facilitate the exercise I'm struck by how similar our top fives turn out to be. Just about every time the same eight or nine general priorities come forth in one form or another. There appears to be a high degree of consensus among nonviolence-oriented folks that our new house is being built with materials such as those which follow. The items on this list are deeply inter-related, and the list is not exhaustive. As Gandhi advised with his own program, we need to add to ours in accordance with the needs and character of our particular locales:

- Undoing oppressions (mass incarceration, mass deportation, human trafficking, homelessness, hate crimes, etc.) and unlearning the root cause "isms" behind those oppressions (racism, sexism, heterosexism, classism, ableism, ageism, religious intolerance, etc.)

- Developing restorative alternatives to unjust systems (education, media, health care, food, immigration, justice, electoral, etc.)
- Radical simplicity, unplugging (growing food, shedding possessions and habits of acquisition, car-free, electricity-free, flush toilet-free, tech gadget-free living)
- Permaculture/healthy local food/food sovereignty
- Community-based alternative energy and energy independence, including alternative transportation
- Gift economics, economic equality, de-jobbing, freedom from landlordism, universal access to basic human needs and services
- Demilitarization, waging peace domestically and internationally
- Honoring, protecting, and connecting with the natural world
- Honoring and cultivating the spiritual dimension

And, though they haven't emerged as common suggestions from workshop participants, I'm going to use facilitator's privilege and suggest four other elements that I believe should be added to the mix:

- Atonement and reparations
- Sobriety support, overcoming addiction and unhealthy dependencies
- Developing and practicing new, more productive forms of group process and decision-making
- Strengthening leadership and followership

I've already made my case for the inclusion of atonement and reparations, and sobriety, but let's take some time with my group process / decision-making and leadership/followership additions. Each of these represents a critical point where the inner personal work we discussed in chapter 2 comes to bear on the health and effectiveness of the collective. That is to say, these are additional key areas where the iceberg's waterline fluctuates between self-purification and constructive program. Let's not be surprised, when it comes to these and other elements of our constructive program, if we find the waterline sometimes lapping up and over the tip of the iceberg too, bringing much to bear on our consideration and implementation of satyagraha.

Group Process and Decision-Making

My friends Ethan and Sarah Wilcox-Hughes established the Possibility Alliance after an intensive stint as apprentices at the Community of the Ark, in Southern France. Ethan and Sarah brought a boatload of powerful insights back home with them from the Ark. (Really. They came back on a boat.) The Gandhi-inspired community was miles ahead of just about everybody in bringing nonviolence to life in the real world, and it served Ethan and Sarah as an invaluable model for their own community-based experiment here in the U.S.

Nevertheless, it is also true that the Ark's interpersonal, group dynamics, and conflict resolution processes, as Ethan and Sarah observed, revealed a basic and critical lack of emotional literacy and communication skills within the community. While the Ark was robust and healthy in its physical, mental, and spiritual dimensions, as a whole the community lacked a deep, shared resolve to undertake the inner, emotional work we talked about in chapter 2. And because that work was left undone, Ethan and Sarah witnessed individuals' old and hidden traumas and ingrained reactive patterns being triggered time and again, leading to the breakdown of group processes on a regular basis. Expert facilitation notwithstanding, nothing sabotages a group's process like the unresolved personal baggage of its members.

Ethan and Sarah immediately recognized that what they were witnessing at the Ark was emblematic of the reality for the entire U.S. social change community, and that this is an enormous area for growth and discernment for all of us, and for all of our various groups. In my experience, this unwelcome understanding initially came home to me within the Quaker community. The Quaker tradition holds a great deal of wisdom on collective, Spirit-led discernment, but that didn't change the fact that at a certain point I became unwilling to expose certain of my spiritual leadings to my particular community's processes of collective discernment. What I eventually came to find was that anything that crossed a certain line on the spectrum of radicality would trigger so many fears and misgivings in folks that, at least from my perspective, our Guiding Spirit would kindly excuse herself. I began to seek accompaniment and accountability elsewhere, from a self-selected group that I knew was prepared to hear me from where I was and which I knew wouldn't become incapacitated, process-wise, by fear.

This kind of dynamic runs rampant in social justice circles. The fear may wear any number of disguises, but it's there, and untold non-profits, intentional communities, and other collectives waste astronomical numbers of hours, words, tears, resources, in meeting after meeting after meeting—sounding familiar?—meetings, it turns out, where radical, innovative visions have come to die. And of course it's not only fear that rears its ugly head in such group situations. Many if not most of us have had multiple painful experiences of dysfunctional and sometimes straight-up violent collective decision-making processes, which have gone sour due to the infiltration of any number of unresolved emotions for any number of participants in our respective groups.

It's humbling but also liberating to acknowledge that, in social terms, group process typically and understandably resembles a minefield. David Rock explains that in addition to our primary needs as human beings—physical safety, food, water, and shelter—five additional social drivers are patently essential for each and all of us: status (our sense of importance relative to others), certainty (the ability to make accurate predictions about our future), autonomy (our fundamental need to have personal control and self-determination over the events of our lives), relatedness (a sense of connectedness, similarity, and safety with those around us), and fairness (our expectation of a baseline of just treatment and results). In collaborative group settings, especially ones which revolve around deeply held values and concerns, decision-making of all stripes—from establishing membership criteria to long-term strategic planning to who's going to wash the dishes—will invariably threaten individuals' sense of security in relation to these core social motivators. And such experiences of real or perceived threat almost always give way to conflict, or its intensification.

Mediation and group process trailblazer Gerry O'Sullivan emphasizes the basic fact that this universally-known cycle impedes our ability to think straight. "The more emotionally intelligent and self-aware we are, the easier it is for us to regulate our emotions and access our rational brain during conflict," she writes. But if we are unable to do this effectively—and this is another hefty plug for self-purification—perceptions of threat to our status, certainty, autonomy, relatedness, or sense of fairness will trigger "a reflex that is more emotional than cognitive in direct proportion to our level of self-awareness and emotional intelligence." In other words, when conflict arises, the less we know ourselves and the nature of our emotions the more likely we are to be rendered more or less reptilian.

In a group context this almost always means stress and division. Some folks will hunker down and dig in to defend their cherished positions, some will try to squeeze a negotiated peace from stones, and others will simply check out. Gerry explains that the purpose of mediation is to guide conflicting parties along a different path. Our well-worn trigger responses, she argues, can and should be used to get to the heart of what's really going on. That is, the discomfort that drives our entrenched defense of our position signals to us that a deeper level of consideration and conversation is needed about the underlying needs and interests driving that position. Practitioners of Nonviolent Communication (NVC) will be entirely familiar with this premise and its great importance in the process of navigating conflict.

Folks, group process and decision-making resembles a minefield because it's a supremely complex undertaking. And let's face it, it's often tackled by individuals who simply aren't prepared. In *Reweaving Our Human Fabric*, Miki Kashtan discusses this critical aspect of our dilemma. She warns of the "tyranny of inclusion." The value of inclusivity, Miki explains, when it's married with a "fear of making decisive moves and offending others," can easily become a robust barrier to productive decision-making. Clearly and by extension, it can also easily become a robust barrier to what renowned Serbian activist-trainer-author, Srdja Popovic, calls, in his characteristically technical language, "Getting shit done."

Facing the challenge of the tyranny of inclusion, Miki makes the case that an unswerving ethic of "everyone mattering" will be imperative. I completely agree, and argue, in addition, that we'll do well to speak more openly to the fact that group process is truly formidable work. We wouldn't expect a hobbyist to make the cut at a tryout for the Philharmonic or the Olympics. Why do we expect that anybody and everybody can navigate the inner and outer labyrinths of high-level group decision-making?

Moving forward, a variety of proven interpersonal communication and group-work modalities are here to support us in our search for a solid balance between inclusivity and efficiency, such as restorative circles, Nonviolent Communication, and Co-Counseling. And, fortunately, Gerry, Miki and other group process pioneers are continually crafting breakthrough analyses based on the innovative group work they facilitate. We've a long way to go, but teacher-practitioners like these are chipping away at it with inspiring one-pointedness and creativity.

Leadership and Followership

We can also consider taking an altogether different approach to such dilemmas. We could, for example, follow the lead of the Indian movement, which very often placed Gandhi in the position of dictatorial shot-caller and voluntarily submitted to his direction. We do see a handful of instances when the Indian National Congress was at odds with Gandhi on some critical decision, and he chose not to coerce them into submission. At a certain point such coercion cut against the grain of his leadership style, not to mention his nonviolence. But for the most part Gandhi was at the helm, and like it or not, the movement was strongest when he was, especially when he went unquestioned and trustingly followed by his crew.

Powerful though he was, Dr. King held a different position here in the U.S. While he was the symbolic, figurehead leader and spokesperson for the national struggle, King and SCLC joined with a constellation of other key leaders and groups in steering the movement. SCLC certainly carried a lot of leadership weight, but not more than SNCC. And groups like the Congress of Racial Equality (CORE) and the NAACP were deeply influential too. So the direction of the movement was determined by a much wider circle of protagonists.

That said, Dr. King's leadership within SCLC is worth talking about. Of course we want to do without the patriarchal and misogynistic elements often reflected in SCLC's black male preacher culture, and sometimes in Dr. King himself, but let's not let that get in the way of the good stuff. Dr. King was a master of synthesis. In short, SCLC leadership would circle up with whatever decision they had to make, with the understanding that Dr. King had the final say. King would elicit the needed points of view, being sure to hear the full spectrum of opinions and ideas. Apparently, Andy Young usually held his position on the conservative extreme of that spectrum, while James Bevel, Hosea Williams, or Jesse Jackson could be counted on to hold down the radical fort at the other end. Then, typically, Dr. King would identify and choose a course that synthesized the mix of views.

Dictatorial? Authoritarian? I tend to think it was actually kingly, no pun intended. Kingly—or queenly of course—in the sense of a mature exercise of earned and honored authority. If you've got the right leaders, why not submit to such authority? We all have our part to play in this grand assignment—let's let the leaders lead, and let's follow them.

I don't offer this illustration to suggest that movements are best served by solitary figurehead leaders, or that we shouldn't be operating within an overall context and culture of dynamic collaboration and *everyone mattering*. Not at all. I'm arguing that shot-calling leadership has its place and that some individuals are excellently suited for it. We'll do well to acknowledge their gifts and practice responsible followership.

One last thing about King and SCLC. I said that King had the final say within his organization, but I want to point out one really important exception. When King came out against the Vietnam War, SCLC, to its shame, distanced itself from him, saying that his pronouncements on the war were his and his alone, and were not representative of the organization. This happened right at the end of King's life, when his popularity was waning, when his radicality and dot-connecting prophecy were becoming more than folks could handle. As the assassins were shaping their plot, King's own organizational base was stepping away from him in a deeply significant way.

King's assassination reminds us that having an individual figurehead leader leaves a movement especially vulnerable. One could argue, and persuasively so, that even now the struggle for freedom in the U.S. has yet to recover from Dr. King's assassination. For all intents and purposes, especially from a nonviolence perspective, the public microphone that fell from King's hands when the bullet struck has yet to be picked back up.

It is also the case, I would argue, that the model of the individual figurehead leader is simply out of step with the spirit of our times. But that does nothing to negate the fact that strong coherent leadership of another form is very much needed. Whenever human beings plunge into the crucible of movement it's a messy affair. This is certainly true for our as yet unformed integral nonviolence submovement. And for the wider, overarching movement of movements now taking shape this will be exponentially so. Only with strong coherent leadership will we be able to build strategy that is creative, adaptive, and effective. Only such leadership will enable decisions and direction to move quickly and efficiently. For these reasons, when it comes to large-scale movement organizing, I'm strongly in favor of intentionally deputized and clearly identifiable leadership, rather than the amorphous type associated with the Occupy Movement, and with some strands of the deeply prophetic and catalytic Black Lives Matter movement.

Naomi Klein echoes the sentiment:

I have, in the past, strongly defended the right of young movements to their amorphous structures—whether that means rejecting identifiable leadership or eschewing programmatic demands. And there is no question that old political habits and structures must be reinvented to reflect new realities, as well as past failures. But I confess that the last five years immersed in climate science has left me impatient. As many are coming to realize, the fetish for structurelessness, the rebellion against any kind of institutionalization, is not a luxury today's transformative movements can afford... The core of the problem comes back to the inescapable fact that has both blocked climate action and accelerated emissions: all of us are living in a world that neoliberalism built, even if we happen to be critics of neoliberalism... In practice that means that, despite endless griping, tweeting, flash mobbing, and occupying, we collectively lack many of the tools that built and sustained transformative movements of the past.

Whereas Klein underscores a lack of "tools" here—the inference being structure and identifiable leadership, my overall emphasis in this book falls on what might best be described as a lack of *depth*—inferring the comprehensive nonviolence remedy I've been describing in these pages. The two analyses are mutually reinforcing, however, and they apply as much to a small special-ized group, such as our emerging integral nonviolence submovement, as to a full-scale mass movement like the one needed to turn the Great Turning. In both cases, the current emergency calls for a balance between the three elements of Gandhi's nonviolence recipe—self-purification, constructive program, and satyagraha—bearing in mind that the mass movement will likely not think of these elements in those terms. Also in both cases, the current emergency, as I've said, calls for solid structure and focused, identi-fiable leadership.

This requires great courage on the part of movement makers—the courage to recognize leaders, to raise them up, to hold them up, to trust them, and to follow them. The raising up and acceptance of leaders, whether at a small, local group level or a national movement level, must be governed not by individual and selfish hankerings, but by a form of brave and healthy collective surrender. A powerful group of leaders, utterly human and imperfect for sure, but fundamentally incorruptible, soulful, and wicked smart, stand ready to lead. We need to call them out and christen them. We need to set a table for them, carve out time, space, and whatever necessary resources for them to vision, strategize, and articulate. And meanwhile, all of us need to be working our self-purification regimens and constructive programs, and getting our affairs in order, so we're good to go when our marching orders come down.

All of the above represents really hard work—individually, but also collectively. This is why I've taken the liberty of adding this and the previous item to the summary list of contemporary constructive program areas. While we're developing our skills and understanding in these realms of group process and leadership/followership, as much as I may wish otherwise, I think this is a case where we need to face the fact that we're not as ready as we'd like to be, and that to a large extent we're going to have to wing it. And winging it, I think, is going to require those of us who have been doing the level of inner work we've been discussing—those of us whose wounds and egos don't sabotage good process—to seek each other out and to draw some difficult boundaries. We're talking about the kind of seriously tough decisions made at big league tryouts and in war rooms, and we're talking about the potential for a lot of hurt feelings. So we all need to start exercising our nonviolent sucking-it-up muscles, while simultaneously rooting ourselves deeply and consistently in the ethic of *everyone mattering* that Miki Kashtan so helpfully places centerstage. Some of the most critical skills we need to hone are naming gifts, deputizing, and building movement structures that enable as many people as possible to find a meaningful entry point into the struggle. The whole operation is going to require immense amounts of love, honesty, and fearlessness, as well as the oversight and accountability-checking of trusted elders who aren't afraid to call it like they see it, and who inspire a healthy and liberating obedience.

We need to field our A-team right now, which means a serious evaluation of track records and preparedness. This is no time to fall captive to the tyranny of inclusion.

———

Clearly, for those of us with enough wiggle room—meaning that Empire isn't kicking in our door just yet—there's no shortage of ways to get busy with constructive program. Our contemporary society is so saturated with oppression and imbalance that we needn't worry over a scarcity of positive things to do. What's more, a great bounty of books and other resources are readily available on each and every one of the areas noted up to now. Better yet, amazing communities and projects are modeling this stuff in the flesh, all over the nation. I'll name just four particularly bright beacons here—each rooted in the Gandhian approach, each working and practicing in their own unique ways: Casa de Paz/Canticle Farm, Oakland, California; Be the Change Project, Reno, Nevada; The Possibility Alliance, La Plata, Missouri; and the New Community Project, Harrisonburg, Virginia. The communities that make up the broad and dispersed Catholic Worker Movement are also immensely valuable go-tos. All of the above changemaking initiatives have done fantastic trailblazing, and along our constructive program way we'll do well to take advantage of all they have to teach us. Guaranteed, they'll be eager to learn from us too.

My mention of these community-based inspirations reminds me that, in addition to discerning where and how we should focus our constructive program energies, an equally pressing question begs our attention:

Are we ourselves part of a community of struggle and uplift with a strong enough network of relationships, talents, and know-how to propel our constructive program efforts beyond the superficial to the truly transformational?

It may take a good deal of trial and error to identify the gifts we are truly called to bring, and best suited to bring, in view of the needs and circumstances of our particular context. But, if we're not part of a community that's capable of transformational work, we need to be. Nobody can build this house alone.

———

A few pages from now we'll begin trekking out to the tip of the iceberg, satyagraha. Before we do it's vital to acknowledge that Gandhi laid far greater emphasis on the necessity of constructive program than on civil disobedience in the political realm. In our efforts to choreograph the best integral nonviolence balancing act to date, we'll do well to deeply consider this key piece of the Gandhian rationale.

Constructive work in the realm of social reform, Gandhi said, was "a hundred times dearer" to him than overtly political work. What's more, Gandhi saw that constructive program would itself bring to light the true purpose of political agitation, and reveal when and where it should be implemented. "In a world of falsehood," Michael Nagler explains, "truth is inherently confrontational. A truly constructive program…will bang into obstructions, even without seeking them." Though at times Gandhi would initiate nonviolent forays with the British Empire, he taught that the ultimate purpose of political action was to remove obstacles placed in the movement's path by the opponent, not in order to weaken that opponent, but to clear the way for the continued regeneration of society. It is for this reason that Michael concludes that constructive program was Gandhi's "main hope." "While nonviolence had an impressive power to protest and disrupt," he writes, "its real power was to create and reconstruct. The tail of protesting wrongs would never wag the dog of building a society."

We've established that the philosophical framework for constructive program is equivalent to that of self-purification. Both spheres of experimentation hinge on the dictates of ahimsa (nonviolence), swadeshi (localism), and heart unity, and the practices of asteya (non-stealing), bread labor, and selfless service. Gandhi concluded, therefore, that self-purification naturally functions as a form of training for the social reform efforts of constructive program. In like manner, constructive program represents training for the third tier of the Gandhian approach, satyagraha, by instilling fearlessness, camaraderie, and commitment to service in the people.

In the foreword to his Constructive Programme treatise, Gandhi writes with specific attention to the civil disobedience component of satyagraha:

Civil Disobedience, mass or individual is an aid to constructive effort and is a full substitute for armed revolt. Training is necessary as well for civil disobedience as for armed revolt. Only the ways are different. Action in either case takes place only when occasion demands. Training for military revolt means learning the use of arms... For civil disobedience it means the Constructive Programme. Therefore, workers will never be on the lookout for civil resistance. They will hold themselves in readiness, if the constructive effort is sought to be defeated.

Fair enough. But here's another rub, and it too is a biggie. Despite a small number of isolated exceptions, collectively we have been and remain in a state of debilitating denial about the extent to which our ability to clear the way for the regeneration of society is impeded by the Domination System (of which we're a part). In fact, this particular sleight of hand, I believe, is the greatest weapon in the Domination System's arsenal. Our communities are in such a state of collusion, and are so fractured, segregated, and distracted that we've missed innumerable telltale signs and proofs that Dr. King was right when he said, just about a half-century ago, that the time had come to move from an era of reform to an era of nonviolent revolution. King's assassination, Malcolm X's assassination, the decimating attacks on the freedom movement carried out by our government's infamous COINTELPRO outfit, not to mention the assassinations of the Kennedy brothers—all of these were instrumental in squashing the revolutionary seedling before it could take root in this country.

And U.S. activism has been in reform mode ever since. A lukewarm reform mode to boot.

Okay, so this is where we again find ourselves acknowledging that the revolution needs to happen and that we're not as ready for it as we'd like to be. When we step back far enough to take in the full measure of the Domination System's death grip—when we take an honest and accurate inventory of the obstacles the Domination System places in our path towards beloved community—we come to see this as true. I mean no disrespect, but can we not hear the Emperor's uproarious laughter when we celebrate the City Council's approval of, say, a new bike lane, or a motion that construction of a new Wal-Mart will be delayed another month for environmental review? Obviously such supposed gains bear no measurable impact on either car culture or Wal-Mart culture, both of which move full steam ahead regardless. And as for the overarching Domination System itself? We're talking about an Emperor with a massive and treacherous playbook, an Emperor who has taken out prophets, presidents, Twin Towers, and nations at will and with complete impunity. Our piecemeal efforts to remove what few and meager obstacles we can, whenever and wherever we can, rarely register even a microscopic blip on the Domination System's radar.

If we're willing to see them, the signs of the times are displayed in plain view. And those signs clearly show that the great treacheries of the past were leading us here all the while, to the great treacheries of today, and to the unprecedented global collapse that is now upon us. Really: We are not facing a doomsday scenario. *The collapse is happening now.* As I write this, Indonesia continues to burn and species continue to disappear at a rate of somewhere between six and eight per hour. As I write this, reputable scientists estimate that the oceans of the world will be devoid of fish as soon as 2048. As I write this, children are dying of starvation and malnutrition at a rate of an estimated twenty-nine thousand per day. As I write this, military conflicts fueled by extremism are escalating, immune to the will of the people and to any efforts at diplomacy, and the world is spending just shy of $5 billion a day on weaponry and war (34 percent of that figure compliments of the U.S.).

For those of us who come at this thing from a Gandhian perspective, it's past time to confess that the Domination System has allowed us just enough crawl space to do just enough constructive program so that we can fool ourselves into believing that it's not yet absolutely necessary for full-fledged resistance. It's really good news, overall, that the new order must be fashioned as the old one remains. But in the age of the Great Turning we need to accept the fact that we can no longer afford to rest, if we ever could, on our constructive program laurels. If we're fearless enough to fully take in the realities of the day, if we're fearless enough to fully take in Naomi Klein's warning in *This Changes Everything*—and if we're clear that the Great Turning is our goal—we recognize that full-scale satyagraha is desperately needed right now, and that it's needed with a force unlike any we've ever seen.

I don't say this in order to demean or negate any of the constructive program efforts and advances we've made. Again, I'm simply pointing out that we've been painfully mistaken in our assessment of how obstructed we actually are in our efforts to build a just and life-sustaining society. I think this is especially the case, unsurprisingly and as we've already discussed, for privileged white nonviolence practitioners like myself, men especially. Those of us in that category have had the luxury to experiment with Gandhi's ideas in rarefied atmospheres that give us a skewed impression of what's possible for the vast majority of people in our society. Remember in "When I Am Arrested," when Gandhi warns his fellow members of Satyagraha Ashram that the spiritual disciplines and apparent good works of their community appear to be turning into "subtle indulgences"? The shoe fits. Many of us have reduced our ecological footprints, we've planted and harvested veggies, we've ridden our bikes, we've built with straw bale, and we've shat in buckets. Many of us have done humanitarian or peace work domestically or inter- nationally. All good, important work that definitely needs doing. Ironic too, because—again I'm speaking here about those of us with unearned white privilege—it's none other than the Domination System's benefits package that has afforded us the opportunity to so experiment with the stuff of radical simplicity and service.

Ultimately, the point I'm aiming for here is that we have yet to take in the bottom-line reality that a bona fide constructive program must be available to all, and that the program we've been working isn't. The extractive, con- sumptive, and passive mindset, tenaciously programmed into everyone in U.S. society by the Domination System—beginning way before Mohandas Gandhi came on the scene on the other side of the planet—combined with our unresolved racial woundedness, and the overwhelmingly powerful, nimble, and white supremacist prison, deportation, and military industrial complexes, among so many other exploitative structures, has made a fully operational, nation-building constructive program virtually inaccessible for the vast majority of our national family.

Surely the Emperor laughs just as raucously to see our national inheritance—our divisions, our separations and segregations—just as evident and present in our supposed efforts to counter the Domination System as they are within that system's own cherished and wily structures. Surely he revels watching the descendants of slave owners proudly composting their grapefruit rinds and converting cooking oil into biodiesel for their outdated Mercedes', while the descendants of slaves take a break from the trenches of class warfare to inject insulin for their fast food-inflicted diabetes.

God bless us for trying, from dipping beeswax candles to getting the death sentence commuted, to anywhere and everywhere in between. And God bless us in our blindness and brokenness. We're so beautiful, just as we are, and just as we're trying to be.

But the time has come for a shift in focus. This Emperor needs a house call. As I emphasized in the introduction, by design and necessity, self-purification and constructive program must continue and must remain the top priorities of our long haul journey. But at this juncture our efforts in these realms need to be taken to a whole new level—a level at which they will pose a real and terminal threat to the violence of the establishment. In short, the time has come to recognize that, as imperfect and incomplete as it's been, the self-purifying and constructive work that so many of us have been carrying out up to now has been noble labor and excellent training. And—at least for the foreseeable future—we've had as much training as we can afford.

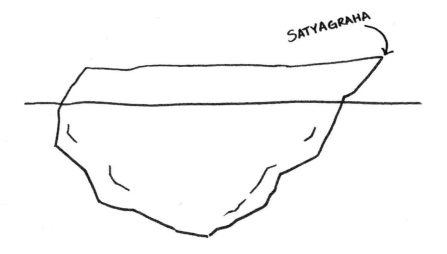

4.
THE TIP OF THE ICEBERG

LA UNIÓN (pt. 1)

WHEN THE INCURSION HAPPENED, my teammate Lily Ray and I had only been in Colombia for a month. Word had passed to the community leaders early in the morning that a group of ten or twelve heavily armed combatants had been seen on one of the many trails leading to La Unión, the little hamlet where we were living and working as international accompaniment volunteers, on behalf of the Fellowship of Reconciliation (FOR). La Unión, a village with a population of 120, is nestled in a gorgeous valley high up in the lush northern Colombian countryside, a little more than an hour's hike from the nearest road. It is one of a constellation of villages that comprise the internationally recognized comunidad de paz (peace community) of San José de Apartadó. During the late nineties, San José was one of dozens of such communities that publicly declared impartiality in the midst of Colombia's decades-long civil war. Characteristic of all peace community declarations was the bold and unapologetic request that all of Colombia's armed actors—official military, paramilitary, and guerrilla—respect their communities as weapon-free, war-free, civilian territories.

As the morning progressed, additional accounts came in, word of mouth, campesino to campesino, confirming the first report, and adding that from all appearances the group en route to the community was most likely a paramilitary unit, and that it was moving toward us at a steady clip. We knew what that meant. "Hay solamente un motivo porque vienen los paracos," the leader of the community's governing council reminded us. "The paramilitaries only come for one reason." Lily and I sent an email updating our project coordinator, Jutta Meier-Weidenbach, who was at the FOR office in San Francisco. Depending on what happened, Jutta would be in charge of sounding the alarm and overseeing our emergency response.

A little more than a year and a half prior, a group like the one that was apparently heading our way had executed six community leaders in broad daylight. The paras rounded up the six men, telling them that they wanted to have a meeting with them. They walked the men to the central plaza of the village, where they ordered them to get down on their knees. Reluctantly, the six leaders did as they were told—their loved ones looking on from a distance. One of the community leaders could be heard speaking with a clear, measured tone, as if trying to reason with the armed men standing above them. The six men then watched the paramilitaries raise their assault rifles. The moment before the shots were fired, the man who had been speaking had begun to rise to his feet.

During my first short weeks in La Unión I formed a strong bond with Yuner, the seven year-old son of that man. In time, Yuner would give me the generous and unexpected honor of naming his pony. To the young boy's smiling approval, I decided on Relámpago. Lightning.

A memorial to the slain leaders—six humble, handpainted wooden crosses—stood in the very spot where they were killed. After the massacre, rather than leaving their homes and their beautiful, fertile land, and thereby forfeiting it to the paramilitary forces, the families of La Unión opted to stay. It was an unusually courageous choice. Massacres like the one La Unión suffered were a primary reason that two million people were internally displaced in

Colombia. In hopes of avoiding such displacement themselves, or another massacre, the community asked FOR to establish an ongoing protective presence there. (Peace Brigades International was already providing such a presence in the peace community's central settlement of San José.) So it was that Lily and I were there, the first team of FOR's Colombia Peace Presence, March 2002.

THE FIRST PRINCIPLE

"Satyagraha," Robert Burrowes tells us, "was Gandhi's attempt to evolve a theory of politics and conflict resolution that could accommodate his moral system." In other words, we're talking about Gandhi's effort to bring to bear on politics and conflict all of the principles we've been discussing up to now, namely Truth, ahimsa, the unity of means and ends, service, heart unity, non-attachment to outcome, and the preservation of human dignity. As we dive headlong into satyagraha, please keep in mind that Gandhi attached particular significance to this latter characteristic of dignity. Satyagraha in the political realm requires astute analysis and systematic design, in terms of tactics, strategy, implementation, and evaluation. In the context of Gandhi's comprehensive nonviolence approach, however, all such considerations remain secondary and in service to the most basic commitment of nonviolence: the defense and preservation of one's self-respect/honor/dignity. The spirit of this core commitment reverberates throughout Gandhi's writings.

The first principle of nonviolent action is that of non-cooperating with anything humiliating.

I cannot conceive a greater loss to a man than the loss of his self-respect.

I would rather have India resort to arms in order to defend her honor than that she should, in a cowardly manner, become or remain a helpless witness to her own dishonor.

To command respect is the first step to swaraj.

My work will be finished if I succeed in carrying conviction to the human family, that every man or woman...is the guardian of his or her self-respect and liberty.

What I did was a very ordinary thing. I declared that the British could not order me around in my own country.

Those moments when our personal dignity is threatened, what I call "Rosa Parks moments," are absolutely critical to the science of satyagraha and to movement-building. What we do with such moments—whether we show up like Ms. Parks did in those brief possibility-laden minutes on her bus ride home—is the cardinal Gandhian pivot point. Rosa Parks moments with the potential to turn into some major political shift may be terribly few in number, but any moment we find our personal dignity under siege, however dramatic or subtle, is a moment when we're out on the tip of the iceberg, a moment when we have an opportunity to generate the nonviolent energy that makes movement possible.

The Domination System's control and ethos so permeates our society and our lives that I've come to believe most of us live in something of a perpetual Rosa Parks moment. The same was certainly the case for Ms. Parks and her peers in the Jim Crow South. It's in the feeling of daily degradation that comes with participating in the life of a society that demeans our lives and life itself as a matter of course. It's in the chronic feeling of impotence and muted rage at the most basic and underlying wrongness of it. Because we live inside such a society, though—a society whose structures and values so deeply and consistently demean us, and because this is more or less all we've known—most of us remain asleep to the fact that our dignity is under constant attack. Our perpetual Rosa Parks moment remains hidden from us, like water from a fish.

If we take Gandhi's words to heart that "the first principle of nonviolent action is that of non-cooperating with anything humiliating," the magnitude of our assignment comes into focus. If we're brave enough to open ourselves to the myriad ways the structures and values of our society and our own collusion with the society humiliate us, we see immediately and without question that we are called to nothing less than full-blown nonviolent revolution. And this is the case whether or not we are personally faced with the kind of heinously overt forms of degradation that we've been taught to associate with oppression.

I mentioned in the introduction that when I first began working with the three-part description of the Gandhian approach I labeled the third tier of the model "political action." But the word political points to the governance and public affairs of one's community, be it local, regional, national, or global, and the nonviolent revolution we're talking about extends a vast distance beyond that. The muscles we put into use in the political realm are exercised each and every time we act in defense of our dignity. Because voluntary self-suffering can reveal truths latent in conflicts both large and small, Gandhi insisted that the application of satyagraha could extend in both micro and macro directions.

As Erik Erikson put it, Gandhi saw satyagraha "as a bridge between the ethics of family life and that of communities and nations." We can recall that, in light of his short temper, jealousy, and domineering habits in the early years of marriage, Gandhi credited his wife Kasturba as his first instructor in the art of soul force. In this we see the principle of swadeshi coming to bear on satyagraha. That is, satyagraha has as much to do with our relationships with those nearest and dearest to us and with day to day perfect strangers, as it does to our relationship with the so-called "powers that be." If we think we can take on the latter without attending to the former, we're in trouble.

———

SATYAGRAHA FUNDAMENTALS (pt. 1)

Here again is Martin Luther King Jr.'s six-part definition of nonviolent resistance:

> Satyagraha:
> 1. is active and courageous, not passive and cowardly;
> 2. seeks reconciliation, not victory over;
> 3. distinguishes injustice from persons behaving unjustly;
> 4. requires the willingness to suffer without retaliating;
> 5. rejects physical and spiritual violence (hate, ill-will, humiliation, deceit, etc.); and,
> 6. is rooted in the conviction that the universe is on the side of justice and truth.

Arguably, the most definitive feature above is number four, which Gandhi put concisely: "The immovable force of satyagraha—suffering without retaliation." There are two principal reasons for this core commitment. First, Gandhi's strict belief in the unity of means and ends precluded any form of violence, as violence would invariably breed further violence and would in turn disrupt progress in the direction of restored dignity and community. Second, the satyagrahi's voluntary nonviolent submission to suffering, if endured for a truthful cause, represented a potent means of conversion for the opponent and for bystanders. If we're courageous enough to go there, it's plain to see that this paradigm-busting axiom—"suffering without retaliation"—when taken to its outermost logical end, fully explains why Gandhi said that with satyagraha "the bravery consists in dying, not in killing."

Robert Burrowes' take on satyagraha helps to illuminate Dr. King's. "*Satyagraha* implies cooperation with the opponent *as a person*," Burrowes states, "[but] noncooperation with the opponent's *role*" within the context of an exploitative social structure. Further, the satyagrahi's commitment to building relationships conducive to mutual growth and reconciliation moves her to remain ever-open to compromise "when basic principles have not been challenged." And, with regards to forging the resolution of a conflict, the satyagrahi seeks "synthesis or transcendence." That is, she seeks a resolution that synthesizes and perhaps even transcends the sum of the elements of truth brought to bear by the parties to the conflict. Each of these observations elucidates Gandhi's definitive contention that "a nonviolent revolution is not a program of seizure of power. It is a program of transformation of relationships, ending in a peaceful transfer of power."

I find it helpful to also consider the way Burrowes characterizes satyagraha as a "principled" approach to nonviolent struggle as opposed to a "pragmatic" approach, though clearly these words are not in fundamental opposition to one another. I have Gandhi's full backing on this point: "The most spiritual act is the most practical in the true sense of the term." (In other words, the means still equal the ends.)

Burrowes argues that satyagraha epitomizes a principled approach to nonviolent struggle by fulfilling five basic criteria:

1. it places a higher priority on ethics than on perceived effectiveness;
2. it views means and ends as indivisible rather than separate;
3. its fundamental view of conflict is that it is a shared problem rather than a case of incompatible interests;
4. its adherents accept suffering rather than inflicting it; and,
5. its adherents are likely to practice nonviolence as a way of life rather than merely as a useful expedient under certain circumstances.

Burrowes offers four further characteristics of satyagraha that mark it as a "revolutionary" nonviolence approach, as opposed to a "reformist" one (another slippery but extremely important dichotomy):

1. its analysis is focused on structural problems in addition to policy problems;

2. it aims for structural changes, rather than merely policy changes;
3. it is strengthened by a constructive program; and,
4. its operational time frame is long-term struggle rather than short or medium-term.

OCCUPY

Several years ago, I heard that an organizing meeting had been scheduled for a public action in my town, in solidarity with a demonstration of some kind that was set to happen in New York City the next day. It had something to do with economic justice and I was curious.

I walked into the room and was immediately handed a quarter sheet flier. "We Are the 99%" was printed at the top of the sheet.

I looked at the slogan for a breath or two, smiled awkwardly, turned around, and walked out of the building. It wasn't an antagonistic thing. It was simply as if I had come with my ball and cleats ready for a soccer game, only to find people pulling out their chess sets.

That was pretty much the extent of my involvement with the Occupy Movement. I did lead a couple of sessions on integral nonviolence for folks from the local Occupy encampment, but I did so as an outsider. I watched the movement as a spectator, applauding the strides for justice, and the passion, courage, and creativity, while waiting for the seeds of the "us vs. them" foundation of the movement to bear their fruit.

As I tell this story, I'm acutely aware of my own admonition against dogmatism. It's super important for me to wrestle with it. I recognize that Occupy did (and still does) some incredibly positive things, and that it set critical energy in motion. I also recognize that some of the nonviolence practitioners I most respect were deeply involved in Occupy, some of whom took on the 99% framing of the movement head on, challenging folks to see that building the movement's identity around the demonization of an entire segment of our national family was not going to serve the long-term struggle for justice. As Miki Kashtan reminds us, bringing an end to the reigning cycle of violence "means, ultimately, finding love for the 1% or the .001% who are truly in power. Everyone. No exceptions." That's nonviolence.

I was struck by how few seemed to recognize that the demonization of the so-called 1% reinforced the warped notion that somehow the ninety-eighth percentile was righteous enough to make the cut. Was Occupy saying that the ninety-eighth percentile was in right relationship with the poor? With the biosphere? How about the eighty-eighth percentile? The fifty-eighth? The thirty-eighth? And at what percentile would the U.S. fall as a whole, in relation to our global family? Another vital and closely related critique of the movement—which was sometimes enunciated, though only tangentially—was that, in essence, Occupy projected the same dead-end demand that characterizes typical left-leaning U.S. activism: Give us a bigger slice of the pie. Far better that we categorically reject the pie baked by the Domination System and celebrate that the Great Turning calls us to work up a whole new recipe.

When I'm really honest with myself, I recognize that this brief story of my experience of Occupy is, at bottom, a story of my own heartbreak and choicelessness. It's a combination I've seen so many times, written across my face and the faces of my closest co-workers-in-struggle. My experience at that inaugural local Occupy meeting was familiar terrain for us—silently, bashfully even, heartbroken, and as choiceless as Michael Meade in the brig in Panama. I knew from the get go that any movement launched with language of division could not have my name on it. And, especially given that our 78 were not assembled, I was equally clear that investing a great deal in an isolated attempt to inject a Gandhian ethic into such a movement would not have been a responsible use of my time and energy. When Occupy began to fray, when the "nonviolence" vs. "diversity of tactics" debate began to escalate and fester, when the movement was unable to make the repressive crackdown on the encampments backfire on itself, I was not surprised. And, honestly, I was glad that in the face of "We Are the 99%" I had directed my energy during those months to the movement to end mass incarceration, a movement, largely thanks to Michelle Alexander, that is grounded in language I can wholly believe in:

> If the movement...fails to cultivate an ethic of genuine care, compassion, and concern for every human being—of every class, race, and nationality—the collapse of mass incarceration will not mean the death of racial caste in America. Inevitably a new system of racialized social control will emerge.

> The failure to acknowledge the humanity and dignity of all persons has lurked at the root of every racial caste system.

> I'm talking about the kind of love that keeps on giving no matter who you are or what you have done. That's the kind of love we need to build this movement.

Whenever I think about the language and ethos of Occupy I recall the name of an inspiring organization headed up by formerly incarcerated organizers and activists, which stands at the forefront of the struggle to dismantle the prison industrial complex: All of Us or None. How's that for an alternative to "We Are the 99%"?

———

```
              Key Concepts Review: Pop Quiz 3
                         (Advanced)
    Choose the best answer:

        (1) self-purification is to Gandhian nonviolence as:

            (a) stickiness is to glue
            (b) melody and rhythm are to music
            (c) soil is to a garden
            (d) all of the above

        (2) constructive program is to self-sufficiency as:

            (a) food is to nourishment
            (b) Bambi is to Godzilla
            (c) thyme is to time
            (d) all of the above

        (3) satyagraha is to an online petition as:

            (a) jet-skiing is to snow-mobiling
            (b) Fred is to Ethel
            (c) a quasar is to an expired triple-a battery
            (d) all of the above
```

SATYAGRAHA FUNDAMENTALS (pt. 2)

When our 78 coheres, our shared agreements for individual and collective discipline out on the tip of the iceberg will no doubt be born of deep reflection and bold, generative dialog. In preparation for that process we stand to learn a lot from a careful review of the recipe Gandhi offered up to India's freedom fighters. Our agreements will certainly differ from these, but—if we're to be true to integral nonviolence—our shared covenant must just as clearly illustrate the essential role of discipline and its inseparability from the art of satyagraha.

POP QUIZ 3 ANSWER KEY: Three cheers and one last smiley face stamp if you went with d, then a, then c. Nicely done.

Qualifications:

Gandhi identified seven qualifications that he held to be essential for every satyagrahi:

1.   He must have a living faith in God, for He is his only Rock.*
2.   He must believe in truth and nonviolence as his creed and therefore have faith in the inherent goodness of human nature which he expects to evoke by his truth and love expressed through his suffering.
3.   He must be leading a chaste life and be ready and willing for the sake of the cause to give up his possessions and his life.
4.   He must be a habitual khadi-wearer and spinner.
5.   He must be a teetotaler and be free from the use of other intoxicants in order that his reason may be unclouded and his mind constant.
6.   He must carry out with a willing heart all the rules of discipline as may be laid down from time to time.
7.   He should carry out the jail rules unless they are specially devised to hurt his self-respect.

Code of Discipline:

Gandhi identified nine points as the appropriate marks of a satyagrahi's conduct during a satyagraha campaign:

1.   Harbor no anger but suffer the anger of the opponent. Refuse to return the assaults of the opponent.
2.   Do not submit to any order given in anger, even though severe punishment is threatened for disobeying.

---

* With regards to this first stated qualification, it's vital to recall Gandhi's broad and inclusive interpretation of what a "living faith in God" might mean, as we discussed in chapter 2.

3. Refrain from insults and swearing.

4. Protect opponents from insult or attack, even at the risk of life.

5. Do not resist arrest nor the attachment of property, unless holding property as a trustee.

6. Refuse to surrender any property held in trust at the risk of life.

7. If taken prisoner, behave in an exemplary manner.

8. As a member of a satyagraha unit, obey the orders of satyagraha leaders, and resign from the unit in the event of serious disagreement.

9. Do not expect guarantees for maintenance of dependents.

Steps:

Gandhian satyagraha campaigns generally ran according to the following steps:

1. an objective investigation of the facts related to the injustice or grievance;

2. dialog and arbitration to attempt a mutual compromise;

3. nonviolence training, spiritual and practical preparation;

4. announcement of the plan of action and adjoining ultimatum (with open invitation to resume arbitration);

5. publicity detailing the reasons for the campaign, and the aims and means of those carrying it out; and,

6. active non-cooperation.

Rules:

These were some of the essential rules to be observed by nonviolent resisters in satyagraha campaigns:

1. Resisters "must rely on themselves" and "keep the initiative,"

without resorting to dependence on outside assistance and with a readiness to adapt and readjust in order to maintain the self-reliant character of the movement.

2. Throughout, resisters must remain "willing to persuade and to enlighten, even as [they remain] ready to be persuaded and enlightened."

3. The satyagrahi should stand ready to assist the opponent "in any unforeseen situation which might rob him of his freedom to remain a counterplayer" in the conflict.

4. The satyagrahi should keep demands consistent, resisting the temptation to expand beyond the "chosen and defined issues."

LA UNIÓN (pt. 2)

There's never a convenient time for a paramilitary incursion, but this day seemed especially awkward. A dear friend and mentor of mine, Jorge Arauz, had arrived only the evening before. It turned out that Lily and my recent arrival in Colombia had coincided with Jorge's own trip south to neighboring Ecuador, the country of his birth. Jorge and I knew each other from the broader U.S. Quaker community and he had agreed to have my back spiritually throughout my time with the FOR project. Needless to say, Jorge's willingness to pay me an in-person visit was an enormous gift to me. This was my first time on the ground as an international accompaniment volunteer—my first time living in a war zone.

And there we were, Lily, Jorge, and I, on the cusp of a paramilitary incursion, watching as the people of La Unión prepared to take to the hills. I would have preferred that the community stayed put, so that our new accompaniment project could be seen to fulfill its purpose. I was confident that paramilitaries would not abduct, hurt, or kill anyone in our presence. Surely their commanders had ordered them to watch their step whenever internationals were looking on, especially internationals sporting t-shirts bearing the logo of a bona fide human rights organization. Because the paramilitaries worked in such close cahoots with the U.S.-sponsored Colombian army, international public opinion was extremely valuable currency for them. In fact, insofar as the paras were concerned, our entire strategy was based on the premise that the negative publicity that we could set in motion, in addition to the support we had garnered from a few dozen congressional offices, would represent a strong enough deterrent to keep them on their best behavior. Upon our arrival in the region, in order to give this strategy some teeth, Lily, Jutta, and I had met with the commander of Colombia's 17th Brigade. And we trusted that the commander had done his job and sent word of our presence through the paramilitary grapevine. Easy for me to say. I see that.

Things were a bit different with the guerrilla. The FARC (Fuerzas Armadas Revolucionarios de Colombia, or Revolutionary Armed Forces of Colombia) and to a much lesser extent the ELN (Ejercito Liberación Nacional, or National Liberation Army) were slippery x-factors for us, and for all the organizations doing what we were doing. We didn't talk about it much, but the guerrilla forces dampened our confidence in the power of international scrutiny. It wasn't that the guerrilla didn't care about international public opinion. They did. At that time, in fact, the FARC was engaged in a formal peace process with the Colombian government—a process which was supported by the international community, and which was drawing a significant amount of attention worldwide. But the bottom line remained. The guerrilla forces were not beholden to the U.S. like the paras and the Colombian army were. So they were especially unpredictable, and it was not uncommon for them to kidnap internationals and influential Colombians for political leverage or ransom. In light of that, before heading to Colombia, Lily and I had signed a form acknowledging our understanding and consent with FOR's policy, modeled after that of Christian Peacemaker Teams, that ransom would not be paid in the event of an abduction, under any circumstances. The precedent that a payment of ransom could set might very well undermine international accompaniment throughout and potentially even beyond Colombia.

Under the circumstances, though, and with an ironic twist, the peace community was our protective presence when it came to the possibility of being kidnapped by the guerrilla. If the peace community's project failed, the FARC in that area would have been hard-pressed to fend off a paramilitary advance on the fertile land of La Unión and its neighboring settlements. We hoped that the FARC's desire to see the peace community succeed would provide enough incentive to dissuade them from kidnapping us.

But, awaiting a paramilitary incursion as we were, rather than a guerrilla incursion, being kidnapped wasn't on my mind. And my strategic preference that the community not run from paramilitaries went unspoken. My job was to accompany the community. And they had decided, well before I ever came on the scene, that in the event of a paramilitary incursion every able-bodied member of the community—which at that point meant everyone—would take to the lush hills surrounding the village. Lily and I were specifically charged with shadowing the community's leaders—who would likely be in the most danger—wherever in the dense forest they might choose to go.

Before long, an incoming report placed the paramilitary unit within minutes of the village, and the community kicked into high gear. In every direction, those who hadn't yet left were racing in and out of their tiny dirt-floored homes, corralling their children and finalizing whatever few choice possessions and small rations of food they were going to take with them.

To my surprise, though, a number of people scattered unevenly among the village's thirty or so dwellings were calmly meandering, with no apparent intention to up and leave. While surveying this confusing scene, I noticed that my friend Jorge, who had zero training in accompaniment and third-party nonviolent intervention, who wasn't wearing an FOR t-shirt, and who looked about as Colombian as a person possibly could, stood by—perfectly calm and composed.

———

ONE STEP FORWARD, ONE STEP BACK

Let's invite two important books to get in on our conversation about the tip of the iceberg: *Blueprint for Revolution*, by Srdja Popovic, and *Why Civil Resistance Works*, by Erica Chenoweth and Maria Stephan. I bring these particular resources up for two reasons. The first is that they both offer invaluable guidance about the inner workings of social movements, couched always in a deep respect for the immense power of ordinary people facing down extreme violence and oppression. The second is that because these two books represent some of the best of contemporary wisdom on the theory and practice of "nonviolent" resistance, and because they have proven quite popular in activist circles, they represent what those of us who practice integral non-violence are up against whenever we choose to step into the public square to clarify what we mean by nonviolence. As we make room for *Blueprint for Revolution* and *Why Civil Resistance Works* in our satyagrahi toolbox, we'll do well to keep in mind their serious limitations.

Srdja Popovic, one of the founders of Otpor! (Resist!), the feisty and inspiring student-led group that galvanized the movement that ousted Serbian dictator Slobodan Milosevic, tells great movement stories and he's super fun to read. He also offers excellent advice on an array of key subjects, including strategizing campaigns, building movement cohesion, adapting to evolving political circumstances, and making oppression backfire on itself. *Blueprint for Revolution* is going to assist us immensely as we implement soul force in real time.

Erica Chenoweth and Maria Stephan's *Why Civil Resistance Works* brings a different set of gifts to the party. The book is a fairly dense scholarly study of anti-regime, anti-occupation, and secession campaigns during the twentieth and early twenty-first centuries. In short, Chenoweth and Stephan have distilled the primary reasons that "nonviolent" campaigns are more consistently successful than violent campaigns. As we chart our own strategy and direction in the realm of satyagraha, their solid research-based findings will greatly strengthen our conversations and discernment.

I'm not going to offer a detailed critique of these authors' treatment of nonviolence itself, or of Gandhi specifically. Suffice it to say that they follow the conventional pattern of leaving anything resembling an iceberg out of the picture, and that this omission is extremely important. These books, after all, among many others, continue to use this slippery word *nonviolence* and to teach the culture about it, which represents a significant problem. One-dimensional caricatures of Gandhi and his nonviolence-inspired vision of what's possible are setting us back in a serious way. Consider one segment near the beginning of *Why Civil Resistance Works*:

> Our perspective does not assume that nonviolent resistance...can melt hearts... We argue that nonviolent campaigns can impose costly sanctions on their opponents... We join a long line of scholars concerned with the strategic effectiveness of different tactical and operational choices.

It is of course an author's prerogative to choose her subject matter. And Erica Chenoweth and Maria Stephan have done a phenomenal job covering their chosen terrain. Their book has been hailed with widespread enthusiasm for finally offering us a thorough presentation, rich with numbers and charts that finally and authoritatively prove that "nonviolence" works better than violence. As valuable as such proof may turn out to be in convincing people who are on the fence about the efficacy of nonviolence, I fear, nonetheless, that such convincement will be a classic case of one step forward, one step back.

The narrative Chenoweth and Stephan share basically ignores Gandhi, and the results are strangely alienating to those of us who live with the means/ends equivalency in our bones. Nonviolence practitioners like us haven't needed anyone to crunch the numbers in order to know where we stand and why we stand there. In fact, from our perspective the number crunching looks a lot like a subservient nod to the paradigm we're looking to scrap. At its core, integral nonviolence is felt, instinctual, and intuitive—and we celebrate that we're able to understand it most profoundly with our heartsense. Please don't misunderstand me to be saying that things like research, strategy, and evaluation are not absolutely essential to our practice of nonviolence. They are. But the purpose of such tools is not to aid us in an effort to "win." My use of metaphors like "suiting up with the team" or "getting in the game" notwithstanding, nonviolent conflict is not a sports match. The purpose of research, strategy, and evaluation is to strengthen our ability to infuse whatever set of circumstances we face with as much love as we possibly can, for the benefit of everyone and everything involved. We research, strategize, and evaluate as part of our attempt to do the right thing, whether or not it's "successful" according to the standards established by the dominant culture.

At bottom, the point I'm making in response to Chenoweth and Stephan's characterization of nonviolence generally, and to their above explanation specifically, is that those who commit themselves to integral nonviolence—that is, to all three dimensions of the Gandhian approach: self-purification, constructive program, and satyagraha—are going to open themselves up to "tactical and operational choices" that would never occur to those who don't. And those choices, I contend, stand to make the difference between regime change and true transformation.

In its own way, *Blueprint for Revolution* promotes the same misleading take on nonviolence. This comes out starkly in Popovic's unabashed and dehumanizing references to opponents as "thugs" and "brutes," but even more significantly, to my reading, in his treatment of what may be the most crucial topic of all: vision.

To his credit, Popovic strongly emphasizes the need to have and communicate a clear vision for the future. And his description of Otpor!'s vision for Serbia's future speaks volumes. In short, he offers up Otpor!'s stated vision as a model illustration, stating that amidst war, ethnic cleansing, and horrific repression, the vision of the student movement was for Serbia to be "a normal country, with cool music." This is Popovic's characteristic tongue in cheek delivery, sure, but it's as thoughtful as it is witty. He explains that for the student movement, "normal country" implicitly meant democracy, and that he—a rock musician himself, at least during his student years—adds the "with cool music" part to drive home the point that Soviet-style censorship epitomized what young Serbs loathed about the way things were in their homeland. I can't help but remember my own long ago visit to the former Soviet Union. During high school I visited Moscow as part of a sister school exchange project. I'll never forget the sheer delight of my young Russian counterparts when I handed over a cassette tape of Pink Floyd's *The Final Cut*, a near impossible find in the U.S.S.R. in 1988. Popovic's Serbia most definitely had the same soul-deadening lockdown vibe. So: to be "a normal country, with cool music." I get it. And I see that the music add-on is a symbol, a powerful symbol, of real freedom in the face of real oppression, humiliation, and death. I'd want that freedom too.

But here's the thing: For all the powerful stories and helpful organizing wisdom in *Blueprint for Revolution*—and *Why Civil Resistance Works* too—and as just and rational as the goal of a "normal country" is, the age of our do-or-die climate emergency absolutely requires a more transcendent vision. Normal countries, very much including normal democracies, are sending the planet over the cliff. We need a vision that connects the dots to reveal that the ever-expanding list of wars, social injustices, and environmental disasters in the world all boil down to a core moral and spiritual crisis, and that all of them are happening within the context of all-out civilizational peril. Because Popovic, Chenoweth, and Stephan don't go there, the social movements and struggles described in their books are horribly compartmentalized (and climate change is basically a parenthesis). The most striking example of this compartmentalization is in Popovic's case study of a struggle for economic equity in Israel, that makes no mention whatsoever of Israel's brutal occupation of Palestine. To be sure, injustice is injustice wherever and however it happens, but at this historical moment we need a dot-connecting vision that tells the whole truth about where we are and what's actually needed to turn this sucker around.

———

ATONEMENT AND REPARATIONS (pt. 3)

Large-scale, militarized conflicts mean large-scale human suffering, and they rightfully draw our attention and profound concern, often across vast oceans and distant borders. As a consequence, however, it's quite easy to lose track of the intimate connection between satyagraha and swadeshi. Largely overshadowed, close to home tensions and smaller scale or less overt forms of violence often take a back seat in many of our minds and many of our actions.

To bring satyagraha closer to home I'd like to briefly revisit part of our discussion in chapter 3. You'll recall that Gandhi's constructive program report card showed mixed results, at best, and that I noted as a particularly stark example that Gandhi's call to trusteeship was an unmitigated flop. Unsurprisingly, the prospect of voluntarily redistributing their wealth to India's poor masses held little appeal for Gandhi's rich contemporaries.

It's intriguing and deeply instructive to observe, however, that Gandhi's disciple Vinoba Bhave, viewed by many as the mahatma's heir apparent, had seemingly miraculous results when he championed trusteeship, beginning just a few short years after his mentor's death. Over the course of fourteen years (1951-1965), Vinoba led a more or less ceaseless crusade called the Bhoodan (land-gift) Movement, which carried him and hundreds of co-workers on walking pilgrimages across the length and breadth of India. The Bhoodan Movement inspired thousands of landowners to freely donate more than four million acres of land holdings to the poor, quite likely the largest instance of nonviolent land redistribution in history.

How did Vinoba get the rich to do this? He asked them. Face to face, in village after village, month after month, he asked the wealthiest people in India to bequeath land to him as a proxy for the poor, as if he were a beloved son due his rightful inheritance. Apparently Vinoba's spiritual stature and his strong association with Gandhi, "the Father of the Nation," imbued his requests with whatever "demand" energy Frederick Douglass and Dr. King believed was always necessary when it came to bringing the rich and powerful to their moral senses. Or, perhaps the Bhoodan Movement gives evidence that Douglass and King underestimated something that the naïve-sounding Gandhi understood about the malleability of the human heart.

Unfortunately, Vinoba's historic achievement on the front end of the movement was largely thwarted by a severe lack of organization on the back end. The massive logistical puzzle that the gifted land represented in real time proved far too much for the ill-equipped movement and inefficient government agencies to handle. In the end, only a small fraction of the land was successfully transferred to poor peasants, a great number of them untouchables, and put to productive use. The Bhoodan Movement, therefore, stands as both an immensely valuable object lesson on the revolutionary potential of bold, love-driven action, and a cautionary tale about the importance of organizational depth and follow through.

When I assert my belief that a sweeping national atonement and reparations campaign should be a top priority of our Great Turning constructive program, I am simultaneously, and by extension, indicating a massive and, at least for many of us, harrowing satyagraha campaign. Massive because of the sheer scale of past due restitution and healing we're after. And harrowing, for the great number of us born into privilege, because we'll be facing some intensely intimidating counterplayers. No, I'm not talking about militarized police forces or policified military forces battening down the mean streets of America. And no, I'm not talking about corporate overlords or despots from the upper echelons of Empire.

Rather, I'm talking about our very own kith and kin, looking into our eyes across the kitchen table.

The repairing that's needed, I believe, will require a colossal wave of boldly courageous family conversations across the nation. Conversations— loving enough, honest enough—to begin short-circuiting and eventually breaking the unquestioned and hardwired cultural customs of family-based inheritance and hoarding.

Self-purification, constructive program, and satyagraha—close to home and all in one—that's atonement and reparations. Perhaps, in honor of

Vinoba Bhave and his audacious trust in human goodness and generosity, we'll simply call it bhoodan.

GRAVITATIONAL PULL

Assuming my usual role as participant-observer, I hovered near the edge of the protest.

A few hundred of us were gathered at the gate of San Quentin to register our dismay that the state was about to kill yet another human being. We were the usual jumble—seasoned community organizers, earnest churchgoers, pissed-off punk "anarchists," left-leaning Bay Area yuppies, a smattering of caustic hecklers. We were all there and accounted for. Definitely take my generalizing with a well-deserved grain of salt, but hear me: It was a circus.

So I stood at the periphery. The further I move into such a tangle of identities, the less comfortable I feel in my own skin. It's a mild form of social phobia that I deal with in any large group, but there's a particular sting to it when said group is doing something I care about. Nevertheless, I was there—again—far enough *in* to be part of, even if far enough *out* to be near the journalists and cameramen.

Scanning the crowd from my safe distance, I caught sight of a young mother with her toddler daughter on her shoulders and her grade school-aged son at her side, holding her hand. I felt the usual wave of gratitude that comes when I see parents exposing their children to stuff that matters. It was already late, and I wondered how long mom would choose to stay at the vigil with her kiddos. Death penalty vigils go up to and then past the 11:59 pm execution. It's a sickening ritual, marked all the way to the end by the faint hope that the Governor will opt for a Godlike last-minute stay. It's hard to picture what those final hours would feel like as the one set to die, and as the elected official with the power to keep that from happening.

I saw a disheveled-looking man with wild eyes carrying an enormous sign above his head. It was a crucifix, the Rated-R Roman Catholic kind, with Jesus, the crown of thorns, the spikes through his wrists and feet, the blood. A phrase was painted boldly above the cross:

as you do to the least of these

And in the distance, right up at the gate I could see and hear a furious young man—*everyone* could see and hear a furious young man—shaking the fence and cussing out the stoic-faced police officers and prison guards on the other side. There seemed to be a method to the young man's madness, for every time I began to wonder how much more of this the officers and guards would tolerate, he would take a break. I could see that he was with a group of friends. If it turned out that they were collectively as enraged as he was, I thought to myself, this had the potential of getting seriously ugly. Little doubt the same thought had occurred to the aforementioned mother, among others. One could feel that classic underlying protest uncertainty lurking. The seasick feeling that comes when people gather for one common reason and a thousand disparate reasons at the same time. In this case, in my experience, the kind of raw violence that just might lead to bloodshed, which was so palpable in the voice of that young man, could also be subtly detected beneath the surface of the unwieldy protest itself.

It's also true, lest we forget, that such raw violence was literally written into the schedule at San Quentin that night, in the form of a pre-meditated killing.

As I continued observing the scene something else eventually grabbed my attention. Actually it was more like the absence of something else. Off to my right-hand side, some twenty or so yards away from the gate, it was as if there was a hole in the crowd, a large empty space where the otherwise tightly-packed activists refused to go. I stood tiptoe to see if I could manage a glimpse of the mysterious space, but I couldn't. Whatever it was gave the crowd a lopsided donut shape. As I kept looking in that direction, something else became apparent to me. It was strange, but it seemed as if the people nearest the donut hole were behaving differently than the rest of the crowd. I couldn't put my finger on it exactly, but they seemed calmer and somehow more grounded, more solid even. And I was struck by the strange realization that the further my gaze fell from the donut hole, the less that calm, solid quality seemed to apply.

I was intrigued. Enough so, in fact, that I shored myself up, bid farewell to my little comfort zone at the edge of the protest, and began making my way through the crowd. As I wove my way toward the hole, I experienced what I had only previously observed. The further I went in that direction, the crowd's energy seemed to shift, by degrees, from frenetic and scattered toward calm and coherent. And, the closer I got to the empty space the more I felt something like a slight gravitational pull in that direction. I made my last few "excuse me" zig zags and finally reached the innermost circle of activists, the men and women standing there at the edge of the emptiness.

I was stunned by what I saw.

That had not been the innermost circle of activists at all. The emptiness was not empty. There on the pavement sat twenty or so men and women, hair-shorn and saffron-robed, eyes gently closed in meditation.

Kerplunk. Another piece fell into place. I had to find my team. These Buddhist monks were making that perfectly clear. I longed for the crisp clarity of it, the naked communication. I longed to be part of a group whose reputation preceded it, and whose demeanor and cohesion confirmed it.

It was plain to see. If it turned out that the friends of the furious young man at the gate decided to join him in rattling the fence and screaming obscenities; and if they started to climb the fence, say, or to throw rocks or Molotov cocktails; and if, say, the men with the clubs and the guns responded with all due diligence; and if the lack of coherence, the chaos at the root of the protest, took over… Whatever happened at that point, however it unfolded from there, no one—not a single person—would have had any doubt about the role played by the men and women in the saffron robes. Every activist, every reporter, every officer and guard, every bystander, every heckler would have known perfectly well what those folks had been about.

As I breathed in their collective prayer, I knew that someday I would suit up with a team that so wore its identity—proudly, humbly, plainly. And so much more than that too. A team that would be as strong and composed at the front end as it would be at the crisis point, infusing donut hole clarity into the process from the organizational get go, and equally strong and composed as well on the back end, ready to sacrifice for the cause, boldly and serenely. And, yes, a team with no qualms about taking its ball and going home, if and when the tyranny of inclusion began to take root, if and when some of our brothers and sisters started hammering in the stakes to erect the circus tent. A team that would say, in effect, and without apology: "This is who we are. This is the kind of witness we get with. Come one, come all, or none at all, this is who we are." A team prepared and longing to be part of a larger movement, but that's not afraid, if need be, to take Gandhi up on his challenge: "The valiant in spirit glory in fighting alone."

APPROACHING THE TIP OF THE ICEBERG

Shoulder to shoulder we continue our trek across the blue-white expanse of the massive glacier. Its tip is still a good ways off, but our boots crunch a steady percussive rhythm. We draw strength from the motion of our bodies, and are lulled by the determined pulse of our steps.

In time, we begin to observe a contour far off in the distance lying crosswise our path. An unexpected disruption in the smooth, otherwise unblemished terrain. Wordlessly, we continue the march, drawing gradually closer to whatever it might be. We walk until it forces us to stop.

We marvel at the deep crevasse. It's roughly hewn edges and deliberately etched corners are the work of the tools and hands of human beings.

We carefully pace the length and breadth of the mazelike crevasse, then stand in wonder at its unmistakably familiar form.

To its right is a second and distinct shape carved just as deeply into the ice. We walk it too, taking stock of its different but equally familiar appearance.

The massive letters, each dug deeply and indelibly across our path, continue into the distance, one after another. We move in silent pilgrimage and slowly absorb the message that's been left for us:

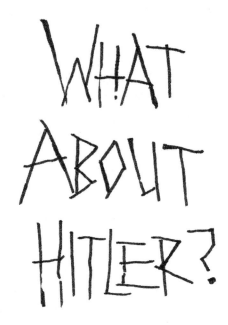

WHAT ABOUT HITLER?

In our collective imagination, he has come to personify humanity's terrifying capacity to be and do evil. His name serves as a placeholder for every example of ultra-extreme violence that challenges us to seriously question the capacity of nonviolence to offer an even remotely satisfactory response:

- Hiroshima/Nagasaki
- The Holocaust
- the Stalin-led purges in the Soviet Union
- the Cambodian genocide carried out by Pol Pot and the Khmer Rouge
- Rwanda
- Sudan
- Burma
- Vietnam
- Iraq: Saddam Hussein's regime, "Desert Storm," a decade of

U.S.-driven UN-backed sanctions, "Shock and Awe," the extreme destabilization and violence since

- Syria
- slavery in the U.S. and worldwide
- genocide against Native Americans, the aboriginal peoples of Australia, Armenians, Bosnians, etc. etc.
- pages and pages of etcs.

ANSWERING THE HITLER QUESTION

Integrity forces me to go there. But in the face of the immeasurable violence-inflicted suffering in our world—past, present, and future—I do so with a profound sense of inadequacy, and a fear of pure insignificance.

The Invisible Hand of Prevention

We owe it to ourselves to be brutally honest: When it comes to countering extreme violence with nonviolence we are horribly unprepared. And we owe the same level of honesty to all those who, in the face of unspeakably horrific violence, challenge us to defend our stance and advocacy on behalf of nonviolence.

To illustrate, we needn't look any further than the first example on the above list. What on earth could nonviolence say or do in defense of the thousands upon thousands of beautiful human beings going about their lives in Hiroshima, August 6, 1945?

The intensity of violence in any given situation determines the intensity of the nonviolence needed to diffuse it. Period. Whether one believes that in a cosmic sense a nonviolent response of some kind could have, and perhaps did, send a small ripple of love into the horror of Hiroshima, integrity demands that we admit, in no uncertain terms, that at this stage in our evolution we are absolutely incapable of matching that level of violence with nonviolence. The atomic bomb dropped from the Enola Gay was both product and pinnacle of an unimaginably complex and gargantuan violence, fed, developed and systematically refined in nations throughout the world over the course of an entire era, and anchored by a global, millenia-old mindset which holds as sacrosanct the myth that violence is redemptive. The bomb came so late in the game it's impossible for us to fully grasp the full process of its evolution and the profundity of the brokenness it represented.

Prevention, the first domain I contemplate when I wrestle with the Hitler question, reminds us of something so self-evident that it feels strange to even mention it: The best way to subvert violence is to keep it from happening in the first place. Granted, it can be difficult to measure things that don't happen. But common sense affirms that nonviolent prevention has kept innumerable catastrophes from unfolding. Its power is undeniable.

When it comes to this level of prevention—that is, the kind that keeps violence from ever emerging—self-purification and constructive program are our finest tools. As Gandhi put it, the foundation-building work of self-purification, "intangible as it seems, is the most potent means of revolutionizing one's environment [and] the straightest way to liberation." And constructive program, by healing social rifts, propagating nonviolent cultural norms and practices, restoring and elevating human dignity, and developing holistic human-scaled infrastructure, establishes nonviolent checks and balances within the community that keep violence at bay without our even noticing. Self-purification and constructive program may not make the headlines for their unparalleled accomplishments in the field of violence-prevention, but they should.

When we don't manage the complete prevention of violence, the next best thing is to keep whatever violence emerges to a minimum level, and nonviolently nip it in the bud. This is the realm of conflict resolution, where things like diplomacy and mediation come into play. Whether the violence occurs at the micro (interpersonal) or macro (international) level, or anywhere in between, this level of prevention is a powerful expression of nonviolence, though it too remains largely unsung in our violence-fascinated, violence-saturated culture.

Next best after that level of prevention is to do whatever it takes to ensure that violence never reaches a level of extremity that outmatches our capacity for nonviolence. This is where we're in the most trouble, and where, in my effort to wholeheartedly respond to the Hitler question, I find myself crossing into a second domain.

Ron Sider's Call

It's a case of the means/ends equivalency coming home to roost. The seeds of so much hatred, misunderstanding, and greed have been planted for so many centuries, and our civilization has been so slow to invest in nonviolence, that we don't have nearly enough fingers to plug all the holes that violence makes. One of the consequences of this, which many of us are growing increasingly aware of and sensitive to, is the way violence and environmental destruction are functioning within high-speed feedback loops, locally and globally. Each time we manage a step forward, it appears that the Domination System has taken ten. It has come to feel that we'll need a quantum leap to catch up.

At the 1984 Mennonite World Conference in Strasbourg, France, theologian Ron Sider delivered a speech that, after a few years gestation, gave birth to Christian Peacemaker Teams (CPT). He was addressing Mennonites but his remarks struck and still strike a chord with nonviolence practitioners of a great many stripes, and I think they have a lot to say to us about quantum leaps:

> Too often we fall into an isolationist pacifism which silently ignores or perhaps profits from injustice and war as long as our boys don't have to fight... To vote for other people's sons and daughters to march off to death while ours safely register as conscientious objectors is the worst

form of confused hypocrisy… Those who have believed in peace through the sword have not hesitated to die. Proudly, courageously, they gave their lives… For their loved ones, for justice, and for peace, they have laid down their lives by the millions… Why do we pacifists think that our way—Jesus's way—to peace will be less costly? Unless we…are ready to start to die by the thousands in dramatic vigorous new exploits for peace and justice, we should sadly confess that we never really meant what we said…

What would happen if we in the Christian church developed a new nonviolent peacekeeping force of 100,000 persons ready to move into violent conflicts and stand peacefully between warring parties in Central America, Northern Ireland, Poland, Southern Africa, the Middle East, and Afghanistan? Frequently we would get killed by the thousands. But everyone assumes that for the sake of peace it is moral and just for soldiers to get killed by the hundreds of thousands, even millions. Do we not have as much courage and faith as soldiers?

The spark of Sider's challenge eventually caught fire in the form of CPT, which joins several other peace team initiatives, such as Witness for Peace, Peace Brigades International, Nonviolent Peaceforce, and Voices for Creative Nonviolence in an earnest and inspiring effort to overcome our collective lack of willingness and preparedness to face war and other forms of extreme violence head on. It's important to point out, however, that the idea Sider articulated so powerfully was not a new one. Toward the end of his life Gandhi was heading in the same direction, laying the groundwork for what he called the Shanti Sena (Peace Army). He drew great inspiration from his friend and comrade, Khan Abdul Ghaffar Khan, the great Pathan nationalist from India's Northwest Frontier Province. In 1929, Ghaffar Khan launched the Khudai Khidmatgars (Servants of God), a nonviolent standing army whose ranks would eventually swell to 100,000—an unprecedented and still unmatched expression of massive, disciplined, and coherent nonviolent strength. In our U.S. context, the tenacious freedom fighter James Bevel, mastermind of the momentous and game-changing Children's March in Birmingham in 1963, impressed a similarly bold vision upon Dr. King and the wider U.S. nonviolence community as early as 1965, when he called for an international peace army to embed itself in Vietnam to throw a wrench in the war machine's wheel. It took King a couple years to catch up with his fiery young interlocutor, but he did. In 1967 King suggested that an unarmed group of six thousand should go to North Vietnam to bring a halt to the treacherous bombing there. King's and Bevel's visions never came to fruition, but they stand as powerful precursors to Ron Sider's 1984 address.

Fast-forwarding to the present, the existence of the aforementioned peace team organizations shows that over time the theory and practice of third-party nonviolent intervention has gained a modicum of respect, interest, and support. We are, nevertheless, forced to admit to some sobering limitations. While spawned by visions of eventually drawing together thousands of frontlines nonviolence practitioners, as Ghaffar Khan did in India's Northwest Frontier, all but one of the aforementioned initiatives most accurately number their ranks in the dozens. The exception, the Nonviolent Peaceforce, has a couple hundred workers. Because of this the contributions of peace teams today represent a drop in the bucket. Don't get me wrong—this work is a hugely important, inspiring, and potentially catalytic drop in the bucket. Nevertheless, compared to the reach and destruction of contemporary violence, it's having a miniscule impact. What's more, generally speaking, the work of these groups typically tends toward the reactive rather than the proactive or generative. That is, peace teams usually and necessarily focus their energy on putting out fires—or trying to keep the very next fire from getting started—rather than orchestrating protracted, targeted resistance against fire itself (i.e., violence) and the structures and cultural forces responsible for so much of it. It would be too much to expect anything different from these organizations, given their size and the scope of their mandates. But it casts light on an extremely important point. While we're falling dreadfully short of Ron Sider's call to pull together a massive peacekeeping force, there is an equally important need for an equally massive force that can proactively initiate engagement with the forces of Empire. Turning the Great Turning is going to require that we subvert the Domination System, not merely lessen the damage and devastation it wreaks.

So, as humbling as it is, we're challenged to imagine a peace army that is capable of standing down the carnage of a Holocaust or a Rwanda. And, until we have rebuilt human culture and systems to be fully animated by the principles of love and nurture, we're challenged to also imagine a force that is capable of deposing the powers that set such catastrophes as the Holocaust and genocide in Rwanda in motion.

At which point, I'll confess, the magnitude of our dilemma and my own feelings of powerlessness threaten to immobilize me, and I find myself asking:

What's the point then? Why are we even talking about this stuff?

For years now I've been working on the assumption that the only logical answer is that we need to come at this thing with a seriously long view perspective. Toward the end of his life, Gandhi emphasized that in understanding the potential and dynamics of large-scale nonviolence, humanity was just getting started. I believe that is still very much the case. In fact, standing face to face with the Hitler question, I've come to think of us as Kindergarteners in the school of satyagraha. And, if indeed we're in Kindergarten, I've figured, then we simply have to do whatever it takes to graduate and move forward. What other choice do we have?

I've seen the experiments of peace team organizations as especially important experiments to support as we head toward and then beyond the first grade. I've learned from ground floor firsthand experience that if we put even a fraction of as much time, energy, and resources into such third-party nonviolent intervention efforts as we do to the forces of militarism we'd see unbelievable advances in large-scale nonviolent engagement.

But, true as that may be, dozens of current and horrifically bloody crises, not to mention the overarching climate change emergency, rudely interrupt us: *"As we head toward first grade!?"* Yes, that's what I said. And no, first grade's not gonna cut it.

"A Formidable Gamble"

Philosopher-author-journalist Albert Camus faced the odds and their true implications, and came up with this:

> Over the expanse of five continents throughout the coming years an endless struggle is going to be pursued between violence and friendly persuasion [I like to think he meant satyagraha], a struggle in which, granted, the former has a thousand times the chances of success than that of the latter. But I have always held that, if he who bases his hopes on human nature is a fool, he who gives up in the face of circumstances is a coward. And henceforth, the only honorable course will be to stake everything on a formidable gamble.

Then there's the great fifteenth century testimony of Thomas á Kempis:

> Love feels no burden,
>> thinks nothing of trouble,
>>> attempts what is above its strength,
>>>> pleads no excuse of impossibility.

And what about Frodo, the noble young Hobbit charged with the most impossible of commissions? Among comrades—yet alone too—he's tasked with leaving all he's known in order to carry the world's burden, the Ring. And carry it he must, an unspeakably perilous distance, to the nightmarish land with the only fire ferocious enough to unmake it.

> ...A great dread fell on him, as if he was awaiting the pronouncement

of some doom that he had long foreseen and vainly hoped might never after all be spoken. An overwhelming longing to rest and remain at peace by Bilbo's side in Rivendell filled all his heart. At last with an effort he spoke, and wondered to hear his own words, as if some other will was using his small voice.

"I will take the Ring," he said, "though I do not know the way."

On a good day it's not difficult for me to remember that mystery still and always reigns. At bottom, my heart resonates with Joanna Macy, when she says: "We don't know how this is going to play out," and when she adds: "And what an utterly amazing time to be alive!"

Unforeseen nonviolent power is waiting to burst forth, I have no doubt. Crisis and catastrophe often bring out the very best in human beings and usher in extraordinary surprises. Heartbreakingly beautiful and inspiring examples abound, each and all deserving of our wholehearted tribute. We've already mentioned a number of them, such as Ghaffar Khan and the Khudai Khid-matgars, the Voices in the Wilderness teams in Iraq, and the Children's March in Birmingham. But there are so many others that we could name: the Chipko Movement in the forests of India, Czechoslovakia's Prague Spring resistance to Soviet occupation, and the U.S. Sanctuary Movement, for instance. Or the many noble and quite literal responses to the Hitler question, carried out as they were during the height of the Nazi regime—such as the collective resistance of the French village of Le Chambon-sur-Lignon, the White Rose student movement, the women's Rosenstrasse Prison Demonstration, and the Danish underground rescue of virtually all of Denmark's Jews.

A massive social movement—here, now, at the cusp of the Great Turning—may inspire a discovery and expression of human potential unlike any we've ever seen, especially if we manage to anchor it with integral nonviolence and the level of courage and commitment modeled by those who carried forth the actions noted above.

Unexpected guides and allies, great and unseen forces, may be conspiring at this very moment to reveal our path to liberation.

And even closer to the heart of it, for me, runs that intuitive hunch that here again we must renounce and abandon the bygone era's success narrative altogether. The paradox is this: We won't be able to wield the full transformative power of nonviolence until we choose it solely because it's good and right to do so, not because we think it will lead to victory—whether we perceive that victory to be on the immediate horizon, or at the end of time.

Our humble and down to earth oracle, Wendell Berry, says the same thing, only better:

> Protest that endures, I think, is moved by a hope far more modest than that of public success: namely, the hope of preserving qualities in one's own heart and spirit that would be destroyed by acquiescence.

Robert Brimlow's Conclusion

Christian philosopher Robert Brimlow has authored an entire book called *What About Hitler?*, which explores the question with unusual courage and honesty. Brimlow pulls this critical thread all the way to its ultimate, logical, and spiritual end. His book crescendos 150 pages in, with a half-page chapter in which he offers his plainspoken response to the Hitler question. Brimlow's conclusion is rooted in his Christian heritage and identity. It is, nevertheless, easy enough to translate for those of us who come at it from a different angle.

> We must live faithfully; we must be humble in our faith and truthful in what we say and do; we must repay evil with good; and we must be peacemakers. This may mean as a result that the evildoers will kill us. Then, we shall also die.

> That's it. There is nothing else—or rather, anything else is only a footnote to this. We are called to live the kingdom as he proclaimed it and be his disciples, come what may. We are, in his words, flowers flourishing

and growing wild today, and tomorrow destined for the furnace. We are God's people, living by faith.

The gospel is clear and simple, and I know what the response to the Hitler question must be. And I desperately want to avoid this conclusion. When my time comes, I may well trot out every nuanced argument I can develop, or seek a way out in St. Thomas Aquinas or Paul Ramsey [just war theory apologists]. This would serve me and my fear, my hypocrisy, and my faithlessness very well. But I would not be telling the truth or living as I ought and as I am called to live.

Brimlow's naked testimony hearkens directly back to Ron Sider's challenging call to a radical acceptance of death as part of the package. In this, Brimlow and Sider are unquestionably Gandhian. "To lay down one's life for what one considers to be right," Gandhi said, "is the core of satyagraha." Unsurprisingly, therefore, Jesus' death on the cross represented the pinnacle of faithfulness to Gandhi. "Jesus was the most active resister known perhaps to history," he said. "This was nonviolence par excellence."

So, what about Hitler?

My own response, in a word, must be this: courage.

When my time comes, and I stand without the armor of my CPT vest or my FOR t-shirt—because I am no longer the peace team volunteer but one of those for whom the Domination System has come—I too may well trot out every nuanced argument I can muster. Or, more likely, I may simply run like hell.

But that doesn't change the call or the aspiration one iota.

"What do you think?" Gandhi asks us. "Wherein is courage required—in blowing others to pieces from behind a cannon, or with a smiling face to approach a cannon to be blown to pieces? Who is the true warrior?"

———

LA UNIÓN (pt. 3)

Lily and I conferred, as Jorge looked on. While the vast majority of the community's members were clearly following protocol and making their way up any number of mountain trails, we agreed that the fifteen or so individuals that were still meandering blocked our going. Several of them were elderly—able-bodied for sure, but slow on their feet and much less at risk. I was frustrated with them, but I sympathized. A few of the people that lingered, however, were younger, a couple of them young men. Under the circumstances, I was straight-up pissed-off at what I perceived as their bravado. I had already gotten a whiff of it on La Unión's makeshift soccer field. But this was no game.

Nevertheless, whyever those who chose to stay had made that choice, we would not leave them.

Three community leaders approached Lily and me. We conveyed our decision to them and encouraged them to get going as quickly as they could. They balked at the idea. Thankfully Lily, whose Spanish was far better than mine, and who had a knack for persuasion, was able to quickly convince them to leave without us.

Just after they did, Jorge gestured subtly and said: "Allí están." There they are.

I looked down the dirt path to the community's main entrance. Fifteen or so combatants, all with assault rifles, were heading toward us. To make sure we were plainly visible we made our way to the center of the path. As the soldiers got closer, Lily and I were able to ascertain several details. First, we could tell from their unguarded body language and from the fact that several of them let their weapons swing unheld at their sides, that these soldiers weren't looking to kill anybody. Second, as they got closer, their ragtag and muddy uniforms let us know that these were definitely not paramilitaries. These were guerrilleros from the FARC. They looked utterly exhausted, and their muddy fatigues reminded me that it had rained the previous night. In my mind's eye I pictured them spending the frigid night in a make-do, cold, and soggy camp, swapping turns sleeping and keeping watch. Third, it was plain to see that all but two or three of them were teenagers, one of whom was a girl no more than fifteen or sixteen years old.

They were surprised to see us. Even in their weary state they couldn't help but show their curiosity and a bit of excitement at the novelty of seeing two white people way out in the hilly Colombian countryside. It's safe to assume that they regarded Jorge as a member of the peace community.

They asked us for water. Lily and I obliged without a second thought. I walked the group to a spigot while Lily went to fetch cups from our kitchen. A little while later, when Lily successfully satellite phoned the San Francisco office, Jutta gently chided us for this humanitarian gesture, reminding us that it was against the community's covenant to aid any of the armed actors in any way. Later that evening, after they returned from their hillside hideouts, we would apologize to the community leaders for this oversight.

The young men, boys, and the girl put down their guns and gear, then set about drinking and refilling, drinking and refilling, their cups of water. As I watched them I began to feel, ever so slightly, the faint beginnings, the slow burn, of rage in my belly. In silence, I began to seethe at the adult world. At adult men, especially, who as a consequence of their own brazen cowardice and stupidity would send the young off into the hills to kill and die.

These tired teenagers, with barely enough energy for the slightest banter among themselves, brought up the courage to ask Lily and me: "¿De dónde son?" Where are you from?

"Los estados unidos," we replied.

"¡América!" And their eyes lit up.

Jorge, meanwhile, had stepped away from us. I watched him as he made his way toward the one member of the unit who was standing apart, some twenty or so yards off. He was older than the others, and I guessed he was their commander. In addition to his weapon, his backpack, and the chains of bullets draped in an X across his chest, he was lugging radio equipment. With one hand he held a headphone to his ear, with the other he negotiated a radio mic and the dials of the receiver. He was trying to establish contact with someone. He was not a large man physically, few Colombians are, but he struck an imposing figure as Jorge, who was even smaller, stepped towards him. The guerrillero lowered the headphone as Jorge drew close.

I couldn't hear a word of their conversation. Observing my friend's posture, however, I was able to absorb a good deal of whatever it was. Throughout the exchange, Jorge's stance revealed quiet self-possession and solidity. Nothing about it was threatening or disrespectful. Nothing about it was apologetic. He stood, authentic and imperturbable.

After a few minutes, Jorge turned from the commander and headed over to Lily and me.

"What was that about?" I asked him softly.

"I wanted to make sure he knew about the peace community's declaration," he said. "And I asked him to move his group along."

Lily and I stole a glance at each other. "Really?" she said.

"Yes. I told him that their presence and their weapons were putting the community in danger, and that we'd appreciate if they'd leave."

Lily and I looked at each other again, not sure what to think or say.

Our uninvited guests had finally quenched their thirst. They began to lean back, sprawl out and relax. I looked back toward the commander. He'd made contact and was speaking into his radio mic. I watched him as he spoke a few sentences, listened to a few sentences, and then clipped his headphone and mic to his belt.

Then, calmly, he approached his dozing charges. "Vamos," he said. Let's go.

Despite a few quiet sighs, the command was met with immediate compliance. The group got to their feet, flung their packs on their backs, and their rifles over their shoulders. One at a time, they handed their cups back to us. "Gracias," they said. The commander indicated the wood-slat gate at the far end of the community. They all fell in line, and hiked out of La Unión.

I stood in a daze of heightened awareness as I watched them go. Only after they had disappeared into the trees beyond the gate did I feel the shock of recalling my greatest personal fear as an international in Colombia: being abducted by the guerrilla.

I took a deep breath and turned to Lily. She took her own deep breath, and we managed a smile for one another. We'd survived our first emergency.

Then I turned to Jorge. He was sitting on a boulder next to the spigot, crying.

He looked me square in the eyes. "That could have been Renata," he said softly. He meant the girl. Jorge's daughter Renata was back home in Philadelphia. She was thirteen or so at the time.

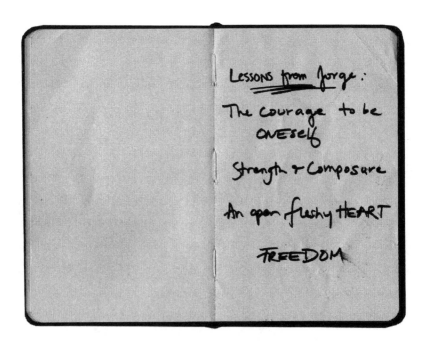

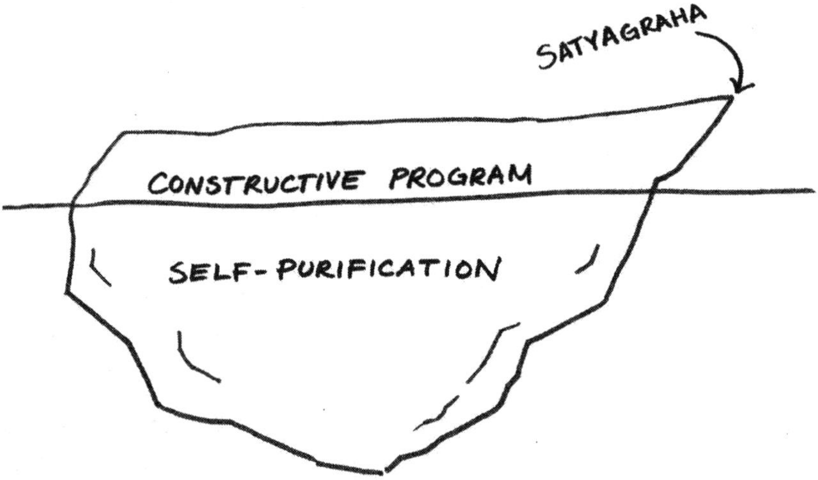
SATYAGRAHA
CONSTRUCTIVE PROGRAM
SELF-PURIFICATION

5.
IN SERVICE TO THE MOVEMENT OF MOVEMENTS

IN THIS CHANGES EVERYTHING, Naomi Klein adds her voice to the ever-expanding chorus of scientists and author-researchers who have demonstrated that the time for global action has most certainly arrived. But what she also shows is that the monumental scale and character of the action needed points to the raising up of more than a movement. As we've touched on at various points throughout this book, the action currently needed points to the raising up of a movement of movements—we might choose to use the acronym MOM—that will be unprecedented in human history. The concept is not new. Some argue, in fact, that we already are a movement of movements, interacting, collaborating, and adapting organically, in a completely decentralized fashion. But I'm talking about something far more intentional and organized than this. I'm talking about the deliberate and focused convergence of our great spectrum of resistance struggles, so that we may move of one accord by bold and careful design. Because such a convergence is still a good ways off, I contend that our movement of movements is in its most incipient phase. We've only just begun to coalesce, and we do so swimming against an incredibly powerful stream.

The Domination System thrives on the segregation of our struggles, and seeks to thwart any serious stride toward their unification. As a painfully clear case in point, consider the trouble Dr. King got himself into when he started connecting the dots between the triplet evils: "We must rapidly begin the shift," he said,

> from a "thing-oriented" society to a "person-oriented" society. When machines and computers, profit motives and property rights are considered more important than people, the giant triplets of racism, materialism, and militarism are incapable of being conquered... A nation that continues year after year to spend more money on military defense than on programs of social uplift is approaching spiritual death... Our only hope today lies in our ability to recapture the revolutionary spirit and go out into a sometimes hostile world declaring eternal hostility to poverty, racism and militarism.

Because of the power wielded by the movement, the establishment was willing to absorb a certain measure of prophetic verbiage and policy upheaval to do with racial integration and voting rights, but the moment Dr. King started pointing at the man behind the curtain, the bullet was loaded. Calling the madness in Vietnam by its true name, setting the stage for the Poor People's Campaign—a nonviolent uprising unlike any the U.S. had ever (and still has never) seen—saying that the time had come for the community of struggle to "see the great distinction between a reform movement and a revolutionary movement," uttering the phrases "guaranteed income for all Americans" and "Democratic Socialism," especially in the absurdly anti-Communist milieu of U.S. society in the late 60s—such statements were out of bounds in a theater owned and operated by the Domination System. King was dead one year after his clearest enunciation of the nature and reach of the triplet evils, and the man behind the curtain continued about his business. And still does.

For our part, here, still near the dawn of the 21st century, we've been holding our posts well, as firefighters basically, each with our own specialization or combination of multiple specializations. Some of us put out fires to do with racism or sexism, some with immigration or police brutality, some with the Israeli occupation or the Syrian refugee crisis, some with drones, some with factory farms and cruelty to animals, some with fracking, some with mountain-top removal, some with the water crisis. We've of course known that these and hundreds more struggles are all interconnected, that they all represent different aspects of our quest to bring a just and life-sustaining society into existence. An untold number of communities and peace and justice-oriented organizations have been created in response to this very understanding, to serve as hubs for cross-fertilization and fellowship across struggles.

But, as we've already established, and as painful as it may be to admit, our big picture evaluation department has been sleeping on the job. For even the most cursory assessment shows that any time a stride for justice is made, the Domination System has just jogged right along, hardly a nick, whistling as it goes. New and worse injustices bubble up somewhere else, or in the same exact spot where the stride for justice was made. We're so familiar with this there's no need to cite examples.

Our reactive firefighting strategy isn't working. Most of us have lived with chronic and often acute feelings of frustration, powerlessness, or despair because of this. Good on us for keeping on, nevertheless. That's a beautiful thing about us. But I and a growing number of changemakers are coming to see that the time has now come for us to heed the call to build our movement of movements. The idea is not simply to cast the widest net possible, it's an invitation to envision anew who we are collectively, and to take full account of what it is we're up against. It's an invitation to honestly assess this critical moment in history, to chart our best course in service to the Great Turning, and to bring all of our work to a whole new level.

We have some terribly important conversations ahead of us—one of the most important of which must center on the question of macro-movement strategy. To help move that crucial conversation forward, I'm going to offer several concrete suggestions. I urge others to thoughtfully and critically assess each of these ideas, to carefully and constructively poke holes in them, to fill in missing spaces, and to offer their own reflections and counter-proposals. In this state of great emergency, we need to close in on our collective strategic needs as quickly as possible. Toward that end, we will not be served by those who relish in dismissing or criticizing from the sidelines. Now's the time for pro-active, supportive, and generative debate. Now's the time for collaboration and initiative. Now's the time to clarify our thinking, to define our intentions, and to lay the groundwork for our best and boldest actions in defense of life. I offer up the following proposals in service to those aims, and in hopes that these ideas might in some way advance the emergence and strengthening of the movement of movements.

May the conversation continue and deepen. And may it move us to resist and to create as never before.

AN OFFERING FOR MOM (pt. 1):
THREE STRANDS OF AN
INTEGRAL NONVIOLENCE SUBMOVEMENT

My first proposal is addressed specifically to those called to comprise an integral nonviolence submovement, which will offer itself in service to the emerging U.S.-wide movement of movements. That is to say, this proposal is for those to whom I have addressed this entire book. Recalling previous discussion in the introduction and the swadeshi section of chapter 1, we can again acknowledge that the U.S. movement of movements will be only one of the great worldwide array of coalitions that will constitute the overarching, global movement of movements. We train our focus on the U.S. in order to make sure our horse stays in front of the cart. We want the building blocks of the overarching movement to be as strong and well-placed as possible. We know that as we grow from strength to greater strength on our home turf, we do so in solidarity with changemakers across the planet. All to say, from here on when I refer to the movement of movements I'm referring to its U.S.

contingent, not its full-blown manifestation on a global scale.

We need to accept that the emerging movement of movements is not going to use the Gandhian Iceberg as its guiding model, at least not any time soon. The societal culture propagated by the Domination System has effectively blocked us from that possibility. Though we can certainly hold out hope that "the bug of nonviolence," as Robért Raymond calls it, is gearing up to bite a great multitude, and though we might rightly choose to hold the forging of a mass Gandhian movement as part of our long-term vision, for now we can see that the Gandhian contingent in the overarching movement will be a tiny minority. This needn't be cause for despair for those of us who have been bitten by the bug and are wedded to integral nonviolence. In this, the movement of movements will mirror freedom struggles the world over. India's 78 and the core leaders of SNCC and SCLC were numerical blips, for example, in the sea of activists that carried forth their respective struggles. But that in no way lessened the singular importance of their contribution.

And that, to put it succinctly, has been the whole point of this book. The hypothesis at the root of all these pages is that those of us who will live out integral nonviolence within the context of the coming struggle will act as leaven within the dough of the movement. As the movement of movements coheres—and as we help it cohere—it will be our task and privilege to inject our radical and disciplined approach and our highest long-term vision of the future into the mix. We'll do this best by protecting the flame of Gandhi's holistic nonviolence understanding, throughout the course of the struggle, from the winds of fear-based compromise and pedestalization that would snuff it out. By so protecting Gandhi's nonviolence understanding—and remember, I'm talking about demonstrating by showing and, in effect, proving the power of the theory in the labs of radical direct action, culture-shifting constructive program, and disciplined self-transformation—chances are good the movement's dough is going to rise. For those of us who have been bitten, though, we'll be good to go whether or not the dough rises. That isn't our chief concern—at least it shouldn't be. Our job is to keep the means in order and to give our full effort.

As mentioned in the introduction, a great many groupings will be needed to build up a strong and balanced integral nonviolence submovement. I am nevertheless limiting my discussion at this point to three. This is not because I see these three potential groups as the most essential overall, but because I believe their coalescence is needed most urgently at this juncture in order to catalyze the formation of our submovement. If created, as with just about everything else described in this book, these groups would be distinct but also deeply interconnected. Certain individuals would certainly serve in multiple groups, and the groups would collaborate closely with one another.

For now, let's call these three proposed groupings the 78, the Constructive Program Corps, and the Group Process and Conflict Transformation Team. Needless to say, the individuals making up these three teams would be steeped in and deeply committed to nonviolence—the integrated, comprehensive, love-based, and revolutionary nonviolence I've done my best to describe in this book.

The 78

"The 78" is not just a nifty rhetorical device. It's my best guess at a realistic estimate, give or take, of how many integral nonviolence practitioners might be ready to sign on for this special role during the opening phase of struggle. Just as the Navy has its inner circle of Navy Seals, if we're going to pull this thing off, I'm wagering that the Great Turning peace armies around the world will each need to have their equivalent of the 78. And, as the struggle persists those 78s will need to steadily expand their ranks.

Anchored by steady practice with self-purification and constructive program, and by the core principles of satyagraha as detailed in chapter 4, the 78 would devise and adopt covenants in terms of qualifications, code of discipline, structure, steps, and rules for the offering of satyagraha in the public sphere. They would train and stand ready for those direct actions deemed faithful expressions of the spirit of the integral nonviolence submovement, and which would be necessary for the advancement of the wider cause. They would initiate nonviolent confrontations with systems and agents of oppression, in order to bring latent, smoldering conflict into the light of day. They would be ready to be deployed as rapid response peace teams in areas of high need and violence. They would cultivate the willingness to face the risks of physical harm, imprisonment, and death, always and ever in service to love and the Great Turning. They would offer to serve the movement of movements at its vanguard.

Social movements the world over have demonstrated that when it comes to galvanizing mass mobilization, nothing compares to direct, self-sacrificial engagement with the forces of Empire. The 78 would be tinder for the fire that is the emerging movement of movements. Their opening forays would help to ignite mass struggle.

Constructive Program Corps

Inspired by the Freedom Schools founded during the civil rights phase of the African American Freedom Movement, I encourage the formation of a Constructive Program Corps dedicated to the emergence of a new constellation of closely connected community-based centers of liberation, resiliency, and renewal across the U.S. The goal and purpose of the centers (some of which are already in-the-making, if not fully operational) would be nothing less than the building up of a new U.S. culture and society. The centers would identify themselves with the same vision that fired the original Freedom School movement, which is to serve as educational and hands-on constructive program spaces where emancipation from oppression and exploitation is sought and gained, where survival, both physical and cultural, is safeguarded, and where the development of our fullest human potential is fostered. This network of grassroots community centers would draw guidance, strength, and a sense of unity from its direct and explicit connection with our nation's movement lineage.

The centers would serve as hubs for community resilience and cultural transition training, and would be designed to ensure that the direct action component of the struggle, with its aim to dismantle violent structures and systems, would be reinforced by the concurrent building up of alternative, nonviolent structures and systems. The Constructive Program Corps would play a special role in identifying and gluing together pre-existing projects that are already pursuing this vision in various forms, and with the spawning and development of more such learning and action centers in rural and urban locations throughout the nation.

Inspired and guided by the vision of the Great Turning, and in close collaboration with pre-existing projects, the Constructive Program Corps would identify and develop trainings and curricula in service to personally and societally transformative learning, and they would assemble teams of skilled, innovative, and nonviolence-oriented community organizers and educators to bring those trainings and curricula to life. The centers would each be bioregion and culture-specific, and they would be accessible and relevant to people of all ages, backgrounds, and walks of life. The great variety of subjects and skills taught and explored at the centers would share the foundation of integral nonviolence. They would include: tools, techniques, and practices for post-oil living, developing post-oil community-based infrastructure, undoing oppressions (racism, sexism, heteronormativity, religious intolerance, etc.), nonviolence and social movement history and practice (including training in the arts of direct action and love-based resistance), gift economics, restorative and transformative justice, group process and dynamics, intergenerational community-building and collaboration, interpersonal communication, overcoming dependencies, health and wholeness (physical, mental, spiritual, and emotional), and leadership/followership development. The Constructive Program Corps would track the specific gifts and expertise that each center has to offer to the wider national network, and would serve as a bridge between centers, encouraging and supporting ongoing cross-fertilization and consultation between them.

Group Process and Conflict Transformation Team

The two aforementioned groups would need the support of a nonviolence cadre with the highest level of skills and expertise in group process and conflict. This team would serve our submovement with ongoing trainings and consultation in the arts of group dynamics and decision-making, interpersonal communication, undoing oppressions, and conflict transformation. It would have the ability to dispatch emergency on-call conflict transformation task forces, to help head off group standoffs or meltdowns that threaten to sabotage the energy and relationships driving the submovement. This team would serve to remind and instruct movement workers to continually seek and find the humanity of the "other," whether that "other" operates within or outside the ranks of the movement. The team would work to forge an anti-ism movement culture, keeping channels open and addressing power imbalances and conflict between, for example, male/female, straight/queer, black/white, atheist/religious, indigenous/settler, etc. etc. This group would teach and model practices for overcoming psychological blocks.

Characteristic of the integral nonviolence submovement, the Group Process and Conflict Transformation Team would offer its gifts in service to the overarching movement of movements, standing ready to be dispatched to assist the wider movement in any way possible. For example, the restorative and transformative justice practices this team would inculcate within the integral nonviolence submovement could serve as resources or models for the overarching movement of movements (not to mention for the society at large). Similarly, this team's ready willingness to support the 78 in their efforts to transform the conflicts they encounter with members of corporations, the military and police, the political system, and the general public, could be extended—at the pleasure of the movement of movements—to any number of other submovements engaged in the struggle.

This team would develop and propose leadership/followership structures for the integral nonviolence submovement as a whole, and for the submovement's three initial constituent groups (the 78, the Constructive Program

Corps, and itself, the Group Process and Conflict Transformation Team).

AN OFFERING FOR MOM (pt. 2):
TOWARDS AN OVERARCHING GAME PLAN

Now I'm going to venture a multilayered proposal for the emerging movement of movements itself. As I do so, I am fully cognizant of yet another paradox: I have asserted, in no uncertain terms, that the Great Turning cannot and will not be a white-led undertaking, and yet I—a white man—am choosing to float a proposal as to how the movement of movements might put its best foot forward.

It's a paradox with which I've grown somewhat familiar, if not entirely comfortable, and which reminds me of one of the most important lessons I've learned while observing my favorite mentors in the field of community organizing. Organizers know what it means to envision and collaborate in service to the emergence or ascension of someone or something other than themselves. It's in that organizing spirit that I offer what follows. My whiteness and the above paradox have given me pause. And, it's also true that several people of color who I deeply trust have encouraged me to bring this vision forward, as an offering. So I am, with the simple hope that it might catalyze deeper conversation about the critically important question of macro-movement strategy.

Movements are living breathing things, unamenable to narrow definitions and rigid expectations. Nonetheless, I contend that the current struggle will be best served by the emergence and coherence of a movement of movements with a clearly articulated movement narrative and vision, and by a high level of identifiable structure, leadership, and strategic planning.

My proposal to the emerging movement of movements has several parts: some suggested language to capture the long-term vision for the movement, my argument for what the movement should choose as its first two direct action focal points, a description of two key national groups whose coalescence and efforts, I believe, would be most crucial during the opening phase of struggle for the newly unified movement, suggested language and concepts for the movement's opening narrative, and a proposed action step to mark the beginning of mass mobilization nationwide.

Long-Term Vision

It should come as no surprise that I encourage the emerging movement of movements to hold the Great Turning as the centerpiece of its overarching vision. Here's some language that might be of use to whomever the movement entrusts to articulate that vision.

> We are a movement of movements, united by love, rooted in nonviolence, driven by our thirst for justice, wholeness, and redemption, and committed to giving our full effort in service to the Great Turning, the epochal shift from our current industrial growth society to a truly just and life-sustaining society.

Two Core Campaigns

I believe that the movement of movements should initiate unified action in the form of two initial and simultaneous campaigns. These campaigns would signal in no uncertain terms that a full-blown nonviolent revolution is underway. I join many others in proposing that one of these first steps must be taking down the fossil fuel industry—the entire entrenched corporate complex of extractive industries that are sending us all over the cliff. Too many trusted analysts have proven the necessity of this step for us to give in to the temptation of denial or to drag our feet. If the vast majority of carbon-emitting resources that are still in the ground do not remain in the ground, we simply won't have the time or space we need to build toward a new and just society. We'll be in the throes of all-out catastrophe, relegated indefinitely to our firefighter posts.

Many are quick to remind us that factory farming and deforestation keep pace with the fossil fuel industry in their devastating contribution to ecological collapse. Because those systems are completely dependent on fossil fuels, however, and given how quickly the climate change clock is ticking, it makes sense strategically to treat them as the next dominoes in the line.

On the spiritual plane, one could say, the food supply for the Domination System is fear, usually showing up in the forms of greed, complacency, and violence. But on the physical plane, the fossil fuel industry represents the food supply for the Domination System. While it's only one component in a massive, complex, and nimble system, it's the one we need to take down in order to buy ourselves the time to keep struggling, learning, and healing.

Simultaneously, as a second and intrinsically related initial step, I believe the movement should launch a national campaign of atonement and reparations for the victims of white supremacy. Our nation has ignored this clear and basic moral obligation for far too long. What's more, the choice to avert environmental catastrophe without operationalizing this second layer of committed action, I believe, would necessarily and inevitably come back to haunt us—in the same way so many remnants of our unfinished business and our unresolved trauma and wrongdoing have haunted us since our nation's beginning. A concerted, strategically devised, citizen-led national campaign of atonement and reparations, though it would only represent one limited mode of action to redress an inconceivable amount of harm and injustice, would mark the beginning of a profound transformation for our society. To undertake such a campaign would signal the advent of an enormous shift, the "national reckoning," the "revolution in American consciousness," that Ta-Nehisi Coates speaks about. The campaign would embody the Great Turning and would be an emblem of the movement's inner integrity. It would bring the white community and communities of color together in a way never before seen, as the healing process and the redistribution of whites' unearned and now-renounced inheritances were made real.

It is crucial to recognize and underscore the essential unity and symbiosis of these two campaigns. The climate crisis that we seek to avert, beginning with our initial attack on the fossil fuel industry, is a direct consequence of white supremacy. And, in the context of the Great Turning, the effort to ameliorate at least some of the harm and wrongdoing done to the human communities victimized by white supremacy, and to begin forging heart unity where bitter and centuries-old division has reigned, cannot be separated from our efforts to offer restitution to the earth itself. In the age of the Great Turning, we are called to extend atonement and reparations not only to oppressed peoples, but to the entire biosphere.

The means=ends formula reminds us, as we consider the immensity of these interwoven proposed steps, that things like the fossil fuel industry and white supremacy cannot and will not be toppled unless the personal and cultural mindsets, values, and habits that uphold them are also brought down. In other words, these campaigns would require that we dismantle the Domination System not only in the external forms it takes at the societal level, but also in the forms it takes in our own hearts and minds, and in the ways we choose to live our lives.

As lofty and far-fetched as they may seem, given the current state of our society and world, the goals raised up by these two campaigns begin to bring the true meaning and realistic demands of the Great Turning into focus. I hope we are, I urge us to be, daring enough to choose them.

In order to draw together our movement of movements, and to begin generating the great power, unity, and sense of direction we'll need to carry forward such momentous campaigns, I propose the formation of two national leadership groups:

National Strategy and Mobilization Team

The national strategy and mobilization team would be charged with developing an overarching and concrete long-term strategy for the movement of movements that would help glue together its various submovements and give them a shared, coherent sense of strategic direction. This team would map current resistance efforts in the U.S., build relationships with the key organizers and leaders in those locales, identify areas of overlap (people, places, campaigns, goals, mission, etc.), and work to weave such areas of overlap together in order to strengthen the collective movement. This team would plan, track, and advise movement campaigns, creatively and deliberately utilizing the submovements' varying strengths and expertise. The team would be capable of teasing out a slew of potential scenarios, plan bs, what ifs, and hail marys.

The members of the national strategy and mobilization team would have proven track records in organizing and implementing campaigns built for deep-rooted structural change, and they would completely understand the inseparable nature of social, political, and environmental action and organizing. A key facet of their work would be gaining a clear understanding of the interlocking structures that uphold the Domination System. Toward this end and by way of example, assuming that the two aforementioned campaigns were adopted by the movement, the strategy and mobilization team would need to give specific initial attention to the role of the fossil fuel industry and the potential means and consequences of its collapse—while simultaneously discerning how to best launch a national campaign of atonement and reparations, given the race/class dynamics of the day.

The members of this national strategy and mobilization team would be deeply rooted in nonviolence, whether or not of the Gandhian ilk, and they would excel in radical, out-of-the-box visioning. They would be characterized by their great teamwork, incorruptibility, and smarts, and they would enjoy the earned trust of seasoned and respected changemakers throughout the U.S.

National Leadership Council

At a critical point Ella Baker knew the moment had come to call together the student leaders that would form the Student Non-Violent Coordinating Committee. At a similarly critical juncture, Dr. King and several of his co-workers discerned that it was time to seize the leadership that had been entrusted to them and to band together as the Southern Christian Leadership Conference. SNCC and SCLC went on to give the freedom struggle a great deal of what it needed in order to cohere—the vision, strategy, language, direction, and inspiration that made possible the forging of a mass national movement. I and many others have come to believe that we desperately need such leadership now.

Despite the presence of powerful, incorruptible, justice-seeking, and love-driven national leaders, we are nevertheless suffering greatly from a vacuum of leadership at the national level. Social, ecological, peace, and justice movements across the nation have raised up incredible individuals as spokespersons and visionaries. We see and hear them in tv and radio interviews. We see their work and words featured in documentary films. We hear them speak when they come through town. We read and discuss their books. We let their visions inspire, challenge, and change us. Though they may not think of it in these terms, we have deputized them to speak to us and for us in this way.

I believe we now need a small and particularly courageous group of such leaders to look up from their important work long enough to see and embrace that they have been deputized in this way, and to recognize that a most unusual opportunity stands before them. Their great privilege to hold the public microphone, and the great trust they have earned from us, their constituencies, affords them the chance and, I believe, the responsibility, to call together a movement of movements unparalleled in human history, and to do so with passion, clarity, and a calm and dignified sense of urgency.

As amazing as it might seem, only one such leader is needed to set this in motion. One leader—sincere and authentic, unwaveringly rooted in love and a commitment to the nonviolent struggle for justice—need only and privately reach out to another such leader, on behalf of our shared struggle. These two leaders could then sit down together, to begin visioning and keeping company under the banner of the Great Turning. When they found that they were in need of more perspectives and voices they could reach out to two more. Like themselves, the leaders they would invite to join their conversation would be consummate team players, quick on their feet, creative, and deeply trusted by the constituencies of the submovements they represent. The four would continue. Then, when needed, they would reach out to four more.

Again, to clarify, I am not picturing that the members of this leadership group, with the potential of perhaps one or two exceptions, would be deeply steeped in Gandhian nonviolence. But they would share at the bare minimum a commitment to an expression of nonviolence that fundamentally eschews any and all forms of physical and verbal violence.

The leadership circle would be multiracial, with whites in a clear minority, and it would represent a beautiful variety of movement constituencies: from Black Lives Matter to climate change, from anti-sexism and trans/gender equality to anti-militarization, from indigenous struggles to the movement against mass deportation, from youth to elders and everywhere in between. To achieve both sufficient diversity and efficiency, I picture a group of somewhere between ten and twenty individuals. More than that would get unwieldy. Significantly less than that would not represent the needed critical mass of hearts and perspectives.

A Unifying Narrative

I believe that the national leadership council's initial purpose should be to develop an opening, unifying narrative for the movement of movements. The words and works of a great many remarkable changemakers, from a great many struggles and backgrounds, would give these leaders a significant head start on such an assignment.

Based on my observations and what I've been able to gather and distill so far, I would suggest that the narrative:

- Explain for the constituencies of all the struggles directly and indirectly represented by this group of leaders why it is now necessary and in the best interest of all them to cohere into one unified movement of movements, and to begin protracted nonviolent struggle to turn the Great Turning.

- Emphasize the centrality of the ancient indigenous understanding and experience of the oneness of creation and the unity of social and ecological balance.

- Assert with conviction and precision that the upcoming and protracted struggle will be a nonviolent struggle, and to unapologetically assert that the encroachment of violence would unquestionably sabotage the effort, that violence epitomizes the worldview against which we are struggling, not to mention that, strategically speaking, it would be utterly untenable and counterproductive.

- Openly acknowledge that heart unity forged across lines of division (race, gender, religion, sexuality, etc.) is a prerequisite of the Great Turning, and that an unwavering commitment to full equality for all persons is a defining mark of the movement of movements' vision and of the individuals determined to see it through.

- Identify two core and intimately interwoven national campaigns as the movement of movement's primary initial pathways toward a just and life-sustaining society: one to take down the fossil fuel industry, and one to concretely enact atonement and reparations for the victims of white supremacy, and for the earth itself. The narrative would clearly explain the necessity and rationale of these core campaigns.

- Clarify that taking down the fossil fuel industry and combating white supremacy are as much matters of personal and community-based transformation as they are resistance to external forces and structures. To topple these deeply entrenched structures means that we each need to topple them in our own life and consciousness. The narrative would describe and introduce the emerging national constellation of constructive program centers as a powerful resource for us as we begin this critical aspect of the work.

- Clearly articulate that this call does not represent a request that all participating submovements put their particular struggles on hold while taking a detour into the interconnected realms of climate change action and atonement and reparations. On the contrary, the underlying point would be that this does not represent a detour. This is each submovement digging a layer deeper into its understanding of the intersectionality of all our complementary struggles and the nature of the common barriers all of our struggles face. This is each submovement working in its own best interest and taking its struggle to a new level.

- Imagine aloud what it would mean to all the participating submovements to be organizing on the other side of a transition that had successfully deposed the fossil fuel industry, and which had enacted sweeping, tangible expressions of atonement and reparations. Such a transition would represent the equivalent of both toppling an imperial oligarchy and beginning an authentic process to redeem the soul of the nation. It would be a political-cultural shift which would open up possibilities for social change unlike any we've ever seen.

- Describe the initial concrete action steps devised by the strategy and mobilization team, as part of their large-scale strategic vision, offering clear instructions as to how individuals, local groups, regional groups, and national groups can best plug into the opening action phase of the struggle.

Launch

Once the movement of movement's opening narrative is prepared and in hand, inclusive of a clear call to action developed by the strategy and mobilization team, I propose that our most respected changemakers in alternative media should invite the national leadership council to take the public microphone, to share the narrative with the nation, and to announce that the opening action phase of the movement of movements has begun. Because of their high profiles and the deep respect that the members of this leadership circle would command, and because of the extraordinary constructive program efforts alternative media pioneers have been putting forth over the course of decades, I would guess that every social change activist in the U.S. would hear of this event within a week's time.

From there, we would take the lead from the national strategy and mobilization team, whose instructions would be disseminated as needed by members of the national leadership council.

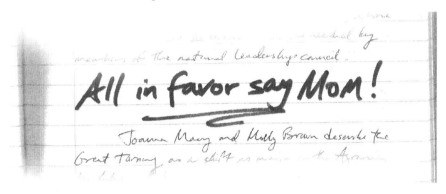

Joanna Macy and Molly Brown describe the Great Turning as a shift as major as the Agrarian Revolution and the Industrial Revolution. The key differences are two, they say. The first is that the Great Turning is going to be intentional and deliberate in a way those other transitions weren't. The second is that this shift needs to happen within a few years, not over the course of generations or centuries. Many small Great Turnings of the personal and community-based variety will be at the heart of the big one, along with—I wholeheartedly believe, as you well know by now—the inspiring willingness to struggle and sacrifice on the part of a submovement made up of several stalwart cadres of seriously trained and deeply committed practitioners of integral nonviolence.

The thing about those of us within the ranks of this submovement is that we'll be good to go however it shakes down, whether the above proposal is followed to the letter, or doesn't go any further than these pages. In the end, my central purpose in sharing the proposal, not to mention everything else in this book, has been to contribute to the coming together of our dispersed little team. When we have found one another and united ourselves in vision and purpose and spirit, we will say to the leadership of whatever mass movement, or movements, or movement of movements that may come on the scene in service of love, justice, and renewal: We stand ready. We're at your service.

And what if no such mass movement energy or structure takes shape?

Then we'll move of our own accord.

Holding all these thoughts, I recently reached out to a dear friend and fellow nonviolence aficionado who I hadn't talked to in a long time. We're the kind of friends whose closeness, for whatever reason, doesn't abate our chronic inability to stay in touch. But our friendship is such, and our commitment to nonviolence is such, that over the years we've both known, without saying it, that we'd both be there when the time of the formidable gamble drew nigh.

We'd be there for each other. We'd be there for our children. "And aren't they all our children?" our wise and compassionate elder Vincent Harding once wrote. We'd be there for the good fight, when the moment came.

When my friend picked up the phone, he sounded mildly shocked to hear my voice, given how long it had been. At the same time, I assure you, there was no note of surprise. And he said to me: "It's time, isn't it?"

NOTES

Epigraph

xiii *"The good news is"*: Naomi Klein, *This Changes Everything*, p. 445.

Introduction

1   *"our greatest failure"*: Anand Mazgaonkar, personal conversation, February 2005, Rajpipla, Gujarat, India.

2   *The Unspeakable*: see Douglass, *JFK and the Unspeakable*, pp. xiii-xix.

4   *Gandhi himself bristled*: Prabhu and Rao, eds., *Mind of Mahatma Gandhi*, p. 11. "Often the title has pained me; and there is not a moment I can recall when it may be said to have tickled me… The Mahatma I must leave to his fate. Though a non-cooperator, I shall gladly subscribe to a Bill to make it criminal for anybody to call me Mahatma and to touch my feet. Where I can impose the law myself, i.e., at the Ashram, the practice is criminal."

5   *When I Am Arrested*: Gandhi, *Non-Violent Resistance*, pp. 223-225.

6   *Kathy Kelly and her friends from Voices*: Kelly, *Other Lands Have Dreams*.

7   *"You're only changed…if you're willing to feel it"*: Dominic Barter, as quoted by Ethan Hughes, personal conversation (phone), November 2015.

8   *It was in the ashram, not Delhi; ashram as "laboratory"*: Brown, *Gandhi*, p. 318.

8   *Sharp and Burrowes probably first to distill these three categories*: Sharp, *Gandhi as a Political Strategist*, p. 8; and Burrowes, *Strategy of Nonviolent Defense*, pp. 101-102.

8   *Joanne Sheehan and John Humphries*: Sheehan, "Gandhi's Constructive Program—and Ours"; and Humphries, "Light Arises Out of Darkness."

9   *"a sacred pilgrimage"*: Gandhi, *Non-Violent Resistance*, pp. 236-237.

9   *"Nonviolence is impossible without self-purification"*: Merton, *Gandhi on Non-Violence*, p. 44.

10 *"Unfortunately a belief has today sprung up"*: Brown, *Gandhi*, p. 229; second half of quote picks up in Gandhi, *All Men are Brothers*, p. 76.

10 *"We brought the English"*: Gandhi, *Hind Swaraj*, p. 57.

11 *Gandhi-Irwin Pact*: Brown, *Gandhi*, pp. 248-250.

11 *"India was now free"*: Fischer, *Life of Mahatma Gandhi*, pp. 274-275.

12 *Roadmap*: see http://www.mettacenter.org/roadmap/.

12 *The Work That Reconnects*: Macy and Brown, *Coming Back to Life*.

13 *The Great Turning*: Ibid., pp. 6-17 (see note ii on p. 6 for discussion of the origins of the term).

13 *when I asked Joanna*: Joanna Macy, personal conversation, January 2015, Oakland, California.

13 *integral nonviolence*: With a nod to philosopher Ken Wilber, Ethan Hughes coined the phrase in 2009, and introduced me to it in a personal conversation (phone) that same year. Ethan had recently finished reading Wilber's *Integral Psychology*.

16   *"Not a single believer"*: Gandhi, *Non-Violent Resistance*, pp. 223-225.

17   *secret side of nonviolence history*: For specific attention to the secret side of women's nonviolence history, see McAllister, *You Can't Kill the Spirit*; and West, "Gendered Legacies of Martin Luther King Jr.'s Leadership."

18   *"holy failure"*; *"In all my efforts"*: Braun, "The Case of the Customized Christ."

19   *"What's worth doing?"*: Brown, *Daring Greatly*, p. 42.

20   *our notions of Gandhi's sainthood*: This section was largely informed by input from Kit Miller, personal conversation (phone), March 23, 2016.

20   *Gandhi's imperial loyalism*: See Waetjen, "Gandhi and Racism."

20   *"We were then marched off"*: Gandhi, *Collected Works*, vol. 8, p. 135; and Lelyveld, *Great Soul*, p. 54.

20   *"In his battle to hold the empire"*: Waetjen, "Gandhi and Racism."

21   *"Gandhi's humanism and moral radar"*: Ibid.

22   *"I see through them"*: Fischer, *Life of Mahatma Gandhi*, p. 425.

22   *"I deceived myself"*: Ibid., p. 473.

22   *"I must confess my bankruptcy"*: Merton, *Gandhi on Non-Violence*, p. 74.

22   *"I failed to recognize"*: Ibid., p. 76.

22   *"In the India that is shaping today"*: Fischer, *Life of Mahatma Gandhi*, p. 470.

23   *Gandhi refuses to attend the ceremony*: Ibid., pp. 473-474.

23   *taking the lives of one million, the displacement of fifteen million*: Gandhi, *Kasturba*, p. 304.

23   *"Would it not be more appropriate to send condolences"*: Fischer, *Life of Mahatma Gandhi*, p. 483.

23   *Dr. King and depression*: Garrow, *Bearing the Cross*, pp. 598-604; Jackson, *From Civil Rights to Human Rights*, pp. 24, 344-345; and Branch, *At Canaan's Edge*, pp. 707-708, 734.

23   *King's nonviolence drawn into question*: See chapter two, "Black Power," in King, Jr., *Where Do We Go From Here*, pp. 23-69, which includes Dr. King's well known assertion (from p. 66): "I would rather be a man of conviction than a man of conformity. Occasionally in life one develops a conviction so precious and meaningful that he will stand on it till the end. This is what I have found in nonviolence." See also Branch, *At Canaan's Edge*, pp. 559, 690-691, 739-741, 770-771.

23   *King's stance on Vietnam...alienated him*: Dyson, *I May Not Get There With You*, pp. 55-64.

23   *King's condemnation of U.S. capitalism...alienated him*: Jackson, *From Civil Rights to Human Rights*, pp. 331-332.

24   *"as a policy," not...as "a life force" and "an article of faith"*: Merton, *Gandhi on Non-Violence*, p. 52, marks the distinction matter-of-factly: "Nonviolence to be a creed has to be all pervasive. I cannot be nonviolent about one activity and violent about others. That would be a policy not a life force." See also: Ibid., p. 75; "My Faith in Non-Violence," pp. 383-384 and "When I Am Arrested," p.223, from Gandhi, *Non-Violent Resistance*.

24   *Gandhi credited this to his own failure*: For one of many statements when Gandhi expressed this sentiment, see previous note for p. 22—"I must confess my bankruptcy..." See also Merton, *Gandhi on Non-Violence*, p. 75: "It is likely...that I was good enough to represent a weak nation, not a strong one. May it not be that a man purer, more courageous, more far-seeing is wanted for the final purpose?"

25   *"Nonviolence is not a garment"*: Ibid., p. 24.

26   *62 individuals control more wealth*: Elliott, "Richest 62 People as Wealthy as Half of World's Population, Says Oxfam."

27   *melted 85 percent of the Arctic's summer ice*: Lindsay and Schweiger, "Arctic Sea Ice Thickness

Loss Determined Using Subsurface, Aircraft, and Satellite Observations."

27   *Atmospheric methane 254 percent of the pre-industrial level*: World Meteorological Organization, "Greenhouse Gas Concentrations Hit Yet Another Record."

27   *[Methane]...now being released by thawing Arctic permafrost*: Wernick, "Thawing Permafrost Could Have Catastrophic Consequences, Scientists Warn."

27   *Because methane is 84 times more potent*: Ocko, "Methane and CO2: Why climate action means addressing both."

27   *"permafrost carbon feedback loop"*: Wernick, "Thawing Permafrost Could Have Catastrophic Consequences, Scientists Warn."

27   *hottest year ever....last 13 of 14 years all record breakers*: National Centers for Environmental Information/National Oceanic and Atmospheric Administration, "Global Analysis - Annual 2015."

27   *Rain in Mecca at 109°, rain in Needles at 115°*: Birchard, "115°F World Record Hot Rain Hits Needles CA & Storm Starts Fire."

27   *if the globe warms by more than 2° Celsius (and corresponding footnote)*: Klein, *This Changes Everything*, pp. 12-15, and the scholarly resources listed in note 14, p. 468; and, regarding the counterclaim that 1.5° Celsius is a more accurate upper limit, see Klein, "Let Them Drown."

27   *565 gigatons of CO²...five times that ready to extract and burn...$90 million per day in exploration...$27 trillion dollars profit*: McKibben, "Global Warming's Terrifying New Math."

27   *fires blazing across Indonesia*: Monbiot, "Indonesia Has Been Burning for Months"; and Claire Phipps, "Indonesian President Visits Haze-Hit Zone as Country Becomes World's Worst Polluter."

28   *150-200 species will become extinct...1,000 times the planet's natural rate*: Vidal, "Protect Nature for World Economic Security, Warns UN Biodiversity Chief."

28   *the only reasonable response must be utterly radical and immediate*: This is a secondhand paraphrase of a statement by Tyler Sheaffer, as conveyed by Ethan Hughes, personal conversation (phone), August 2015.

28   *"the threshold"*: Osbon, ed., *Reflections on the Art of Living*, p. 78.

28   *"The Hero's Journey"*: Ibid., pp. 71-82; and "The Adventure of the Hero," from Campbell, *The Hero With a Thousand Faces*, pp. 49-251. Thanks to Adam Campbell and Ethan Hughes for directing me to Joseph Campbell, personal conversations (phone) and letters, Fall 2015.

28   *"the wasteland"*: Obson, ed., *Reflections on the Art of Living*, pp. 72-73.

29   *"You come then to the final experience"*: Ibid., p. 79.

29   *"astray entirely"*: Ibid., p. 74.

30   *Domination System*: Wink, *Engaging the Powers*.

30   *I read This Changes Everything*: Klein, *This Changes Everything*. In between *Engaging the Powers* and *This Changes Everything*, three other books deeply impacted my understanding of the ways and reach of the Domination System: David Ray Griffin's courageous exposé of the systematic deceit and treachery surrounding the events of 9/11, *The New Pearl Harbor*; James Douglass' in depth and spiritually-driven excavation of the intricate machinations and the core meaning of the assassination of President Kennedy, *JFK and the Unspeakable*; and Michelle Alexander's unparalleled and prophetic study of race and criminal justice in the U.S., *The New Jim Crow*.

30   *Klein's book, one of many that have done this*: For example, McKibben, *The End of Nature*;

Kolbert, *The Sixth Extinction*; Pearce, *With Speed and Violence*; and Flannery, *The Weather Makers*.

33 *Picture this:* This roster of nonviolence cadres, pp. 33-34, borrows heavily from Ethan Hughes' and Robért Raymond's growing catalog of "Peace Archetypes," which Ethan and I discussed in personal conversations (phone) and letters, Fall 2015. The Peace Archetypes are Ethan and Robért's refashioning and expansion of the formulation first devised by Johan Galtung in 1976. See Galtung, "Three Approaches to Peace," pp. 282-304. Ethan reports that he and Robért were introduced to Galtung's "archetypes" by way of Elise Boulding's writings. See Boulding, *Cultures of Peace*.

36 *because of the central role the U.S. plays*: This is a paraphrase of a comment by Miki Kashtan, personal conversation (phone), May 2016.

Chapter 1: The Ice

39 *beloved community*: Simpson, "Changing the Face of the Enemy"; King, Jr., *Stride Toward Freedom*, pp. 90-91; and Cone, *Martin and Malcolm*, p. 66.

39 *"to redeem the soul of America"*: Fairclough, *To Redeem the Soul of America*, p. 32; and Cone, *Martin and Malcolm*, p. 66.

39 *strong steady voice of Michelle Alexander*: Alexander, *The New Jim Crow*.

40 *Susan Burton and A New Way of Life*: Moore-Backman, "A New Way of Life and the New Underground Railroad" [radio documentary].

40 *"Susan's building a new underground railroad"*: Michelle Alexander, personal conversation (phone), Winter 2013.

40 *shifting tides brought on by World War II*: Lelyveld, *Great Soul*, pp. 276-277; and Dalton, *Mahatma Gandhi*, pp. 196-197.

41 *"to see God face to face"*: Gandhi, *Autobiography*, p. xxvi.

41 *sarvodaya*: See "Vision of a New World," from Mathai, *Mahatma Gandhi's World-View*, pp. 151-234.

41 *Ruby Sales*: Harding, "Ruby Sales Biography."

41 *murder of Jonathan Daniels*: Ibid.; and Branch, *At Canaan's Edge*, p. 346.

42 *spiritual accompaniment of Sojourner Truth*: Harding, "Ruby Sales Biography."

42 *SpiritHouse*: http://www.spirithouseproject.org.

42 *"long distance runner for justice"*: http://spirithouseproject.org/aboutruby-extended.cfm.

42 *I had the opportunity to interview Ruby*: Ruby Sales, interview, October 26, 2009, Ft. Benning, Georgia.

44 *"greatest and most active force in the world"*: Merton, *Gandhi on Non-Violence*, p. 44.

45 *Eknath Easwaran, ahimsa, flawless*: Miki Kashtan, *Reweaving Our Human Fabric*, p. 27.

45 *"When all violence subsides"*: Easwaran, *Gandhi the Man*, p. 53.

45 *"human nature, in its essence"*: Merton, *Gandhi on Non-Violence*, p. 25.

45 *"highest expression of the soul"*: Ibid., p. 24.

45 *"The more you develop it in your being"*: Ibid., p. 26.

45 *"mightier than the mightiest weapon"*: Prabhu and Rao, eds., *Mind of Mahatma Gandhi*, p. 122.

45 *"invincible"*: Gandhi, *Non-Violence in Peace & War: Vol. I*, p. 354.

45 *"knows no defeat"*: Merton, *Gandhi on Non-Violence*, p. 45.

45 *"You just don't see what's coming at you"*: Nagler, *Search for a Nonviolent Future*, p. 102.

46 *"law of love"*: For example, Merton, *Gandhi on Non-Violence*, p. 45.

46 *the same way the law of gravity is a law*: See "My Faith in Non-Violence," from Gandhi, *Non-Violent Resistance*, pp. 383-384.

46 *heart unity*: Nagler, *Search for a Nonviolent Future*, pp. 173-176, 270-271.

47 *"unenforceable obligations"*: King, Jr., *Where Do We Go From Here?* pp. 106-107.

47 *Constructive Programme*: Mathai, *Mahatma Gandhi's World-View*, pp. 255-260; and Gandhi, *Constructive Programme*.

47 *"before they dare think of freedom"*: Fischer, *Life of Mahatma Gandhi*, p. 223.

48 *mass incarceration*: As of December 2015, Prison Policy Initiative estimates that 2.3 million Americans are incarcerated. See http://www.prisonpolicy.org/reports/pie2015.html.

48 *Black Lives Matter*: See http://blacklivesmatter.com; and Foran, "A Year of Black Lives Matter."

48 *mass deportation*: See the American Immigration Council's analysis of the United States' 368,644 deportations/removals in 2013, "Misplaced Priorities: Most Immigrants Deported by ICE in 2013 Were a Threat to No One."

48 *unparalleled economic inequality*: For a breakdown of disparity in the US see Fitz, "Economic Inequality: It's Far Worse Than You Think," which includes the following statistics: "The top 20% of US households own more than 84% of the wealth, and the bottom 40% combine for a paltry 0.3%. The Walton family, for example, has more wealth than 42% of American families combined." For global disparity, see Elliott, "Richest 62 People as Wealthy as Half of World's Population, Says Oxfam," which states that "Oxfam said that the wealth of the poorest 50% dropped by 41% between 2010 and 2015...In the same period, the wealth of the richest 62 people increased by $500bn (£350bn) to $1.76tn."

48 *rampant human trafficking*: Current estimates place the number of trafficked persons at 21 million worldwide, with 1.5 million of them in North America. See Hagen, "5 Things You Didn't Know About Human Trafficking." And, according to Hagopian, "Global Human Trafficking, a Modern Form of Slavery," 22 percent of human trafficking victims are forced into sexual exploitation, 68 percent into forced labor in the private sector, and 10 percent into forms of state-imposed forced labor. 5.5 million or 26 percent of all modern slaves are children under 18, the majority being girls forced into the sex trade.

48 *homelessness*: The National Alliance to End Homelessness estimates that in January 2015, 564,708 people were homeless in the United States. See http://www.endhomelessness.org/pages/snapshot_of_homelessness.

48 *"Truth is God"*: Gandhi, *All Men are Brothers*, pp. 63-64.

49 *This interpretation is featured in Fate and Destiny*: Meade, *Fate and Destiny*, pp. 60-82. Special thanks to Max Kee for introducing me to Meade's work.

49 *"There was a basic problem," "foolish or mean-spirited or clearly ignorant," "a crucial mistake"*: Ibid., p. 63.

50 *"I began a descent," "wasn't present in any normal sense"*: Ibid., p. 65.

50 *"the inner voice"*: See an excellent summary in Prabhu and Rao, eds., *Mind of Mahatma Gandhi*, pp. 31-34.

51 *"the heart of his own religion"*: Gandhi, *All Men are Brothers*, p. 65.

51 *all life is one*: Mathai, *Mahatma Gandhi's World-View*, pp. 88-89.

52 *Truth and nonviolence must must remain aspirations*: Ibid., p. 68.

52 *"Perfect nonviolence whilst you are inhabiting the body"*: Gandhi, *All Men are Brothers*, p. 83.

52 *"What is Truth?"*: Ibid., pp. 64-65.

53 *"nothing passive about Gandhi"*: Fischer, *Life of Mahatma Gandhi*, p. 77.
53 *Gandhi's speech on September 11, 1906*: Ibid., p. 76.
54 *King's six-part definition*: King, Jr., *Stride Toward Freedom*, pp. 90-95.
54 *"sometimes made Gandhi sound naïve"*: Fischer, *Life of Mahatma Gandhi*, p. 81.
55 *"In spite of everything"*: Frank, *Diary of a Young Girl*, p. 333.
56 *willing to be persuaded*: Erikson, *Gandhi's Truth*, p. 416.
56 *all parties hold a piece of the Truth*: Bondurant, *Conquest of Violence*, pp. 15-35.
56 *"A nonviolent revolution"*: Merton, *Gandhi on Non-Violence*, p. 28.
56 *The home setting*: Ibid., p. 66.
56 *"No one knew better than Kasturba"*: Gandhi, *Kasturba*, p. 212.
57 *MEANS=ENDS*: Gandhi, *All Men are Brothers*, pp. 74-76.
57 *"one thing about violence/nonviolence"*: Nagler, *Search for a Nonviolent Future*, p. 128.
58 *"the more ancient place"*: Luke Anderson, personal conversation, Winter 2013, Chico, California.
59 *the Bhagavad Gita*: Fischer, *Life of Mahatma Gandhi*, pp. 29-37; Easwaran, *Gandhi the Man*, pp. 105-123; and Prabhu and Rao, eds., *Mind of Mahatma Gandhi*, pp. 94-95. See the text of the Gita along with Gandhi's own commentary in Gandhi and Strohmeier, ed., *The Bhagavad Gita According to Gandhi*.
59 *"By detachment I mean"*: Easwaran, *Gandhi the Man*, p. 105.
59 *on the lookout for lows and highs*: Gandhi and Strohmeier, ed., *The Bhagavad Gita According to Gandhi*, pp. 14-24.
60 *"globalism in reverse"*: Nagler, *Search for a Nonviolent Future*, p. 169.
61 *"ocular demonstration"*: Ibid., p. 184; and Gandhi, *Non-Violence in Peace & War: Vol. I*, pp. 121-124.
61 *Martin Luther King at seven*: Nagler, *Search for a Nonviolent Future*, p. 184.
61 *"a man's first duty is to his neighbor"*: Mathai, *Mahatma Gandhi's World-View*, p. 141.
61 *the state would eventually wither away*: Ibid., p. 258.
61 *example of a barber*: Gandhi, *Vows and Observances*, pp. 42-43.
62 *"innumerable machine-made things...my answer can be only one"*: Gandhi, *Hind Swaraj*, p. 82.
63 *"swaraj stood above all for freedom"*: Burns, *Transforming Leadership*, p. 155.
64 *"The tendency to ignore the Negro's contribution"*: King, Jr. "Where Do We Go From Here?" [keynote address], p. 246.
64 *"axiomatic that life is sacred"*: Nagler, *Search for a Nonviolent Future*, p. 267.
65 *"from the lower to the higher self"*: Mathai, *Mahatma Gandhi's World-View*, p. 239.
65 *"The individual is the key"*: Ibid., p. 154.
65 *personalism*: Garrow, *Bearing the Cross*, p. 44.
65 *"This was Gandhi's refrain"*: Fischer, *Life of Mahatma Gandhi*, p. 260.
66 *never meant to perpetuate a spirituality disconnected*: Ibid., p. 340; Mathai, *Mahatma Gandhi's World-View*, p. 154; and Brown, *Gandhi*, p. 83.
66 *SARVODAYA*: See "Vision of a New World Order: Sarvodaya," in Mathai, *Mahatma Gandhi's World-View*, pp. 151-234.
67 *"If there is to be a livable world"*: Macy and Brown, *Coming Back to Life*, p. 4.
67 *Industrial Growth Society*: Ibid., p. 2, footnote *i*, where Macy and Brown explain the term and credit it to Sigmund Kwaloy.
67 *they sometimes use the word revolution*: Ibid., p. 34, for example.

Chapter 2: Under Water

72   *the rare privilege of interviewing Harry Belafonte*: Harry Belafonte, interview, February 27, 2010, New York.

73   *to personify a purified and liberated India*: In my research notes the phrase "to personify a purified India," in quotes, is attributed to Erik Erikson, from his book *Gandhi's Truth*. Unfortunately, however, I failed to note a page number. I've pored over the book in search of the statement, to no avail. Perhaps the phrase was my own summation of Erikson's analysis in pp. 265-267. If not, I'll be grateful to whomever can accurately confirm the original source of the statement.

73   *"Apply everything to yourself"*: Gandhi, *Collected Works*, vol. 10, p. 477.

73   *self-purification isn't about achieving a certain spiritual state*: Brown, *Gandhi*, p. 83; Fischer, *Life of Mahatma Gandhi*, p. 340; and Mathai, *Mahatma Gandhi's World-View*, p. 154.

73   *fearlessness*: Gandhi, *Vows and Observances*, pp. 32, 43-44, 135-137.

74   *"Millions had read Ruskin and Thoreau"*: Fischer, *Life of Mahatma Gandhi*, pp. 88-89.

74   *"Renounce and enjoy"*: as quoted in Bill McKibben, "The End of Growth," p. 53.

75   *"Renounce and rejoice"*: Eknath Easwaran, ed., *Bhagavad Gita*, p. 123.

76   *"The measure of our purification"*: Gandhi, *Non-Violent Resistance*, pp. 280-281.

76   *"It is through action that we come to know who we are"*: CT Vivian, Keynote Address, Gandhi-King Conference, October 24, 2009, Memphis, Tennessee.

76   *"For more than a century of slavery"*: King, Jr., *Trumpet of Conscience*, pp. 16-17.

77   *"Without self-purification"*: Prabhu and Rao, eds., *Mind of Mahatma Gandhi*, p. 225.

77   *"Nonviolence was not simply a political tactic"*: Merton, *Gandhi on Non-Violence*, p. 6.

78   *no evidence that Gandhi ever uttered that statement*: Brian Morton, "False Words Were Never Spoken."

78   *"I can indicate no royal road"*: Fischer, *Life of Mahatma Gandhi*, p. 340.

79   *"I must not flatter myself"*: Ibid., p. 493.

80   *"As food is necessary for the body"*: Ibid., p. 87.

80   *"Prayer is the greatest binding force"*: Gandhi, *Prayer*, p. 34.

80   *"I have not the shadow of a doubt"*: Ibid., p. 27.

80   *"Prayer is the first and last lesson"*: Prabhu and Rao, eds., *Mind of Mahatma Gandhi*, p. 87.

80   *" 'the key of the morning and the bolt of the evening' "*: Ibid., p. 87.

80   *communal prayer held both morning and evening*: See Michael Nagler's introduction to Gandhi, *Book of Prayers*, pp. 13-14.

80   *one hour of spinning at the wheel*: Fischer, *Life of Mahatma Gandhi*, pp. 212-213, 232, 430.

80   *spinning as "sacrament"*: Ibid., p. 192.

80   *ramanama*: Gandhi, *Ramanama*, pp. 30-33; and *Prayer*, pp. 151-166.

80   *Rambha*: Gandhi, *Autobiography*, pp. 31-32; and *Prayer*, pp. 14-15.

81   *"staff of life"*: Easwaran, *Gandhi the Man*, p. 117.

81   *"what eyes are for the outer world"*: Fischer, *Life of Mahatma Gandhi*, p. 233.

81   *"There is no prayer without fasting"*: Gandhi, *Prayer*, p. 111.

81   *fasts for a great variety of physical and emotional ailments*: Fischer, *Life of Mahatma Gandhi*, p. 233.

81   *fasting as form of political and social witness*: Douglass, *Non-Violent Cross*, pp. 72-75, which includes a lengthy quote from Amiya Chakravarty, *A Saint at Work*, p. 23ff. See also Sharp, *Gandhi Wields the Weapon of Moral Power*, pp. 258-260; and Fischer, *Life of Mahatma Gandhi*,

p. 222.

81 *"last weapon of a Satyagrahi"*: Gandhi, *Non-Violent Resistance*, p. 314.

81 *reverence for the great plurality of religious paths…"equality of religions"*: Gandhi, *Vows and Observances*, pp. 141-145.

82 *"Far be it from me to suggest"*: Ibid., p. 364.

82 *including atheists*: Mathai, *Mahatma Gandhi's World-View*, pp. 65-66. See also the fascinating exchange between Gandhi and an atheist Gandhian, in Gora, *An Atheist with Gandhi*.

82 *The Summer Day*: Oliver, *House of Light*, p. 60.

83 *"I am not a man of learning"*: Gandhi, *Prayer*, p. 42.

84 *prayer as Gandhi understood and practiced it*: Ibid., pp. 13-20.

84 *"One smouldering night"*: Frady, *Martin Luther King, Jr.*, p. 3.

85 *Movement scholar Clayborne Carson's landmark book*: Carson, *In Struggle*.

85 *"As Bernice Reagon…recalled"*: Ibid., p. 59.

86 *Michael Lerner, the Network of Spiritual Progressives, "awe, wonder, and radical amazement"*: See the Network of Spiritual Progressives, "Our Values and Vision"—http://www.spiritualprogressives.org/newsite/?page_id=303

86 *"not some utopian ideal"*: Lerner, "After Paris."

87 *"Not until we have reduced ourselves"*: Prabhu and Rao, eds., *Mind of Mahatma Gandhi*, p. 90.

88 *"I saw it in his anxiety"*: Harry Belafonte, interview, February 27, 2010, New York,.

89 *"The hearing of the Voice"*: Prabhu and Rao, eds., *Mind of Mahatma Gandhi*, pp. 33-34.

89 *"a ceaseless effort"*: Ibid., p. 31.

90 *the more widespread gift economics becomes*: See "Transition to Gift Economy," in Eisenstein, *Sacred Economics*, pp. 317-329; and to learn about the gift economics approaches of two current U.S.-based projects, East Point Peace Academy and the Possibility Alliance, see http://eastpointpeace.org/gifteconomics/ and http://urbanwwoofer.blogspot.com/2012/10/permaculture-training-and-gift-economy.html, respectively.

91 *only an India that was physically healthy*: See Gandhi, *Collected Works*, vol. 72, p. 380.

92 *The Sky's Sheets*: St. Teresa of Avila, as featured in Ladinksy, *Love Poems from God*, p. 295.

93 *The recent writings of Brené Brown*: Brown, *Daring Greatly* and *Rising Strong*.

94 *The Possibility Alliance, vulnerability-avoidance, unspoken shame, psychological blocks*: Ethan Hughes, personal conversations (phone) and letters, Fall 2015.

95 *a great many other resources represent coherent and powerful companions for us:* Here are two more such resources, which are currently in the works: *Recipes for the Beloved Community* proposes a model for thriving community life that includes personal wholeness, communal bondedness, and direct action. The bulk of the book focuses on skills for living in community, such as balancing self-care with self-giving, noticing and dismantling oppression, and building communal connection. Authors Jenny Truax and Carolyn Griffeth are old-timers of the St. Louis Catholic Worker community, and the book reflects the simplicity and edginess of the CW movement. Much of their material can be downloaded directly from the Karen House Catholic Worker website: http://newsite.karenhousecw.org. Jenny and Carloyn can also be contacted to lead workshops on such topics: 314-588-8351. And, in *The Possibility Handbook*, Ethan Hughes and his collaborator Scott Mann explore the ways to become an "Agent of Possibility" by embodying nonviolence, permaculture, and manifesting our passion. Find out more at: http://www.thepermaculturepodcast.com/book. Ethan can be contacted at the Possibility Alliance: 660-332-4094; and Scott can be reached by phone, 717-827-6266, or email: scott@thepermaculturepodcast.com.

95   *unwillingness to dig into one place*: This section was largely informed by Ethan Hughes, personal conversations (phone) and letters, Fall 2015.

97   *ideology of chosenness*: See Brueggemann, *Reality, Grief, Hope*.

99   *there were ten million people in this land*: United to End Genocide, "Atrocities Against Native Americans."

99   *"predicated on the torture of black fathers"*: Coates, "Case for Reparations."

99   *the enslavement of upwards of four million Africans*: Gates Jr., "Slavery, by the Numbers."

100 *what Gandhi recognized about the people of India*: Prabhu and Rao, eds., *Mind of Mahatma Gandhi*, pp. 471-472; and Gandhi, *Constructive Programme*, pp. 10-11.

100 *emotions and sense desires were expansive reservoirs*: Brown, *Gandhi*, pp. 85-86; Prabhu and Rao, eds., *Mind of Mahatma Gandhi*, pp. 272-278; Easwaran, *Gandhi the Man*, p. 74; Gandhi, *All Men are Brothers*, pp. 100-102; Fischer, *Life of Mahatma Gandhi*, pp. 34-36, 73, 240; and Lelyveld, *Great Soul*, p. 18.

101 *a good friend of mine...strict fast from cars*: Tyler Sheaffer, personal conversation, Fall 2014, Chico, California.

102 *areas where Gandhi's teaching betrays serious limitations*: In addition to the areas discussed in this section, and those previously mentioned in the introduction, two other important realms also raise question.

When it comes to the challenging work of parenting as committed changemakers, ample evidence suggests we'd do well to look beyond Gandhi for truly inspiring models. As a man who sought to live as though the whole world was his family, Gandhi apparently over-reached in his eagerness to not favor or appear to favor his own children above others. His kids suffered from this and other well-meaning but poorly executed tendencies of their perfectionistic father (see Fischer, *Life of Mahatma Gandhi*, pp. 206-211; Brown, *Gandhi*, pp. 41, 201; Lelyveld, *Great Soul*, p. 87; Erikson, *Gandhi's Truth*, pp. 319-321; and Gandhi, *Autobiography*, pp. 311-312). The eldest boy, Harilal, undoubtedly suffered the most (see Fischer, *Life of Mahatma Gandhi*, pp. 206-211; and Lelyveld, *Great Soul*, p. 87).

Gandhi the husband raises some doubts too, though my reading thus far has not cleared the way to a solid verdict. From Gandhi's own admission, he made some major mistakes as Kasturba's life partner, and through our cultural looking-glass their mode as helpmates is often difficult to understand and relate to. The two were married at the age of thirteen, a reality and social custom that Gandhi railed against throughout his adult life (see Fischer, *Life of Mahatma Gandhi*, pp. 16-17). And of course we've traveled a great distance since their time in terms of understanding, though clearly not adequately mitigating, unhealthy and oppressive gender and power dynamics. But one can never know the true quality of a couple's covenant, their intimacy, and their friendship from a distance of great remove. The same can and should be said of Gandhi's parenting also, though for me personally his role as spouse remains the more enigmatic of the two. It is, perhaps, the Gandhis' grandson, Arun, who writes most poignantly about the hills and valleys of his grandparents' relationship. If interested, I commend you to his book, *Kasturba*, to traverse the 60-plus years of their fascinating union.

103 *Gandhi's own unresolved psychological trauma*: Brown, *Gandhi*, pp. 85-86; Erikson, *Gandhi's Truth*, pp. 229-254; and Lelyveld, *Great Soul*, pp. 272-274. See also "Gandhi and Women," from Kakar, *Intimate Relations*, pp. 85-128.

103 *Gandhi's childhood marriage and early sex-related traumatic experiences*: Brown, *Gandhi*, pp. 21, 86; Kakar, *Intimate Relations*, pp. 86-94; and Fischer, *Life of Mahatma Gandhi*, pp. 16-18.

103 *his denigrating comments about sex*: For a few examples, see Prabhu and Rao, eds., *Mind of Mahatma Gandhi*, pp. 278-279, 283.

103 *his homoerotic correspondence with Hermann Kallenbach*: Lelyveld, *Great Soul*, pp. 88-97.

103 *sleeping naked with naked young women*: Brown, *Gandhi*, pp. 377-378; Gandhi, *Gandhi*, pp. 548-555; Erikson, *Gandhi's Truth*, pp. 403-406; and Lelyveld, *Great Soul*, pp. 303-308.

103 *Erikson's treatment of the subject*: Erikson, *Gandhi's Truth*, pp. 229-254.

103 *"Your precocious sexual life"*: Ibid., p. 237.

103 *"Not once in all your writings"*: Ibid., p. 236.

104 *the palate was the most difficult and important source*: Mathai, *Mahatma Gandhi's World-View*, p. 130; and Gandhi, *Vows and Observances*, pp. 128-130.

105 *his advice was to eat only when hungry*: Gandhi, *Vows and Observances*, pp. 128-129.

106 *Gandhi and vegetarianism*: Erikson, *Gandhi's Truth*, pp. 144-151; and Fischer, *Life of Mahatma Gandhi*, pp. 25-26.

106 *no nutritional requirements that a plant-based diet could not meet*: Gandhi, *Collected Works*, vol. 83, p. 231.

106 *goat milk*: Ibid. See also Fischer, *Life of Mahatma Gandhi*, p. 159; Erikson, *Gandhi's Truth*, pp. 381-383; and Gandhi, *Autobiography*, pp. 272-273.

106 *meat-eating friends who were better nonviolence practitioners*: Merton, *Gandhi on Non-Violence*, p. 68.

106 *"the one supreme lesson to conserve my anger"*: Gandhi, *All Men are Brothers*, p. 99.

106 *"Anger wells up in my breast"*: Gandhi, *Non-Violent Resistance*, p. 71.

107 *"It is not that I do not get angry"*: Gandhi, *All Men are Brothers*, p. 99.

107 *"the aging Mahatma seemed to the public a tranquil spirit"*: Brown, *Gandhi*, p. 284.

107 *"a visionary haunted by his own inadequacies"*: Ibid., p. 285.

107 *"one of the benefits of his frequent silences"*: Ibid.

107 *"fretting and foaming"*: Fischer, *Life of Mahatma Gandhi*, p. 233.

107 *"a useless question"*: Gandhi, *All Men are Brothers*, p. 99.

108 *"a short madness"*: Prabhu and Rao, eds., *Mind of Mahatma Gandhi*, p. 35.

108 *compassion for individuals, righteous indignation for unjust conditions*: A similar version of this formulation was shared with me by Kazu Haga, personal conversation, January 2016, Ben Lomond, California.

108 *"The standard of purity"*: Gandhi, *Non-Violent Resistance*, p. 71.

109 *"If I could persuade myself"*: Prabhu and Rao, eds., *Mind of Mahatma Gandhi*, p. 224.

109 *"It is an obsession"*: Ibid., p. 244.

109 *"I cannot imagine better worship"*: Ibid., p. 224.

109 *life expectancy in India was 27 years old*: Fischer, *Life of Mahatma Gandhi*, p. 363.

110 *Asteya*: Gandhi, *Vows and Observances*, pp. 130-133.

110 *"You with a second coat in your closet"*: Attributed to St. Basil (329-379), as quoted in Ethan Hughes, "Disruptive Peacemaking," pp. 51-52.

110 *"Divine law gives to man"*: Gandhi, *Vows and Observances*, p. 133.

110 *"the earth has enough to satisfy"*: Mathai, *Mahatma Gandhi's World-View*, p. 187.

110 *Gandhi made asteya one of the vows*: Hitched to the vow of asteya was its twin observance, aparigraha, non-possessiveness, the spiritual basis and life-orientation that makes non-stealing possible. See Gandhi, *Vows and Observances*, p. 133-135.

110 *"Only the destitute"*: Crossan, *The Essential Jesus*, p. 58.

110 *"Only those without bread"*: Ibid., p. 63.

111 *an expensive evening suit and nothing less than a top-hat*: Gandhi, *Gandhi*: p. 31.

111 *the loincloth had become his principle garment*: Fischer, *Life of Mahatma Gandhi*, p. 193.

111 *"an English villa at the beach"*: Ibid., p. 59.

111 *Gandhi lived in a mud hut*: Gandhi, *Gandhi*, pp. 380-381.

111 *Gandhi's preference was to ride third class*: Fischer, *Life of Mahatma Gandhi*, p. 227

111 *no longer able to travel "like a poor man"*: Ibid.

111 *a "crank" with "quack" remedies*: For example, Gandhi, *Autobiography*, p. 453, and Fischer, *Life of Mahatma Gandhi*, p. 216.

111 *suspicious of Western medicine*: Prabhu and Rao, eds., *Mind of Mahatma Gandhi*, pp. 395-396, 484-485.

111 *nature cure*: For a helpful summation of Gandhi's nature cure philosophy, see "Key to Health," in Gandhi, *Collected Works*, vol. 83, pp. 224-273. See also Fischer, *Life of Mahatma Gandhi*, pp. 216, 413-414; Prabhu and Rao, eds., *Mind of Mahatma Gandhi*, pp. 393-396; and Brown, *Gandhi*, pp. 361-362.

111 *more faith in prevention*: See "Key to Health," in Gandhi, *Collected Works*, vol. 83, pp. 224-273.

111 *"earth, sun, ether, light, and water"*: Ibid, vol. 91, p. 416.

111 *"body, mind and soul"*: Gandhi, *Non-Violence in Peace and War, Vol. II*, p. 120.

111 *repetition of the mantra, "sovereign remedy"*: Gandhi, *Ramanama*, pp. 30-33.

112 *"a brisk walk in the open"*: Gandhi, *Collected Works*, vol. 83, p. 241.

112 *a serious challenge to keep up with Gandhi*: Gandhi, *Gandhi*, p. 309; Easwaran, *Gandhi the Man*, p. 137; and Erikson, *Gandhi's Truth*, p. 108.

113 *500 lbs of fossil fuels, 47 lbs. of chemicals, and 1.5 tons of water*: UNEP, "E-waste, the Hidden Side of IT Equipment's Manufacturing and Use."

113 *Seven hundred different materials and chemicals...between 25 and 50 countries, up to 200,000 miles of transport*: Ethan Hughes, "Love is the Highest Technology," p. 4.

113 *disposing and "recycling" it*: Ibid.

114 *e-waste was 41.8 million metric tons*: Kuehr, Baldé, Wang and Huisman, *Global E-Waste Monitor 2014*.

114 *"The time we once knew"*: Strand, *Waking Up to the Dark*. p. 52.

114 *"To turn out the lights"*: Ibid., p. 51.

114 *"the one remaining revolutionary act"*: Ibid., p. 53.

115 *"I refuse to be dazzled"*: Prabhu and Rao, eds., *Mind of Mahatma Gandhi*, p. 236.

115 *"I would not weep"*: Ibid., p. 234.

115 *"What I object to is the 'craze' "*: Ibid., p. 235.

115 *"converting men into machines"*: Ibid., p. 235

116 *"God forbid"*: Ibid., p. 242.

116 *"A time is coming"*: Ibid., p. 233.

116 *"an onslaught on India"*: Ibid., p. 241.

116 *"You cannot build nonviolence"*: Merton, *Gandhi on Non-Violence*, p. 54.

116 *"If India became the slave"*: Ibid.

116 *Edward Snowden*: See Bamford, "Edward Snowden, the Untold Story."

116 *Chelsea Manning*: Listen to the Amnesty International UK podcast, "In Their Own Words: Chelsea Manning."

117 *bread labor, Tolstoy, and Bondarev*: Mathai, *Mahatma Gandhi's World-View*, pp. 135-137; and Brown, *Gandhi*, p. 89. For more on Timofej Bondarev see also http://www.molokane. org/subbotniki/Russia/Siberia/2005_Donskov.html.

117 *"Work with your hands"*: See "The Principle is the Unity of Life: A Conversation with Lanza del Vasto," from Wink, ed., *Peace Is the Way*, pp. 76-81.

118 *as our ancestors before us did*: Gandhi, *Hind Swaraj*, p. 82; and Brown, *Gandhi*, p. 90.

118 *high tech printing press*: Gandhi, *Hind Swaraj*, pp. 83-84.

118 *"Every time he used a train"*: Brown, *Gandhi*, p. 88.

118 *"The theory is there"*: Ibid., pp. 88-89.

119 *ceaseless quest to steer his nation*: See Mathai, *Mahatma Gandhi's World-View*, pp. 187-196.

Chapter 3: Above Water

121 *Gandhi needed a strategy for clear communication*: Fischer, *Life of Mahatma Gandhi*, pp. 245-246. Accounts of Gandhi's constructive program hand demonstration offer an inspiring picture—albeit, perhaps, a bit romantic. Maybe Gandhi's status as "our greatest failure" was actually the outcome of all those massive crowds playing telephone with his instructions. (I'm guessing the truth probably lies somewhere in between.) Gandhi's close friend and co-worker Charlie Andrews describes his own use of the same strategy when working "among the villagers." See Andrews, *Mahatma Gandhi*, p. 238.

123 *"an enlightened anarchy...based on pure moral authority"*: Mathai, *Mahatma Gandhi's World-View*, p. 204. See also Merton, *Gandhi on Non-Violence*, p. 55, where Gandhi also says that "the ideally nonviolent state will be an ordered anarchy."

123 *"Real swaraj will come"*: Mathai, *Mahatma Gandhi's World-View*, p. 258; and Fischer, *Life of Mahatma Gandhi*, p. 225.

123 *"The postponement of social reform"*: Mathai, *Mahatma Gandhi's World-View*, p. 257.

124 *an unsafe, run-down house*: Sharp, *Gandhi as a Political Strategist*, pp. 80-81.

124 *"Our contribution to the progress of the world"*: Gandhi, *All Men are Brothers*, p. 134.

125 *"It [community organizing] doesn't make good copy"*: Bob Moses, as quoted in Albert and Hoffman, *We Shall Overcome*, p. 74.

125 *Freedom Schools*: Clayborne Carson, *In Struggle*, pp. 109-110.

125 *"an educational experience"*: Ibid., p. 110.

125 *Howard Zinn, "solutions for poverty"*: Jackson, *From Civil Rights to Human Rights*, p. 206.

125 *"normal academic subjects, contemporary issues..."*: Carson, *In Struggle*, p. 109.

125 *Clark, Cotton, Robinson, Young, and the Citizen Education Program*: Jackson, *From Civil Rights to Human Rights*, pp. 108-110, 145-146, 235-236; and Branch, *Parting the Waters*, pp. 263-64, 646.

126 *the historic black colleges and the black church*: For a fascinating description of the movement intersection of these two oases, see Morris, "Black Southern Student Sit-In Movement," pp. 744-767. See also Lowe, "An Oasis of Freedom in a Closed Society." Regarding the black church specifically, the following summary of its role as an autonomous "haven of refuge" is from Miller, *Voice of Deliverance*, p. 27: "For many decades the black pulpit served indisputably as a weekly power station transmitting strength and endurance to an exploited people... The African-American church also provided a haven of refuge. Because the church was the only large institution that blacks operated entirely by themselves, it served as the institutional center of black life. Between services that sometimes lasted for hours, churches functioned as music schools, concert halls, recreation clubs, educational centers, and sites for political debates and town meetings. Whenever whites

stripped blacks of their humanity, the church offered dignity. A black woman might work as a maid her entire life, but she could maintain her self-respect by coordinating a youth program or teaching Sunday School. Congregations also served as extended families. Churches cared for members bereaved and widowed, and churchmen served as father figures for boys growing up without a father."

126 *a healthy and sometimes messy tension*: Jensen and Hammerback, "Working in Quiet Places"; and Carson, "African-American Leadership and Mass Mobilization" and "Between Contending Forces."

126 *Ella Baker*: Carson, *In Struggle*, pp. 19-20, 24-26, 30; and "Learning from Ella," in Moses and Cobb Jr., *Radical Equations*, pp. 23-57.

127 *"nonviolence has to be rooted in the local scene"*: James Lawson, interview, November 23, 2009, Los Angeles.

128 *most significant...was voter registration*: For a persuasive in-depth illustration see Carson, *In Struggle*.

128 *tenant union organizing, farm cooperatives, business development initiatives, tutoring programs, credit unions, SCLC's Operation Breadbasket*: King, Jr., *"Where Do We Go From Here?"* [keynote address].

128 *the Freedom Singers*: Carson, *In Struggle*, p. 64.

128 *the Free Southern Theater*: Ibid., p. 120.

129 *Gandhi's Constructive Programme listed*: Gandhi, *Constructive Programme*; and Mathai, *Mahatma Gandhi's World-View*, pp. 255-256.

130 *Improvement of cattle*: See Prabhu and Rao, eds., *Mind of Mahatma Gandhi*, pp. 387-390; and Gandhi, *Vows and Observances*, pp. 107-109.

131 *"I went to Gandhi's room and found him spinning"*: Fischer, *The Life of Mahatma Gandhi*, p. 430.

131 *"God whispered into my ear"*: Gandhi, *Collected Works*, vol. 74, pp. 160-161.

131 *Michael Nagler treats khadi excellently*: Nagler, *Search for a Nonviolent Future*, pp. 160-196. See also Mathai, *Mahatma Gandhi's World-View*, pp. 255-260; and King, *Mahatma Gandhi and Martin Luther King Jr.*, pp. 35-38.

131 *Constructive Programme had "an overall design"*: Nagler, *Search for a Nonviolent Future*, p. 166.

131 *"Khadi connotes the beginning of economic freedom"*: Gandhi, *Constructive Programme*, p. 11.

132 *"Wearing their beliefs on their bodies"*: Nagler, *Search for a Nonviolent Future*, p. 170.

132 *the documentary film, A Force More Powerful*: York, *A Force More Powerful* [documentary film].

132 *"other village industries"*: Gandhi, *Constructive Programme*, p. 15; and Mathai, *Mahatma Gandhi's World-View*, pp. 255-256.

132 *"What are they holding over us?"*: Ron Toppi, personal conversations, 2013, Chico, California.

134 *"The last true revolutionary act"*: Strand, *Waking Up to the Dark*, pp. 50-51.

134 *"Turn out the lights"*: Ibid., p. 54.

134 *"Let there be darkness"*: Ibid., p. 50.

135 *Gandhi was deeply pained...by alcohol dependency and abuse*: Prabhu and Rao, eds., *Mind of Mahatma Gandhi*, pp. 471-472; and Gandhi, *Constructive Programme*, p. 8.

135 *guess who had a monopoly?*: See Blocker, Fahey, and Tyrrell, *Alcohol and Temperance in Modern History*, pp. 309-311.

135 *India's rampant addiction to opium and other intoxicants*: Gandhi, *Collected Works*, vol. 83, pp. 239-243.

136 *First World Lifestyles Anonymous*: Learn about a similar 12-step-inspired group, Recovery from the Dominant Culture, in Leviton, "Dangerous Love," pp.14-15. See also Glendinning,

My Name is Chellis and I'm in Recovery From Western Civilization.

136 *A.A. and other 12-step programs*: See *Alcoholics Anonymous ("Big Book")*.

138 *separate electorates, Gandhi's fast unto death*: Gandhi, *Gandhi*, pp. 346-350; Brown, *Gandhi*, pp. 265-268; and Fischer, *Life of Mahatma Gandhi*, pp. 306-321. For a less romanticized account, see Lelyveld, *Great Soul*, pp. 224-236.

138 *the recent re-release*: Ambedkar, *Annihilation of Caste*, featuring Arundhati Roy's introducton, "The Doctor and the Saint."

139 *"If I could tear [my heart] open"*: Prabhu and Rao, eds., *Mind of Mahatma Gandhi*, p. 398.

139 *"I hug the belief"*: Ibid., p. 3.

139 *Michelle Alexander presents a powerful contemporary analogue*: Alexander, *The New Jim Crow*, pp. 244-251. Here's a snapshot of her commentary on affirmative action and "racial bribes," from page 249: "Diversity-driven affirmative action programs seem to be the epitome of racial justice purchased on the cheap. They create the appearance of racial equity without the reality and do so at no great cost, without fundamentally altering any of the structures that create racial inequality in the first place. Perhaps the best illustration of this fact is that, thanks in part to affirmative action, police departments and law enforcement agencies nationwide have come to look more like America than ever, at precisely the moment that they have waged a war on the ghetto poor and played a leading role in the systematic mass incarceration of people of color. The color of police chiefs across the country has changed, but the role of the police in our society has not."

140 *"rank irreligion"*: This rendering of Gandhi's assessment of untouchability is from Mathai, *Mahatma Gandhi's World-View*, p. 134.

140 *"segregation gone mad"*: This rendering is borrowed from Fischer, *Life of Mahatma Gandhi*, p. 142.

140 *Hindu-Muslim friendship, "the firm rock"*: Ibid., p. 217. See also Prabhu and Rao, eds., *Mind of Mahatma Gandhi*, pp. 398-402. All the major Gandhi biographies are replete with examples of his steadfast advocacy for Hindu-Muslim unity.

140 *oppression of Indian women, and girls*: Brown, *Gandhi: Prisoner of Hope*, pp. 208-213; Fischer, *Life of Mahatma Gandhi*, pp. 228, 241-242, 456; Mathai, *Mahatma Gandhi's World-View*, pp. 172-178; Prabhu and Rao, eds., *Mind of Mahatma Gandhi*, p. 281; and Gandhi, *Constructive Programme*, pp. 18-19. For a variety of Gandhi's statements on the equality of the sexes, see also King, *Mahatma Gandhi and Martin Luther King Jr*, pp. 330-331.

140 *particular leaders, all formerly incarcerated, of the movement to end mass incarceration*: Listen to several of them in Moore-Backman, "The Formerly Incarcerated and Convicted People's Movement" [radio documentary].

141 *Naomi Klein and co.*: For example, McKibben, *The End of Nature;* Kolbert, *The Sixth Extinction;* Pearce, *With Speed and Violence;* and Flannery, *The Weather Makers*.

141 *the soon-to-be majority*: For a window into this facet of the United States' racial landscape, and so much else relevant to the reality and dynamics of white privilege, see Wise, *Dear White America*, or anything/everything else by him.

142 *two-plus million locked in cages*: As of December 2015, Prison Policy Initiative estimates that 2.3 million Americans are incarcerated. See http://www.prisonpolicy.org/reports/pie2015.html.

142 *hundreds of thousands of the world's 21 million trafficked human beings*: Current estimates place the number of trafficked persons at 21 million worldwide, with 1.5 million of them in North America. See Hagen, "5 Things You Didn't Know About Human Trafficking."

142   *average of 350,000 deported every year*: This average corresponds to 2011-2015. See U.S. Immigration and Customs Enforcement, "FY 2015 ICE Immigration Removals," https://www.ice.gov/removal-statistics.

142   *well over half a million living on the streets*: The National Alliance to End Homelessness, estimates that in January 2015, 564,708 people were homeless in the United States. See http://www.endhomelessness.org/pages/snapshot_of_homelessness.

142   *"Swaraj is a meaningless term"*: Prabhu and Rao, eds., *Mind of Mahatma Gandhi*, p. 107.

142   *"I would far rather Hinduism died"*: Ibid., p. 108.

142   *"Before they dare think of freedom"*: Fischer, *Life of Mahatma Gandhi*, p. 223.

143   *"To paraphrase a Biblical verse"*: Ibid.

143   *"we seek not to destroy the capitalist"*: Prabhu and Rao, eds., *Mind of Mahatma Gandhi*, p. 257.

143   *"An economics that inculcates Mammon worship"*: Ibid., p. 264.

144   *The return to the human-scaled village-based economic model*: Mathai, *Mahatma Gandhi's World-View*, pp. 187-190.

144   *trusteeship*: Ibid., pp. 257-263.

144   *"The contrast between the palaces of New Delhi"*: Fischer, *Life of Mahatma Gandhi*, pp. 327-328.

144   *"Trusteeship provides a means of transforming the present capitalist order"*: Prabhu and Rao, eds., *Mind of Mahatma Gandhi*, p. 262. The editors attach this footnote to this quotation: "This 'simple, practical trusteeship formula' was drawn up by Kishorlal Mashruwala and Narahari Parikn and approved, with a few changes, by Gandhiji."

145   *Even though we gained legislative and judicial victories*: King, Jr., "Dr. King's Speech," (Frogmore, South Carolina), p. 6.

145   *"cost the nation something...something is wrong with capitalism"*: Ibid., p. 14.

146   *the redistribution of wealth he was proposing*: Ibid.; see also Smith, "The Radicalization of Martin Luther King, Jr.," pp. 275-276.

146   *5 percent using 25 percent of the world's resources*: Estimates vary, with the 5% figure commonly rounding up from the more accurate population figure of 4.5%. The 5%/25% ratio would appear to represent a ballpark midpoint. Annie Leonard's short film, *The Story of Stuff*, places it at 5%/30%, while the Global Footprint Network, see University of Michigan, "U.S. Environmental Footprint," concludes that it would take five Earths (that would correlate to 5%/20%) to support the current world population if everyone's consumption patterns were similar to the average person in the U.S. We should also note that this same 5% to 25% ratio also applies to U.S. incarceration rates. See American Friends Service Committee, "Facts about the mass incarceration of people of color in the U.S."

146   *with such an egregiously unjust baseline intact*: This sentence is a paraphrase of a comment by Ethan Hughes, personal conversation (phone), April 2016.

147   *gift economics*: This section was largely informed by input from Ethan Hughes, personal conversations (phone) and letters, Fall 2015. See "Transition to Gift Economy," in Eisenstein, *Sacred Economics*, pp. 317-329; and to learn about the gift economics approaches of two current U.S.-based projects, East Point Peace Academy and the Possibility Alliance, see http://eastpointpeace.org/gifteconomics/ and http://urbanwwoofer.blogspot.com/2012/10/permaculture-train¬ing-and-gift-economy.html, respectively.

147   *"The Sun Never Says"*: Ladinsky, *The Gift*, p. 34.

149   *"What I'm talking about is more than recompense"*: Coates, "The Case for Reparations."

149   *Like "simple living" and "voluntary poverty"*: This and the next paragraph are based on insights

shared with me by Carolyn Griffeth, personal conversations (phone) and correspondence, March 2016.

150 *"Plunder has matured"*: Coates, *Between the World and Me*, pp. 150-151.

151 *"The white man literally sought to annihilate"*: King, Jr., "Frogmore Speech," p. 7.

151 *"The common phrase, 'The only good Indian is a dead Indian'"*: King, Jr., *Where Do We Go From Here?*, p. 85.

151 *the collision of two opposed worldviews*: Klein, *This Changes Everything*, pp. 393-396, 444-446.

151 *cases of reconciliation between indigenous and non-Native*: Ibid., pp. 373-374, 380-384.

152 *pioneers of white allyship*: The first time I heard someone lifting up the names and example of such leaders, and pointing to the fact that their stories and contributions rarely find their way into the history books or public discourse, was at a talk by Tim Wise, titled "They Want Their Country Back, Racial Nostalgia and White Anxiety in an Era of Change," Sierra College, Rocklin, California, January 19, 2012.

152 *Anne Braden*: See "Anne Braden: Organizing 'The Other America.' "

152 *Bob Zellner*: Zellner, *The Wrong Side of Murder Creek*.

152 *Dottie Zellner*: See Zellner, "My Real Vocation," in Holsaert et al, *Hands on the Freedom Plow*, pp. 311-325.

152 *Stan Levison*: Kamin, *Dangerous Friendship*.

152 *Andrew Goodman*: Bullard, *Free At Last*, p. 70.

152 *Mickey Schwerner*: Ibid.

152 *Rita Schwerner Bender*: Hannah-Jones, "A Brutal Loss, but an Enduring Conviction."

152 *Jonathan Daniels*: Bullard, *Free At Last*, p. 86.

152 *Jim Zwerg*: See "Jim Zwerg: Appleton's Freedom Rider." Zwerg also appears in Nelson, *Freedom Riders* [documentary film]. See the segment of the film that features him at http://www.voyageurmagazine.org/feature/feature2.html.

152 *Viola Liuzzo*: Bullard, *Free At Last*, p. 80.

152 *James Reeb*: Ibid., p. 78.

153 *unpaid wages...somewhere between $6.5 to $10 trillion*: Cussen-Anglada, "On Whiteness," p. 3.

153 *1.5 billion acres of land was stolen from Native Americans*: DeGraaf, "How the West was Stolen."

153 *"Reparations are ill-suited to address the harm"*: Sanchez, "Justice for Native Americans Rests in Restoring Relationship with the Land, Not Reparations."

154 *congressional bill HR40*: Coates, "Case for Reparations."

156 *"What if the captives cannot be set free"*: Katy Chandler, personal correspondence, Summer 2015.

157 *spinning had taken hold in 5,000 Indian villages*: Lelyveld, *Great Soul*, p. 261.

157 *Constructive Programme met with resistance*: Ibid., p. 259

157 *outright ridicule*: Dalton, *Mahatma Gandhi*, p. 61; Fischer, *Life of Mahatma Gandhi*, p. 231; and Lelyveld, *Great Soul*, p. 178.

157 *"The response was nil"*: Fischer, *Life of Mahatma Gandhi*, p. 328.

157 *"power concedes nothing without a demand"*: Frederick Douglass, as quoted in Alexander, *The New Jim Crow*, p. 258.

157 *"freedom is not something that is voluntarily given"*: Carson, ed., *Autobiography of Martin Luther King Jr.*, p. 353.

158 *"a common defect"*: Lelyveld, *Great Soul*, p. 261.

158 *In the epilogue*: Brown, *Gandhi*, pp. 385-394.

159 *"Millions like me may fail"*: Merton, *Gandhi on Non-Violence*, p. 75.

159 *Mathai and Nagler present a picture that contradicts Lelyveld and Brown*: Mathai, *Mahatma Gandhi's World-View*; Nagler, *Search for a Nonviolent Future*.

160 *"As Gandhi advised with his own program"*: As explained in the Foreword of Gandhi, *Constructive Programme*, p. 3.

162 *Ethan and Sarah Wilcox-Hughes and the Community of the Ark*: Ethan Hughes and Sarah Wilcox-Hughes, personal conversations and correspondence, 2005-present.

162 *Quaker wisdom on collective, spirit-led discernment*: Morley, *Beyond Consensus*.

163 *David Rock and five social drivers*: Rock, *Your Brain at Work*, pp. 195-197, 199.

164 *"The more emotionally intelligent and self-aware"*: Gerry O'Sullivan, personal conversation, January 2016, Hebron, Palestine. Gerry is currently writing a book on mediation and mediation questions. See www.osullivansolutons.ie for details.

164 *Nonviolent Communication*: Rosenberg, *Nonviolent Communication*; and https://www.cnvc.org/.

164 *"'tyranny of inclusion'...fear of making decisive moves"*: Kashtan, *Reweaving Our Human Fabric*, p. 142.

165 *"Getting shit done"*: Popovic, *Blueprint for Revolution*, p. 231.

165 *"everyone mattering"*: Kashtan, *Reweaving Our Human Fabric*, pp. 142, 150-151.

165 *Co-Counseling*: See https://www.rc.org/

165 *Gandhi in the position of dictatorial shot-caller*: In his interview on *Democracy Now*, June 5, 2012, Norman Finkelstein discusses this aspect candidly; See also Finkelstein, *What Gandhi Says about Nonviolence, Resistance and Courage*.

165 *he chose not to coerce them into submission*: For a cogent discussion see Fischer, *Life of Mahatma Gandhi*, pp. 358-360.

166 *Dr. King was a master of synthesis*: Garrow, *Bearing the Cross*, pp. 464-465. According to Andy Young: "He [King] would want somebody to express as radical a view as possible and somebody to express as conservative a view as possible...He figured...the wider variety of opinions you got, the better chance you had of extracting the truth from that."

166 *Young on the conservative end; Bevel, Williams, or Jackson at the other end*: Michael Eric Dyson, *I May Not Get There With You*, pp. 55-64. "Ironically," Dyson adds, "Young was more dedicated to King's latter-day vision of democratic socialism than any of the more radical staffers."

166 *let's let the leaders lead, and let's follow them*: For a helpful story about a group surrendering to mature "dictatorship," with a collective evaluation process tagged on at the end, see Kashtan, *Reweaving Our Human Fabric*, p. 157.

167 *SCLC distanced itself organizationally from him on Vietnam question*: Dyson, *I May Not Get There With You*, p. 55.

167 *the U.S. has yet to recover from Dr. King's assassination*: I first heard this assertion by James Lawson in the video segment, "Civil Rights pioneer Rev. James Lawson returns to Vanderbilt," produced by Vanderbilt University, and then explored the theme further in my interview with him, November 23, 2009, Los Angeles.

167 *the public microphone that fell from King's hands*: The seed for this conclusion was planted by Ruby Sales in my interview with her, October 26, 2009, Ft. Benning, Georgia.

167 *"I have, in the past, strongly defended"*: Klein, *This Changes Everything*, p. 158.

170 *a great bounty of books and other resources*: See the previous note corresponding to p. 95 for two such resources, both forthcoming: *Recipes for the Beloved Community* and *The Possibility Handbook*. These books promise to offer a wealth of insight and information about all of

these and more constructive program areas.

170 *Casa de Paz/Canticle Farm*: https://canticlefarm.wordpress.com.

170 *Be the Change Project*: 775 348 2505; kisacksen@gmail.com.

170 *The Possibility Alliance*: 28408 Frontier Lane, La Plata, MO 63549; 660 332 4094.

170 *New Community Project*: https://ncpharrisonburg.wordpress.com.

170 *Catholic Worker Movement*: Karen House Catholic Worker in St. Louis has an excellent list of books and other resources about the movement. See http://karenhousecw.org/CatholicWorkerBooks.html. See also http://www.catholicworker.org/.

171 *"a hundred times dearer"*: Gandhi, *All Men are Brothers*, p. 154; and Mathai, *Mahatma Gandhi's World-View*, p. 259.

171 *"In a world of falsehood"*: Nagler, *Search for a Nonviolent Future*, p. 172.

171 *"main hope"*: Ibid., p. 162.

171 *"an impressive power to protest"*: Ibid.

171 *"self-purification...as training...for constructive program"*: Brown, *Gandhi*, p. 229.

172 *"Civil Disobedience...is a full substitute for armed revolt"*: Gandhi, *Constructive Programme*, p. 3.

172 *Dr. King was right when he said the time had come to move from an era of reform*: Vincent Harding, "King and Revolution"; and Michelle Alexander, *The New Jim Crow*, p. 259.

172 *key assassinations of the 60s*: For a harrowing window into the impacts of those assassinations on the "revolutionary seedling" see Douglass, *JFK and the Unspeakable* and "The Martin Luther King Conspiracy Exposed in Memphis." See also Pepper, *An Act of State*; and, *The 13th Juror*. At the time of this writing, James Douglass is working on his long-awaited and in-depth study of the assassinations of Dr. King, Malcolm X, and Robert Kennedy, to be published by Orbis Books.

172 *COINTELPRO*: Branch, *At Canaan's Edge*, pp. 660, 708-709.

173 *Indonesia continues to burn*: Monbiot, "Indonesia Has Been Burning for Months"; and Phipps, "Indonesian President Visits Haze-Hit Zone as Country Becomes World's Worst Polluter."

173 *species continue to disappear...somewhere between six and eight per hour*: Vidal, "Protect Nature for World Economic Security, Warns UN Biodiversity Chief."

173 *the oceans of the world will be devoid of fish*: Dean, "Study Sees 'Global Collapse' of Fish Species."

173 *children dying at an estimated rate of 29,000 per day*: UNICEF, "Millenium Development Goals: 4. Reduce Child Mortality."

173 *just shy of $5 billion a day on weaponry and war (34 percent of that compliments of the U.S.)*: Bajpai, "Military Spending: U.S. Versus Everywhere Else."

Chapter 4: The Tip of the Iceberg

177 *peace community of San José de Apartadó*: Courtheyn, "San José de Apartadó: Lessons from Colombia's Peace Community."

179 *Peace Brigades International*: http://www.peacebrigades.org/; http://pbicolombia.org/.

179 *FOR's Colombia Peace Presence*: https://peacepresence.org/.

179 *"Satyagraha was Gandhi's attempt"*: Burrowes, *Strategy of Nonviolent Defense*, p. 108.

179 *"The first principle of nonviolent action"*: Merton, *Gandhi on Non-Violence*, p. 29.

179 *"I cannot conceive a greater loss"*: Fischer, *Life of Mahatma Gandhi*, p. 110.

179 *"I would rather have India resort to arms"*: Prabhu and Rao, eds., *Mind of Mahatma Gandhi*, p. 142.

180 *"To command respect is the first step to Swaraj"*: Fischer, *Life of Mahatma Gandhi*, p. 260.

180 *"What I did was a very ordinary thing"*: Ibid., p. 153.

180 *"My work will be finished"*: Prabhu and Rao, eds., *Mind of Mahatma Gandhi*, p. 22.

180 *The chronic feeling of impotence and muted rage*: For Dr. King's searing description of such feelings, see King, Jr., "Letter from Birmingham City Jail."

181 *satyagraha could extend in both micro and macro directions*: Merton, *Gandhi on Non-Violence*, p. 66; and Gandhi, *Hind Swaraj*, p. 68.

181 *"a bridge between the ethics of family life"*: Erikson, *Gandhi's Truth*, p. 413.

181 *Kasturba as Gandhi's first instructor in the art of soul force*: Gandhi, *Kasturba*, p. 212.

182 *King's six-part definition*: King, Jr., *Stride Toward Freedom*, pp. 90-95.

182 *"The immovable force of satyagraha"*: Merton, *Gandhi on Non-Violence*, p. 46.

182 *violence would breed further violence*: See Dr. King's description of violence as a descending spiral, King, Jr., *Where Do We Go From Here*, pp. 64-65.

182 *a potent means of conversion*: The process of "double conversion" pertaining to Gandhi is explored in Erikson, *Gandhi's Truth*, pp. 437-38; pertaining to King, see Simpson, "Changing the Face of the Enemy"; and pertaining to both Gandhi and King, Philip Hefner, "Spiritual Transformation and Nonviolent Action," pp. 264-273.

182 *"the bravery consists in dying"*: Merton, *Gandhi on Non-Violence*, p. 26.

182 *"Satyagraha implies cooperation"*: Burrowes, *Strategy of Nonviolent Defense*, p. 108.

183 *"when basic principles have not been challenged"*: Ibid.

183 *"synthesis or transcendence"*: Ibid.

183 *"a nonviolent revolution"*: Merton, *Gandhi on Non-Violence*, p. 28.

183 *satyagraha as a "principled" approach*: Burrowes, *Strategy of Nonviolent Defense*, pp. 98-101.

183 *"The most spiritual act"*: Gandhi, *All Men are Brothers*, p. 69.

183 *five basic criteria*: See table 1, "Nonviolence Criteria," in Burrowes, *Strategy of Nonviolent Defense*, p. 100.

183 *four further characteristics of satyagraha as revolutionary approach*: Ibid.

184 *some took on the 99 percent framing of the movement head on*: Pancho Ramos-Stierle, for example, who said, among other things, "We're the 99 percent, facilitating the healing, facilitating the awakening of the 100 percent," on *Democracy Now*, November 18, 2011, http://www.democracynow.org/2011/11/18/occupy_oakland_protester_pancho_ramos_stierle; and Kazu Haga, whose words echoed Dr. King, "The struggle is not against the 1 percent; the struggle is not between the 1 percent and the 99 percent; the struggle is between the 100 percent and injustice. If we use violence and intimidation to get what we want, that's what's going to be reflected in the world that we create," in O'Brien et al, "Nonviolence vs. 'Diversity of Tactics' in the Occupy Movement."

185 *"Everyone. No exceptions."*: Kashtan, *Reweaving Our Human Fabric*, p. 250.

185 *Give us a bigger slice of the pie*: This observation was shared with me by Ethan Hughes, personal conversation (phone), Fall 2015.

185 *a story of my own heartbreak*: Special thanks to Tyler Sheaffer for pointing this out to me in a personal conversation (phone), Summer 2015.

185 *Michael Meade in the brig in Panama*: Meade, *Fate and Destiny*, p. 65.

185 *"nonviolence" vs. "diversity of tactics" debate*: See Kashtan, *Reweaving Our Human Fabric*, pp. 254-255; and O'Brien et al, "Nonviolence vs. 'Diversity of Tactics' in the Occupy

Movement."

185 *unable to make the crackdown backfire*: See "Make Oppression Backfire," in Popovic, *Blueprint for Revolution*, pp. 125-150; and Kashtan, *Reweaving Our Human Fabric*, pp. 257-258.

186 *"care, compassion, and concern for every human being"*: Alexander, *The New Jim Crow*, p. 258.

186 *"The failure to acknowledge the humanity"; "I'm talking about the kind of love"*: Michelle Alexander, from her speech at Riverside Church, May 21, 2011, New York.

186 *All of Us or None*: http://www.prisonerswithchildren.org/our-projects/allofus-or-none/.

188 *Qualifications*: Gandhi, *Non-Violent Resistance*, p. 87.

188 *"living faith in God" (and corresponding footnote)*: Ibid., p. 364; and Mathai, *Mahatma Gandhi's World-View*, pp. 65-66.

188 *Code of Discipline*: Bondurant, *Conquest of Violence*, pp. 39-40.

189 *Steps*: Erikson, *Gandhi's Truth*, pp. 414-415.

189 *Rules*: Ibid., pp. 416-417.

193 *Let's invite two important books*: Popovic, *Blueprint for Revolution*; and Chenoweth and Stephan, *Why Civil Resistance Works*.

193 *Otpor!*: Popovic, *Blueprint for Revolution*; and York, *Bringing Down a Dictator* [documentary film].

194 *"Our perspective does not assume"*: Chenoweth and Stephan, *Why Civil Resistance Works*, p. 18.

194 *at its core, integral nonviolence is felt*: a paraphrase of a comment by Ethan Hughes, personal conversation (phone), Fall 2015.

195 *"thugs" and "brutes"*: for example, Popovic, *Blueprint for Revolution*, pp. ix, 8.

195 *"a normal country, with cool music"*: Ibid., p. 70.

196 *Popovic's case study of a struggle in Israel*: Ibid., pp. 30-36.

197 *Vinoba Bhave and the Bhoodan Movement*: Cholkar, "Bhoodan-Gramdan Movement."

198 *The massive logistical puzzle*: Ibid.

200 *The state was about to kill yet another human being*: Donald Beardslee, executed January 19, 2005.

202 *"The valiant in spirit"*: Easwaran, *Gandhi the Man*, p. 92.

205 *Hiroshima, August 6, 1945*: On the subject of Hiroshima, Gandhi is at his most irrepressibly other-paradigmed. His interview with Margaret Bourke-White, American photographer and *Life* magazine correspondent, is recounted in Gandhi, *Collected Works*, vol. 98, p. 329:

> *Did he still cherish the wish and hope to live the full span of life [which Gandhi held to be 125 years]?*
>
> *He had lost that wish, Gandhiji said, in view of the prevailing darkness. He was, however, groping for light. If things took a turn for the better and the people responded to his call and co-operated to usher in a new era of peace and amity, he would again wish—indeed, he would be "commanded" to wish to live the full span.*
>
> *"Would you advise America to give up the manufacture of atom bombs?" she finally asked.*
>
> *"Most certainly. As things are, the war ended disastrously and the victors are vanquished by jealousy and lust for power. Already a third war is being canvassed, which may prove even more disastrous. Ahimsa is a mightier weapon by far than the atom bomb. Even if the people of Hiroshima could have died in their thousands with prayer and goodwill in their hearts, the situation would have been transformed as if by a miracle…"*
>
> *"How would you meet the atom bomb…with non-violence?"*
>
> *"I will not go underground. I will not go into shelter. I will come out in the open and let the pilot see I have not a trace of ill will against him. The pilot will not see our faces from his great height, I know. But the longing in our hearts—that he will not come to harm—would reach up to him and his eyes*

would be opened. If those thousands who were done to death in Hiroshima...had died with that prayer-ful action—died openly with that prayer in their hearts—their sacrifice would not have gone in vain." I don't pretend to conceive of the potential consequences of 300,000 people praying in unison in such a situation, with 140,000 of them destined to die. The image of Gandhi coming "out in the open" under the pilot and the bomb, for me, is simply and powerfully representative of the fact that at this stage humanity is nowhere near ready to engage such extreme violence with nonviolence, by way of the particular type of "prayerful action" Gandhi suggested or any other.

205 *The intensity of violence...determines the intensity of the nonviolence needed*: For an excellent discussion on this point, see "'Work' Versus Work," in Nagler, *Search for a Nonviolent Future*, pp. 87-130.

206 *"intangible as it seems"*: Gandhi, *All Men are Brothers*, p. 76.

207 *Ron Sider, Christian Peacemaker Teams, "Too often we fall"*: Loney, *Captivity*, pp. 6-9. Loney is one of four CPTers taken hostage in Iraq in 2005. *Captivity* is an unusually courageous, openhearted, and challenging book. With great humility and insight, Loney explores tough questions and offers tough answers about nonviolence in the face of deadly threat and extreme dehumanization. Learn more about CPT at http://cpt.org/.

208 *Witness for Peace*: http://www.witnessforpeace.org/.

208 *Peace Brigades International*: http://peacebrigades.org/.

208 *Nonviolent Peaceforce*: http://www.nonviolentpeaceforce.org/.

208 *Voices for Creative Nonviolence*: http://vcnv.org/.

208 *Shanti Sena*: See Gandhi, *Collected Works*, vol. 73, pp. 23-34, where he writes: "By this time, i.e., after seventeen years' practice of nonviolence, the Congress should be able to put forth a nonviolent army of volunteers numbering not a few thousands but lacs who would be equal to every occasion where the police and the military are required... They would be constantly engaged in constructive activities that make riots impossible. Theirs will be the duty of seeking occasions for bringing warring communities together, carrying on peace propaganda, engaging in activities that would bring and keep them in touch with every single person, male and female, adult and child, in their parish or division. Such an army should be ready to cope with any emergency, and in order to still the frenzy of mobs, should risk their lives in numbers sufficient for the purpose."

208 *Badshah Kahn and the Khudai Khidmatgars*: Easwaran, *Nonviolent Soldier of Islam*.

208 *Whose ranks would eventually swell to 100,000*: Ibid., p. 16.

209 *James Bevel...Children's March*: Branch, *Pillar of Fire*, pp. 75-78. See also Houston, *Mighty Times: The Children's March* [documentary film], a heartwarming, inspirational account of this critical turning point in the Southern Freedom Struggle.

209 *as early as 1965...[Bevel] called for an international peace army*: Branch, *At Canaan's Edge*, pp. 286.

209 *King suggested that an unarmed group of 6,000 should go*: Jackson, *From Civil Rights to Human Rights*, p. 322.

210 *I've come to think of us as Kindergarteners in the school of satyagraha*: In York, *A Force More Powerful* [documentary film], the narrator (Ben Kingsley) states that Gandhi once said: "My technique of nonviolent struggle is in the same stage as electricity in Edison's time—to be refined and developed." My research has uncovered no such statement, though it certainly rings as wholly consistent with Gandhi's view.

210 *if we put even a fraction of as much time, energy, and resources*: Considering the financial resources

alone brings this into stark relief. From July 2014 to June 2015, Nonviolent Peaceforce, the largest organization engaged in third-party nonviolent intervention, spent approximately $11.5 million. Christian Peacemaker Teams' current annual budget is approximately $1 million. The United States annual military spending for 2014 was $600 billion, give or take.

211 *"Over the expanse of five continents"*: Albert Camus, from his essay "Neither Victims nor Executioners," as quoted in Kelly, *Other Lands Have Dreams*, pp. 10-11.

211 *"Love feels no burden"*: Thomas à Kempis, *The Imitation of Christ* (c. 1418), book 3, chapter 6. See Easwaran, *Seeing With the Eyes of Love*, p. 255.

211 *"A great dread fell on him"*: Tolkien, *The Fellowship of the Ring*, p. 303.

212 *"We don't know how this is going to play out"*: As stated by Joanna Macy during a "Work That Reconnects" workshop, January 2015, Oakland, California.

212 *the Chipko Movement*: See Weber, *Hugging the Trees*.

212 *Prague Spring*: See Nagler, *Search for a Nonviolent Future*, pp. 117-120, 234-235.

212 *The U.S. Sanctuary Movement*: See Davidson, *Convictions of the Heart*.

212 *Le Chambon-sur-Lignon*: See Grose, *A Good Place to Hide*.

212 *the White Rose student movement*: See Freedman, *We Will Not Be Silent*.

212 *women's Rosenstrasse Prison Demonstration*: See Stoltzfus, *Resistance of the Heart*.

212 *the Danish underground rescue*: See Lampe, *Hitler's Savage Canary*.

213 *"Protest that endures"*: From "A Poem of Difficult Hope," in Berry, *What Are People For?*, p. 62.

213 *"We must live faithfully"*: Brimlow, *What About Hitler?*, p. 151.

214 *"To lay down one's life"*: Merton, *Gandhi on Non-Violence*, p. 29.

214 *"Jesus was the most active resister"*: Ibid., p. 40.

214 *"What do you think? Wherein is courage required?"*: Gandhi, *Hind Swaraj*, p. 71.

Chapter 5: In Service to the Movement of Movements

221 *Naomi Klein, This Changes Everything, the raising up of a movement of movements*: See "Not an 'Issue,' a Frame" in *This Changes Everything*, chapter 4, pp. 152-160, where Klein contends that the climate crisis represents a potential "political game changer, a unifier of...disparate issues and movements," which can all work in concert in the "grand project of building a nontoxic, shockproof economy before it's too late," and where she quotes Yotam Marom saying, "The fight for the climate isn't a separate movement, it's both a challenge and an opportunity for all of our movements...We don't need a separate climate movement; we need to seize the climate moment." In *This Changes Everything* Klein doesn't explicitly issue a clarion call for the building up of a movement of movements, and the primary goal she identifies for movement workers is a new sane and sustainable post-capitalism economy, but her narrative is nonetheless deeply resonant with the vision of a coherent, deliberately organized movement of movements committed to turning the Great Turning. See also and/or listen to Klein, "Let Them Drown."

221 *Some argue that we already are a movement of movements*: See, for example, Rivera Sun, "We Are a Movement of Movements."

222 *"We must rapidly begin the shift...A nation that continues year after year...Our only hope"*: King, Jr., "A Time to Break Silence," pp. 240, 242.

222 *the madness in Vietnam*: Ibid., pp. 231-244.

222 *Poor People's Campaign*: Treated excellently in "Power to Poor People," in Jackson, *From Civil Rights to Human Rights*, pp. 329-350.

222 *"the great distinction between a reform movement and a revolutionary movement"*: As quoted in Alexander, *The New Jim Crow*, p. 259.

222 *"guaranteed income for all Americans"*: King, Jr., *Where Do We Go From Here*, pp. 170-175. See also Jackson, *From Civil Rights to Human Rights*, pp. 272-273; and Dyson, *I May Not Get There With You*, p. 83.

222 *"Democratic Socialism"*: Jackson, *From Civil Rights to Human Rights*, p. 271.

224 *THREE STRANDS OF AN INTEGRAL NONVIOLENCE SUBMOVEMENT:* The sketches of these three proposed groups were largely informed by input from Tom Benevento and Ethan Hughes, personal conversations (phone), Fall 2015-Spring 2016.

225 *"the bug of nonviolence"*: Robért Raymond is co-founder of the Community of l'Arche de Gwenves. He is quoted here secondhand, by way of Ethan Hughes in a personal conversation, Summer 2007, Community of the Ark, La Borie Noble, France.

227 *Inspired by the Freedom Schools*: See discussion in chapter 3, pp. 125-128, and corresponding notes.

231 *fossil fuel industry*: the corporate complex, propelled by our consumption and collusion, which is driving climate change—from fracking to coal-mining to tar sands pipelines to offshore drilling, etc. In *This Changes Everything*, Naomi Klein's use of the more encompassing terms "extractive industries" and "extractivism" is instructive.

231 *Too many trusted analysts*: Ibid. The research of a large cross-section of these analysts is summarized and carefully cited throughout Naomi Klein's *This Changes Everything*.

232 *factory farming and deforestation keep pace with the fossil fuel industry*: See Cowspiracy, "The Facts."

232 *"national reckoning"*; *"revolution in American consciousness"*: Coates, *Case for Reparations*.

235 *At a critical point Ella Baker knew*: Carson, *In Struggle*, pp. 19-20, 24-26.

235 *Dr. King and several of his co-workers discerned*: Fairclough, *To Redeem the Soul of America*, pp. 29-33. Fairclough reveals that King and his Southern-based colleagues were largely spurred to this discernment and action by Northern-based organizers Bayard Rustin, Ella Baker, and Stan Levison. See also, "The Birth of SCLC, 1957-1959," in Garrow, *Bearing the Cross*, pp. 83-125.

237 *violence...strategically speaking, would be utterly untenable*: Dr. King explains precisely why, in Carson, *Autobiography of Martin Luther King Jr.*, pp. 328-330.

239 *as major as the Agrarian and Industrial Revolutions*: Macy and Brown, *Coming Back to Life*, p. 4.

240 *I recently reached out to a dear friend*: Tom Benevento, personal conversation (phone), June 2015.

240 *"And aren't they all our children?"*: Vincent Harding, from his foreword to *The New Jim Crow Study Guide and Call to Action*, p. viii.

SOURCES

Albert, Peter J., and Ronald Hoffman, editors. *We Shall Overcome: Martin Luther King, Jr., and the Black Freedom Struggle*. New York: Da Capo Press, 1993.

Alcoholics Anonymous ("Big Book," 4th Edition). New York: AA World Services, 2001.

Alexander, Michelle. *The New Jim Crow: Mass Incarceration in the Age of Colorblindness*. New York: New Press, 2012.

Ambedkar, B.R. *Annihilation of Caste*. Brooklyn: Verso, 2014.

American Friends Service Committee. "Facts about the mass incarceration of people of color in the U.S." June 19, 2013.

American Immigration Council, "Misplaced Priorities: Most Immigrants Deported by ICE in 2013 Were a Threat to No One." *Just Facts*. March 28, 2014.

Amnesty International UK, "In Their Own Words: Chelsea Manning" [audio podcast]. February 3, 2016.

Andrews, Charles F. *Mahatma Gandhi: His Life and Ideas*. Woodstock, VT: SkyLight Paths, 2003.

"Anne Braden: Organizing 'The Other America'." *Veterans of Hope Pamphlet Series*, 2(2). Denver: Veterans of Hope, 2004.

Bajpai, Prableen. "Military Spending: U.S. Versus Everywhere Else." Investopedia, June 10, 2015.

Bamford, James. "Edward Snowden, the Untold Story." *WIRED*, September 2014.

Berry, Wendell. *What Are People For?* Berkeley: Counterpoint, 2010.

Birchard, George. "115°F World Record Hot Rain Hits Needles CA & Storm Starts Fire." *Daily Kos*, August 15, 2012.

Blocker, Jack S., David M. Fahey and Ian R. Tyrrell. *Alcohol and Temperance in Modern History: An International Encyclopedia, Volume 1*. Santa Barbara, CA: ABC-CLIO, 2003.

Bondurant, Joan V. *Conquest of Violence: The Gandhian Philosophy of Conflict*. Princeton, NJ: Princeton University Press, 1988.

Boulding, Elise. *Cultures of Peace: The Hidden Side of History*. New York: Syracuse University Press, 2000.

Branch, Taylor. *At Canaan's Edge: America in the King years, 1965-68*. New York: Simon and Schuster, 2006.

———. *Parting the Waters: America in the King Years, 1954-63*. New York: Simon and Schuster, 1988.

———. *Pillar of Fire: America in the King Years, 1963-65*. New York: Simon and Schuster, 1999.

Braun, Will. "The Case of the Customized Christ." *Geez Magazine*, 16, Winter 2009, pp. 34-35.

Brimlow, Robert. *What About Hitler: Wrestling with Jesus's Call to Nonviolence in an Evil World*. Grand Rapids, MI: Brazos, 2006.

Brown, Brené. *Daring Greatly: How the Courage to Be Vulnerable Transforms the Way We Live, Love, Parent, and Lead*. New York: Avery, 2012.

———. *Rising Strong: The Reckoning. The Rumble. The Revolution*. New York: Spiegel and Grau, 2015.

Brown, Judith. *Gandhi: Prisoner of Hope*. New Haven: Yale University Press, 1989.

Brown, Michael. *The Presence Process: A Journey Into Present Moment Awareness*, Revised Edition. Vancouver: Namaste, 2010.

Brueggemann, Walter. *Reality, Grief, Hope: Three Urgent Prophetic Tasks.* Grand Rapids, MI: Eerdmans, 2014.

Bullard, Sara. *Free At Last: A History of the Civil Rights Movement and Those Who Died in the Struggle.* New York: Oxford University Press, 1989.

Burns, James MacGregor. *Transforming Leadership.* New York: Atlantic Monthly Press, 2003.

Burrowes, Robert J. *The Strategy of Nonviolent Defense: A Gandhian Approach.* Albany, NY: State University of New York, 1996.

Campbell, Joseph. *The Hero With a Thousand Faces.* New York: MJF, 1949.

Carson, Clayborne. "African-American Leadership and Mass Mobilization." *The Black Scholar,* 24(4), 2001, pp. 2-7.

———. "Between Contending Forces: Martin Luther King, Jr., and the African American Freedom Struggle." *OAH Magazine of History,* 19(1), 2005, pp. 17-21.

———. *In Struggle: SNCC and the Black Awakening of the 1960s.* Cambridge, MA: Harvard University Press, 1981.

Carson, Clayborne, editor. *The Autobiography of Martin Luther King Jr.* New York: Warner, 1998.

Center for Sustainable Systems, University of Michigan. "U.S. Environmental Footprint Factsheet." Pub. No. CSS08-08, October 2015.

Chakravarty, Amiya. *A Saint at Work: A View of Gandhi's Work and Message.* Philadelphia: Young Friends Movement of the Philadelphia Yearly Meetings, 1950.

Chenoweth, Erica, and Maria Stephan. *Why Civil Resistance Works: The Strategic Logic of Nonviolent Conflict.* New York: Colombia University Press, 2011.

Cholkar, Parag. "Bhoodan-Gramdan Movement: An Overview." *Gandhi Sevagram Ashram,* Wardha, India.

Coates, Ta-Nehisi. "The Case for Reparations." *The Atlantic,* June 2014.

———. *Between the World and Me.* New York: Spiegel & Grau, 2015.

Cone, James. *Martin and Malcolm: A Dream or a Nightmare.* Maryknoll, NY: Orbis, 1991.

Courtheyn, Chris. "San José de Apartadó: Lessons from Colombia's Peace Community." *Upside Down World,* April 15, 2015.

Cowspiracy. "The Facts." cowspiracy.com/facts/.

Crossan, John Dominic. *The Essential Jesus: Original Sayings and Earliest Images.* Edison, NJ: Castle, 1994.

Cussen-Anglada, Brenna. "On Whiteness." *Dubuque Catholic Worker Newsletter,* Summer 2015.

Dalton, Dennis. *Mahatma Gandhi: Nonviolent Power in Action.* New York: Columbia, 1993.

Davidson, Miriam. *Convictions of the Heart: Jim Corbett and the Sanctuary Movement.* Tucson, AZ: University of Arizona Press, 1988.

Dean, Cornelia. "Study Sees 'Global Collapse' of Fish Species." *New York Times,* November 3, 2006.

DeGraaf, Mia. "How the West was Stolen: Scale of Native American Dispossession Revealed in Striking Time-Lapse Video." DailyMail.com, January 8, 2015.

Douglass, James W. "The Martin Luther King Conspiracy Exposed in Memphis." *Probe Magazine,* 7:4, May-June 2000.

———. *JFK and the Unspeakable: Why He Died and Why It Matters.* Maryknoll, NY: Orbis, 2008.

———. *The Non-Violent Cross: A Theology of Revolution and Peace.* New York: Macmillan, 1966.

Dyson, Michael Eric. *I May Not Get There With You: The True Martin Luther King Jr.* New York: Free Press, 2000.

Easwaran, Eknath. *Gandhi the Man.* Tomales, CA: Nilgiri Press, 1997.

————. *Nonviolent Soldier of Islam: Badshah Khan, A Man to Match His Mountains*. Tomales, CA: Nilgiri Press, 1999.

————. *Seeing With the Eyes of Love: Eknath Easwaran on the Imitation of Christ*. Tomales, CA: Nilgiri Press, 1996.

Easwaran, Eknath, editor. *The Bhagavad Gita*. Tomales, CA: Nilgiri Press, 2007.

————. *The Upanishads*. Tomales, CA: Nilgiri Press, 2007.

Eisenstein, Charles. *Sacred Economics: Money, Gift, and Society in the Age of Transition*. Berkeley, CA: Evolver/North Atlantic, 2011.

Elliott, Larry. "Richest 62 People as Wealthy as Half of World's Population, Says Oxfam." *The Guardian*, January 18, 2016.

Erikson, Erik H. *Gandhi's Truth: On the Origins of Militant Nonviolence*. New York: Norton, 1969.

Fairclough, Adam. *To Redeem the Soul of America: The Southern Christian Leadership Conference and Martin Luther King Jr.* Athens, GA: University of Georgia Press, 1987.

Finkelstein, Norman. *What Gandhi Says About Nonviolence, Resistance and Courage*. New York: OR Books, 2012.

Fischer, Louis. *The Life of Mahatma Gandhi*. New York: Harper and Row, 1950.

Fitz, Nicholas. "Economic Inequality: It's Far Worse Than You Think." *Scientific American*, March 31, 2015.

Flannery, Tim. *The Weather Makers: How Man Is Changing the Climate and What It Means for Life on Earth*. New York: Grove Press, 2007.

Foran, Clare. "A Year of Black Lives Matter." *The Atlantic*, Dec. 31, 2015.

Frady, Marshall. *Martin Luther King, Jr.: A Life*. New York: Penguin, 2002.

Frank, Anne. *The Diary of a Young Girl*. New York: Bantam, 1997.

Freedman, Russell. *We Will Not Be Silent: The White Rose Student Resistance Movement That Defied Adolf Hitler*. New York: Clarion, 2016.

Galtung, Johan. "Three Approaches to Peace: Peacekeeping, Peacemaking, and Peacebuilding." In *Peace, War and Defense: Essays in Peace Research, Vol. II*. Copenhagen: Christian Ejlers, 1976, pp. 282-304.

Gandhi, Arun. *Kasturba: a Life*. New Delhi: Penguin, 2000.

Gandhi, Mohandas K. *All Men are Brothers*. New York, UNESCO, 1972.

————. *An Autobiography: The Story of My Experiments with Truth*. Boston: Beacon, 1993.

————. *Book of Prayers*. Berkeley: Berkeley Hills Books, 1999.

————. *The Collected Works of Mahatma Gandhi (Electronic Book)*. New Delhi: Publications Division Government of India, 1999.

————. *Constructive Programme: Its Meaning and Place*. Ahmedabad: Navajivan, 1945.

————. *Hind Swaraj; or, Indian Home Rule*. Ahmedabad: Navajivan, 1938.

————. *Non-Violence in Peace & War: Volume I*. Ahmedabad: Navajivan, 1942.

————. *Non-Violence in Peace and War, Volume II*. Ahmedabad: Navajivan, 1949.

————. *Non-Violent Resistance (Satyagraha)*. New York: Dover, 2001.

————. *Prayer*. Berkeley: Berkeley Hills, 2000.

————. *Ramanama*. Ahmedabad: Navajivan, 1949.

————. *Vows and Observances*. Berkeley: Berkeley Hills, 1999.

Gandhi, Mohandas K. and John Strohmeier, editor. *The Bhagavad Gita According to Gandhi*. Berkeley, CA: Berkeley Hills Books, 2000.

Gandhi, Rajmohan. *Gandhi: The Man, His People, and the Empire*. Berkeley: University of California Press, 2008.

Garrow, David J. *Bearing the Cross: Martin Luther King, Jr., and the Southern Christian Leadership Conference*. New York: HarperCollins, 2004.

Gates Jr., Henry Louis. "Slavery, by the Numbers." *The Root*, February 10, 2014.

Glendinning, Chellis. *My Name is Chellis and I'm in Recovery From Western Civilization*. Boston: Shambhala, 2007.

Gora (G. Ramachandra Rao). *An Atheist with Gandhi*. Ahmedabad: Navajivan, 1971.

Griffin, David Ray. *The New Pearl Harbor: Disturbing Questions About the Bush Administration and 9/11*. Northampton, MA: Interlink Pub Group, 2004.

Grose, Peter. *A Good Place to Hide: How One French Village Saved Thousands of Lives During World War II*. New York: Pegasus, 2016.

Hagen, Jamie. "5 Things You Didn't Know About Human Trafficking." *Rolling Stone*, August 19, 2014.

Hagopian, Joachim. "Global Human Trafficking, a Modern Form of Slavery." *Global Research*, May 18, 2015.

Hannah-Jones, Nikole. "A Brutal Loss, but an Enduring Conviction." *ProPublica: Dispatches From Freedom Summer*, July 22, 2014.

Harding, Vincent. "King and Revolution," *The Progressive*, 47(4), 1983, pp.16-17.

———. "Ruby Sales Biography," *Veterans of Hope Project*, 2000.

Harding, Vincent, with Michelle Alexander and Chris Moore-Backman. *The New Jim Crow Study Guide and Call to Action*. Denver: Veterans of Hope, 2013.

Hefner, Philip. "Spiritual Transformation and Nonviolent Action: Interpreting Mahatma Gandhi and Martin Luther King, Jr." *Currents in Theology and Mission*, 31(2), 2004, pp. 264-273.

Houston, Robert, director. *Mighty Times: The Children's March* [documentary film]. United States: Teaching Tolerance, 2004.

Hughes, Ethan. "Disruptive Peacemaking: Living Out God's Impossible Standard." *Plough Quarterly*, Summer 2015, pp. 50-56.

———. "Love is the Highest Technology." *The Round Table*, Winter 2011, pp. 3-6.

Humphries, John. "Light Arises Out of Darkness: Prophetic Witness as Spiritual and Political Practice." In *Radical Witness: Four Talks on Faith Made Manifest in the World*, S. Spencer, ed. Boston: Beacon Hill Friends House, 2009.

Jackson, Thomas F. *From Civil Rights to Human Rights: Martin Luther King, Jr., and the Struggle for Economic Justice*. Philadelphia: University of Pennsylvania Press, 2007.

Jensen, Richard, and John Hammerback. "Working in 'Quiet Places': The Community Organizing Rhetoric of Robert Parris Moses." *Howard Journal of Communications*, 11(1), 2000, pp. 1-18.

"Jim Zwerg: Appleton's Freedom Rider." *Voyageur Magazine*, 25(2), Winter/Spring 2009.

Kakar, Sudhir. *Intimate Relations: Exploring Indian Sexuality*. New Delhi: Penguin, 1990.

Kamin, Ben. *Dangerous Friendship: Stanley Levison, Martin Luther King Jr., and the Kennedy Brothers*. East Lansing, Michigan: Michigan State, 2014.

Kashtan, Miki. *Reweaving Our Human Fabric: Working Together to Create a Nonviolent Future*. Oakland: Fearless Heart, 2015.

———. *Spinning Threads of Radical Aliveness: Transcending the Legacy of Separation in Our Individual Lives*. Oakland: Fearless Heart, 2014.

Kelly, Kathy. *Other Lands Have Dreams*. Petrolia, CA: Counterpunch, 2005.

King, Mary. *Mahatma Gandhi and Martin Luther King Jr: The Power of Nonviolent Action*. New Delhi,

India: Mehta/Indian Council for Cultural Relations, 1999.

King, Jr., Martin Luther. "The Current Crisis in Race Relations." In *A Testament of Hope: The Essential Writings and Speeches of Martin Luther King, Jr.* James M. Washington, ed. San Francisco: HarperSanFrancisco, 1986, pp. 87-88.

———. "Dr. King's Speech" (Address to SCLC staff, Frogmore, South Carolina, November 14, 1966). Atlanta, GA: King Library and Archives.

———. "Letter from Birmingham City Jail." In *A Testament of Hope: The Essential Writings and Speeches of Martin Luther King, Jr.* James M. Washington, ed. San Francisco: Harper-SanFrancisco, 1986, pp. 289-302.

———. "A Time to Break Silence." In *A Testament of Hope: The Essential Writings and Speeches of Martin Luther King, Jr.* James M. Washington, ed. San Francisco: HarperSanFrancisco, 1986), pp. 231-252.

———. "Where Do We Go From Here?" (Keynote address, 11th Annual SCLC Convention, Atlanta, GA, May 1967) In *A Testament of Hope: The Essential Writings and Speeches of Martin Luther King, Jr.* James M. Washington, ed. San Francisco: HarperSanFrancisco, 1986, pp. 245-252.

———. *Stride Toward Freedom: The Montgomery Story.* New York: Beacon Press, 1958.

———. *The Trumpet of Conscience.* New York: Harper and Row, 1968.

———. *Where Do We Go From Here: Chaos or Community?* New York: Harper and Row, 1967.

Klein, Naomi. "Let Them Drown: The Violence of Othering in a Warming World." *London Review of Books*, 38(11), 2 June 2016, pp. 11-14.

———. *This Changes Everything: Capitalism vs. the Climate.* New York: Simon and Schuster, 2014.

Kolbert, Elizabeth. *The Sixth Extinction.* New York: Picador, 2015.

Kuehr, Ruediger, Cornelis Peter Baldé, Feng Wang, and Jaco Huisman. *The Global E-Waste Monitor 2014.* Bonn, Germany: United Nations University, IAS – SCYCLE, 2015.

Ladinksy, Daniel, translator. *Love Poems from God: Twelve Sacred Voices from the East and West.* New York: Penguin, 2002.

———. *The Gift: Poems by Hafiz.* New York: Penguin, 1999.

Lampe, David. *Hitler's Savage Canary: A History of Danish Resistance in World War II.* New York: Arcade, 2014.

Lelyveld, Joseph. *Great Soul: Mahatma Gandhi and His Struggle with India.* New York: Vintage, 2011.

Leonard, Annie. *The Story of Stuff* [film]. United States: Free Range Studios, 2007.

Lerner, Michael. "After Paris: A World That Has Lost Its Ethical Direction and Spiritual Foundation (and a Media that Cheer Leads for Fear and Militarism)." *The Huffington Post*, November 16, 2015.

Leviton, Mark. "Dangerous Love: Reverend Lynice Pinkard On the Revolutionary Act of Living The Gospels." *The Sun Magazine*, 466, October 2014.

Lindsay, R., and A. Schweiger. "Arctic Sea Ice Thickness Loss Determined Using Subsurface, Aircraft, and Satellite Observations." *The Cryosphere*, 2015.

Loney, James. *Captivity: 118 Days in Iraq and the Struggle for a World Without War.* Toronto: Knopf Canada, 2011.

Lowe, Maria R. "An 'Oasis of Freedom' in a 'Closed Society': The Development of Tougaloo College as a Free Space in Mississippi's Civil Rights Movement, 1960 to 1964." *Journal of Historical Sociology*, 20(4), December 2007, pp. 486-520.

Macy, Joanna, and Molly Brown, *Coming Back to Life: The Updated Guide to the Work That Reconnects.* Gabriola Island, BC: New Society, 2014.

Mathai, M.P. *Mahatma Gandhi's World-View.* New Delhi: Gandhi Peace Foundation, 2000.

McAllister, Pam. *You Can't Kill the Spirit (Barbara Deming Series: Stories of Women and Nonviolent Action).* Philadelphia, PA: New Society, 1988.

Bill McKibben. "Global Warming's Terrifying New Math." *Rolling Stone,* July 19, 2012.

———. "The End of Growth." *Mother Jones,* November/December, 1999.

———. *The End of Nature.* New York: Random House, 2006.

Meade, Michael. *Fate and Destiny: The Two Agreements of the Soul.* Seattle: GreenFire Press, 2010.

Merton, Thomas, editor. *Gandhi on Non-Violence.* New York: New Directions, 1964.

Miller, Keith D. *Voice of Deliverance: The Language of Martin Luther King, Jr. and Its Sources.* New York: Free Press, 1992.

Monbiot, George. "Indonesia Has Been Burning for Months. So Why is the World Still Looking Away?" *The Guardian Weekly,* 193(22), November 6-12, 2015, p. 12.

Moore-Backman, Chris, producer. "The Formerly Incarcerated and Convicted People's Movement: The Struggle for Freedom and Transformation Continues" [radio documentary]. *Bringing Down the New Jim Crow: A Radio Documentary Series,* April 2014.

———. "A New Way of Life and the New Underground Railroad: Making a Break for Freedom During the Era of Mass Incarceration" [radio documentary]. *Bringing Down the New Jim Crow: A Radio Documentary Series,* June 2013.

Morley, Barry. *Beyond Consensus: Salvaging Sense of the Meeting (Pendle Hill Pamphlet 307).* Wallingford, PA: Pendle Hill, 2003.

Morris, Aldon. "Black Southern Student Sit-In Movement: An Analysis of Internal Organization." *American Sociological Review,* Vol. 46, December 1981, pp. 744-767.

Morton, Brian. "Falser Words Were Never Spoken." *New York Times,* Aug. 29, 2011.

Moses, Robert P., and Charles E. Cobb, Jr. *Radical Equations: Civil Rights from Mississippi to the Algebra Project.* Boston: Beacon Press, 2001.

Nagler, Michael. *The Search for a Nonviolent Future: A Promise of Peace for Ourselves, Our Families, and Our World.* Maui, HI: Inner Ocean, 2004.

National Centers for Environmental Information/National Oceanic and Atmospheric Administration. "Global Analysis—Annual 2015." Report: December 2015.

Nelson, Stanley, director. *Freedom Riders* [documentary film]. United States: Firelight Media/PBS American Experience, 2010.

O'Brien, Sean, Phil Lawson, Matthew Edwards, Kazu Haga, Melissa Merin, Josh Shepherd, Paolo, and Starhawk, "Nonviolence vs. 'Diversity of Tactics' in the Occupy Movement." *Tikkun,* March 29, 2012.

Ocko, Ilisa. "Methane and CO2: Why climate action means addressing both." *Environmental Defense Fund,* August 12, 2015.

Oliver, Mary. *House of Light.* Boston: Beacon, 1990.

Osbon, Diane, editor, *Reflections on the Art of Living: A Joseph Campbell Companion.* New York: HarperCollins, 1991.

Pearce, Fred. *With Speed and Violence: Why Scientists Fear Tipping Points in Climate Change.* Boston: Beacon, 2007.

Pepper, William F. *An Act of State: The Execution of Martin Luther King.* New York: Verso, 2008.

Phipps, Claire. "Indonesian President Visits Haze-Hit Zone as Country Becomes World's Worst Polluter." *The Guardian Weekly,* 193(22), November 6-12, 2015, p. 12.

Popovic, Srdja. *Blueprint for Revolution: How to Use Rice Pudding, Lego Men, and Other Nonviolent Techniques to Galvanize Communities, Overthrow Dictators, or Simply Change the World.* New

York: Spiegel & Grau, 2015.

Prabhu, R.K., and U.R. Rao, editors, *The Mind of Mahatma Gandhi*. Ahmedabad: Navajivan, 1967.

Rock, David. *Your Brain at Work*. New York: Harper Collins, 2009.

Rosenberg, Marshall. *Nonviolent Communication: A Language of Life*. Encinitas, CA: PuddleDancer Press, 2003.

Roy, Arundhati. "The Doctor and the Saint." *In Annihilation of Caste*, B.R. Ambedkar. Brooklyn: Verso, 2014.

Sanchez, Mary. "Justice for Native Americans Rests in Restoring Relationship with the Land, Not Reparations." *The Kansas City Star*, June 15, 2014.

Sharp, Gene. *Gandhi as a Political Strategist, with Essays on Ethics and Politics*. Boston: Extending Horizons, 1979.

———. *Gandhi Wields the Weapon of Moral Power: Three Case Histories*. Ahmedabad: Navajivan, 1960.

Sheehan, Joanne. "Gandhi's Constructive Program—and Ours." *Peacework*, 368, 2006.

Simpson, Gary M. "Changing the Face of the Enemy: Martin Luther King, Jr., and the Beloved Community." *Word and World*, 28(1), Winter 2008.

Smith, Kenneth L. "The Radicalization of Martin Luther King, Jr.: The Last Three Years." *Journal of Ecumenical Studies*, 26(2), Spring 1989, pp. 270-288.

Stoltzfus, Nathan. *Resistance of the Heart: Intermarriage and the Rosenstrasse Protest in Nazi Germany*. New York: Norton, 1996.

Strand, Clark. *Waking Up to the Dark: Ancient Wisdom for a Sleepless Age*. New York: Spiegel and Grau, 2015.

Sun, Rivera. "We Are a Movement of Movements," *RiveraSun.com*, February 14, 2014.

The Thirteenth Juror: The Official Transcript of the Martin Luther King Assassination Conspiracy Trial. MLK the Truth, 1999.

Tolkein, J.R.R. *The Fellowship of the Ring: The Lord of the Rings Part One*. New York: Mariner Books, 2012.

Tolle, Eckart. *A New Earth: Awakening to Your Life's Purpose*. New York: Penguin, 2005.

UNEP. "E-waste, the Hidden Side of IT Equipment's Manufacturing and Use." *United Nations Environment Programme: Environment Alert Bulletin*, January 2005.

UNICEF, "Millenium Development Goals: 4. Reduce Child Mortality." *UNICEF.org/mdg/childmortality.html*.

United to End Genocide. "Atrocities Against Native Americans," *EndGenocide.org/learn*.

Vanderbilt University, *Civil Rights Pioneer Rev. James Lawson Returns to Vanderbilt* [video segment]. United States: Vanderbilt, 2007.

Vidal, John, environment editor. "Protect Nature for World Economic Security, Warns UN Biodiversity Chief," *The Guardian* (U.S. Edition), August 16, 2010.

Waetjen, Thembisa. "Gandhi and Racism." *Backstories*, July 27, 2015.

Weber, Thomas. *Hugging the Trees: The Story of the Chipko Movement*. New York: Penguin, 1989.

Wernick, Adam. "Thawing Permafrost Could Have Catastrophic Consequences, Scientists Warn." *Living On Earth/Public Radio International*, June 24, 2015.

West, Traci. "Gendered Legacies of Martin Luther King Jr.'s Leadership," *Theology Today*, 65, 2008, pp. 41-56.

Whitty, Julia. "10 Key Findings from a Rapidly Acidifying Arctic Ocean." *Mother Jones*, May 7, 2013.

Wilber, Ken. *Integral Psychology: Consciousness, Spirit, Psychology, Therapy.* Boston: Shambhala, 2000.

Wink, Walter. *Engaging the Powers: Discernment and Resistance in a World of Domination.* Minneapolis: Fortress Press, 1992.

Wink, Walter, editor. *Peace Is the Way: Writings on Nonviolence from the Fellowship of Reconciliation.* Maryknoll, NY: Orbis, 2000.

Wise, Tim. *Dear White America: Letter to a New Minority.* San Francisco: City Lights, 2012.

World Meteorological Organization. "Greenhouse Gas Concentrations Hit Yet Another Record" [Press Release]. November 9, 2015.

York, Steve, producer and director, *Bringing Down a Dictator* [documentary film]. United States: York Zimmerman Inc., 2001.

———. *A Force More Powerful* [documentary film: episode 1/part 2 "India"]. United States: York Zimmerman Inc., 2000.

Zellner, Bob, with Constance Curry. *The Wrong Side of Murder Creek: A White Southerner in the Freedom Movement.* Montgomery, AL: NewSouth, 2008.

Zellner, Dorothy. "My Real Vocation." In *Hands on the Freedom Plow: Personal Accounts by Women in SNCC,* Faith S. Holsaert, Martha Prescod Norman Noonan, Judy Richardson, Betty Garman Robinson, Jean Smith Young, and Dorothy M. Zellner, eds. Chicago: University of Illinois, 2012, pp. 311-325.

INDEX

ACKNOWLEDGMENTS

AN AMAZING CIRCLE OF READERS offered invaluable guidance and accompaniment over the course of this project. Thanks especially to Ethan Hughes for his steadfast encouragement and deeply influential input. With the exception of Gandhi and King, nobody has left a stronger imprint on these pages. Special thanks as well to Katy Chandler-Isacksen, who so graciously helped me find the book buried deep beneath my first draft. And to Melanie Edwards, beloved friend and sudden editor, whose boundless, unshakable support carried me through on several occasions. To the many others who read and weighed in on portions or complete drafts of my manuscript-in-progress, I also offer my heartfelt appreciation: Carin Anderson, Tom Benevento, Kazu Haga, Kit Miller, Tyler Sheaffer, Julie Estep, Kyle Chandler-Isacksen, Michelle Alexander, Daniel Hunter, Jason Winton, Jim Douglass, Kathy Kelly, Pancho Ramos, Anne Symens-Bucher, Maya Schenwar, Patricia Moore, John Lindsay-Poland, Gerry O'Sullivan, Joanna Macy, Miki Kashtan, and David Hartsough.

Time and space to write the book were made financially and materially possible, gift economics style, by Peaceworkers, the Possibility Alliance, Marcia and John McCarley, Andrea Hamilton, Monica Moore, Patricia Moore, Sue Hilderbrand, Michael Chambers and Jen Durbin, Jennifer Jeffries, Jim Anderson, Susan Chandler, Rich and Jeanne Backman, Julie and Gary Estep, Anne Marie Larsen, and Ian Sawyer. I am deeply grateful for your kindness and generosity.

Warm thanks to Sarena Kirk for her excellent drawings, and to Vanessa Mendozzi for her wonderful design and infinite patience.

Love to all.

bkow 89493

61576934R00179

Made in the USA
Lexington, KY
14 March 2017